# Mainline Economics

## ADVANCED STUDIES IN POLITICAL ECONOMY

*Series Editors: Virgil Henry Storr and Stefanie Haeffele-Balch*

The Advanced Studies in Political Economy series consists of republished as well as newly commissioned work that seeks to understand the underpinnings of a free society through the foundations of the Austrian, Virginia, and Bloomington schools of political economy. Through this series, the Mercatus Center at George Mason University aims to further the exploration and discussion of the dynamics of social change by making this research available to students and scholars.

Don Lavoie, *Rivalry and Central Planning: The Socialist Calculation Debate Reconsidered*

Don Lavoie, *National Economic Planning: What Is Left?*

Peter J. Boettke, Stefanie Haeffele-Balch, and Virgil Henry Storr, eds., *Mainline Economics: Six Nobel Lectures in the Tradition of Adam Smith*

# $\mathcal{M}$AINLINE
# ECONOMICS

## SIX NOBEL LECTURES
### *in the* TRADITION *of* ADAM SMITH

*Edited by*

PETER J. BOETTKE,
STEFANIE HAEFFELE-BALCH,
*and* VIRGIL HENRY STORR

MERCATUS CENTER
George Mason University

Arlington, Virginia

## ABOUT THE MERCATUS CENTER AT GEORGE MASON UNIVERSITY

The Mercatus Center at George Mason University is the world's premier university source for market-oriented ideas—bridging the gap between academic ideas and real-world problems.

A university-based research center, Mercatus advances knowledge about how markets work to improve people's lives by training graduate students, conducting research, and applying economics to offer solutions to society's most pressing problems.

Our mission is to generate knowledge and understanding of the institutions that affect the freedom to prosper and to find sustainable solutions that overcome the barriers preventing individuals from living free, prosperous, and peaceful lives.

Founded in 1980, the Mercatus Center is located on George Mason University's Arlington and Fairfax campuses.

Mercatus Center at George Mason University
3434 Washington Blvd., 4th Floor
Arlington, Virginia 22201
www.mercatus.org

# CONTENTS

# INTRODUCTION: WHAT IS MAINLINE ECONOMICS?

PETER J. BOETTKE, STEFANIE HAEFFELE-BALCH,
AND VIRGIL HENRY STORR

Adam Smith made important contributions to political economy, moral philosophy, political science, and legal philosophy. Additionally, he wrote interesting pieces on everything from astronomy and stage acting to rhetoric. Despite the breadth of his scholarship and the significance of his influence in multiple disciplines, Smith is deservedly referred to as the father of modern economics. He asked and attempted to answer what has continued to be the central question in economics: Why are some nations rich and others poor?

In his primary contribution to political economy, *An Inquiry into the Nature and Causes of the Wealth of Nations*, as well as in several of his other works, especially *The Theory of Moral Sentiments* and *Lectures on Jurisprudence*, Smith explored the nature and consequences of economic exchange and the influence of informal and formal institutions on exchange relationships.

Smith offers a straightforward recipe for economic development in *The Wealth of Nations*. This recipe is captured in Smith's famous dictum regarding the importance of "peace, easy taxes, and the tolerable administration of justice." The richest societies are those societies that benefit from the gains to productivity that result from the division of labor. According to Smith ([1776] 1981: 13), "the greatest improvement in the productive powers of labour, and the greater part of the skill, dexterity, and judgment with which it is any where directed, or applied, seem to have been the effects of the division of labour." It is, Smith argues, our propensity to trade that gives occasion to the division of labor. It is our propensity to "truck, barter, and exchange" that allows both for you to satisfy your need for food and for me to satisfy my need for farming instruments even when you have focused solely on developing farming instruments and I have focused all of my efforts on farming. "As it is the power of exchanging that gives occasion to the division of labour," Smith (ibid.: 31) explains, "so to the extent of this division must always be limited by that power, or, in other words, by the extent of the market." The richest societies are, therefore, those whose formal and informal institutions allow for and protect an open and expansive market sphere.

In addition to articulating the key question in modern economics and offering a compelling and still well-regarded answer to that question, Adam Smith also anticipated and inspired a number of the major theoretical developments in several branches of economics, including price theory, market process economics, economic development, industrial organization, public economics, institutional economics, experimental economics, and behavioral economics. But, while many economists will trace the profession back to the tomes of Adam Smith and admit to finding inspiration in Smith for their theoretical and empirical projects, it is sometimes quite difficult to identify Smith's direct influence in many of the branches of modern economics. In fact, the propositions regarding the nature of human action, the place of institutions, and the role of government articulated by the mainstream of economics has sometimes deviated quite significantly from those advanced by the mainline of economics that descended from Adam Smith.

There are, however, several economists whose research is grounded in the Smithian mainline of economics. The Nobel Laureates in Economics whose addresses are collected in this volume—F. A. Hayek, James M. Buchanan, Ronald H. Coase, Douglass C. North, Vernon L. Smith, and Elinor C. Ostrom—represent key figures in the mainline of economics.

## Mainline Political Economy

Peter Boettke has written elsewhere about the distinction between mainline and mainstream economics.[1] "Mainline," he (2012: xvii) explains, "is defined as a set of positive propositions about social order that were held in common from Adam Smith onward, but mainstream economics is a sociological concept related to what is currently fashionable among the scientific elite of the profession."

The economists in the mainline are attempting to address the questions advanced by Smith and are working to critically engage and advance the propositions that Smith introduced. This is not to suggest that mainline economists are always self-consciously engaged in a history of thought or hermeneutical exercise to interpret or reinterpret Smith.[2] This is also not to suggest that the mainline economists always agree with any particular aspect of Smith's analysis or with Smith's conclusions. Instead, it is meant to suggest that you can identify Smithian themes in their theoretical and empirical work.

Mainstream economics, on the other hand, is the dominant economics at any given time. It is the brand of economics practiced by most professional economists in any particular period. The economists in the mainstream, thus, represent the leading figures in economic science at any given time. They hold positions at the most prestigious institutions, and they publish in the most prestigious academic journals.

Those economists outside the most prestigious places who take their scientific cues, as it were, from those at the most prestigious settings, would also be considered mainstream economists.

It is important to note that there have been significant shifts over time in what constitutes mainstream economics. For instance, the Keynesian revolution in macroeconomics gave rise to the Neoclassical Synthesis, which in turn lost ground to the Neo-Keynesians, who were then replaced by monetarism and New Classical Economics, which gave way to New Keynesian Economics, which has lost ground to the New Neoclassical Synthesis. The same has happened in institutional economics, where the Old Institutionalism of Thorstein Veblen has been replaced by the New Institutional Economics of North.

It is also important to note that mainline economics sometimes represents the mainstream and sometimes it does not. As Boettke (ibid.) notes, "Often the mainline and the mainstream dovetail, but at other times they deviate from one another." Keynes' theory, for instance, replaced an older mainline monetary theory advanced by Knut Wicksell, Hayek, and others as the mainstream view. Similarly, as noted above, the institutionalism of Veblen was replaced by the mainline institutional views of North.

Arguably, there are at least three propositions regarding the nature of human action and the role of institutions that mainline economics critically adopt and advance: (1) there are limits to the benevolence that individuals can rely on and therefore they face cognitive and epistemic limits as they negotiate the social world, but (2) formal and informal institutions guide and direct human activity, and, so (3) social cooperation is possible without central direction. Stated another way, by relying on the emergent and human-devised rules of conduct, agents possessing both the capacities and the failings of the typical human being can nonetheless work together to achieve their individual and collective goals.

Human beings can be imperfectly benevolent. As Smith argues in the "butcher, brewer, baker" passage in *The Wealth of Nations*, civilized society forces us to rely on the cooperation and assistance of countless others who are outside our narrow circle of family and friends. Think, for instance, of the large number of individuals involved in the production of the simple woolen coat that the day laborer wears.[3] Consequently, we cannot rely on others' benevolence alone when attempting to convince them to act on our behalf. We are more likely to succeed, Smith explains, by relying on their self-love than by relying on their kindness. "It is not from the benevolence of the butcher, the brewer, or the baker, that we expect our dinner," Smith ([1776] 1981: 27) writes, "but from their regard to their own interest. We address ourselves, not to their humanity but to their self-love, and never talk to them of our own necessities but of their advantages." Although individuals are far from selfish on Smith's account, and do not slavishly pursue their narrow interests without limits, they are rightfully self-interested. As Smith ([1759] 1982: 213) explains in *The Theory of Moral Sentiments*, prudence is a virtue.[4]

While human beings cannot rely solely on the benevolence of individuals to assist them, they also cannot rely on a central authority arranging human society and directing others in such a way that everyone's needs are met. Human beings can also never know enough to devise and control such a system. Smith's ridicule of the "man of system" is quite telling in this regard. "The man of system," Smith (ibid.: 234) writes, "is apt to be very wise in his own conceit." And, as Smith (ibid.: 235) continues, the man of system

> seems to imagine that he can arrange the members of a great society with as much ease as the hand arranges the different pieces upon a chess-board. He does not consider that the pieces of the hand have no other principle of motion besides that which the

hand impresses upon them; but that, in the chess-board of human society, every single piece has a principle of motion of its own, altogether different from that which the legislature might choose to impress on them.

The man of system inexorably faces what Don Lavoie ([1985] 2015; [1985] 2016) has characterized as a "knowledge problem." Every human being has a principle of motion of her own that the central authority could never know, much less marshal to control human society.

That we must cooperate with countless others to satisfy our needs, and that these others cannot be made to do so by some central authority nor compelled to do so because of their intimate connection to us, need not paralyze us. Individuals are able to negotiate the social world because there are formal and informal rules of just conduct on which they can rely.

Institutions matter for Smith. As Smith ([1776] 1981: 910) notes, "commerce and manufactures can seldom flourish long in any state which does not enjoy a regular administration of justice, in which the people do not feel themselves secure in the possession of their property, in which the faith of contracts is not supported by law, and in which the authority of the state is not supposed to be regularly employed in enforcing the payment of debts from all those who are able to pay." Consider, also, Smith's discussion of how different institutional arrangements in two universities can actually alter the quality of teaching in those settings (ibid.: 760). While teachers in Scotland were paid primarily from fees from students, teachers in Oxford were paid from endowments and were prohibited from receiving fees from their pupils. As such, in Scottish universities (such as Glasgow), teachers could incur monetary losses if student enrollment dropped, whereas in Oxford, teachers were paid the same whether their lectures were well attended or not.

According to Smith, professors cared more about teaching in Scottish universities than they did at Oxford. "In the university of Oxford," Smith (ibid.: 761) asserts, perhaps hyperbolically, "the greater part of the public professors have for these many years, given up altogether the pretense of teaching" because professor pay there was divorced from performance. By examining the incentives of the different institutional structures, Smith was able to understand why a commitment to teaching and providing quality lectures varied across universities.[5]

Similarly, Smith has also argued that norms govern the behavior of individuals. For instance, he described how norms of fair play affect the way that we compete with one another and how we view the competitive behavior of others. As Smith ([1759] 1982: 83) explains,

> In the race for wealth, and honours, and preferments, he may run as hard as he can, and strain every nerve and every muscle, in order to outstrip all his competitors. But if he should justle, or throw down any of them, the indulgence of the spectators is entirely at an end. It is a violation of fair play, which they cannot admit of. This man is to them, in every respect, as good as he: they do not enter into that self–love by which he prefers himself so much to this other, and cannot go along with the motive from which he hurt him.

We are comfortable with people competing to the best of their abilities, trying as hard as they can, and seeking whatever advantage that they can secure so long as they act within the rules. But, we are not willing to endorse individuals who are willing to cheat to win. And, most of us cannot so prefer ourselves over others that we cheat to win without our internal compasses "humbl[ing] the arrogance of [our] self-love, and bring[ing] it down to something which other men can go along with" (ibid.).

Individuals with imperfect benevolence, cognition, and knowledge are able to cooperate with the aid of formal rules and social norms. Additionally, this cooperation and the social order that results, Smith has demonstrated, can and does occur without the direction of a central authority.

Indeed, as Smith famously argued, individuals pursuing their own goals are led as if by an "invisible hand" to satisfy the desires and to improve the lives of others. Commenting on the efficacy of efforts to regulate commerce with the aim of supporting domestic industries, Smith ([1776] 1981: 453) argued in *The Wealth of Nations* that "no regulation of commerce can increase the quantity of industry in any society beyond what its capital can maintain. It can only divert a part of it into a direction into which it might not otherwise have gone; and it is by no means certain that this artificial direction is likely to be more advantageous to the society than that into which it would have gone of its own accord."

The maximum size of a society's economy, as it were, is driven by certain market fundamentals (that is, the extent of the market, the level of productivity, the size of its capital stock, and so on). Moreover, while efforts to direct the economy through regulation can change its course (perhaps for the worse) toward certain industries and away from others, regulation cannot expand the domestic economy beyond certain natural limits. In fact, as Smith writes, domestic entrepreneurs attempting to advance their own interests, rather than regulation, is what drives economic growth. According to Smith (ibid.: 456),

> every individual necessarily labours to render the annual revenue
> of the society as great as he can. He generally, indeed, neither
> intends to promote the public interest, nor knows how much he
> is promoting it. ... by directing that industry in such a manner as
> its produce may be of the greatest value, he intends only his own

gain, and he is in this, as in many other cases, led by an invisible hand to promote an end which was no part of his intention.

And, as Smith (ibid.: 454) wrote, "Every individual is continually exerting himself to find out the most and every man's interest leads him to seek that employment of capital which is most advantageous to the society. It is his own advantage, indeed, and not that of the society, which he has in view. But the study of his own advantage naturally, or rather necessarily leads him to prefer that employment which is most advantageous to the society." It is not the visible hand of regulation but the invisible hand of the market that directs entrepreneurial efforts in socially beneficial directions.[6]

In *The Theory of Moral Sentiments*, Smith's reference to the invisible hand speaks to the likelihood that the advantages of the rich can, must, and will (eventually) be shared with even the poorest in a commercial society. The constant striving for riches leads to economic growth and might lead to inequality in certain respects, but the trend is always toward equality regarding the necessaries of life. As Smith ([1759] 1982: 184–185) wrote,

> The produce of the soil maintains at all times nearly that number of inhabitants which it is capable of maintaining. The rich only select from the heap what is most precious and agreeable. They consume little more than the poor; and in spite of their natural selfishness and rapacity, though they mean only their own conveniency, though the sole end which they propose from the labours of all the thousands whom they employ be the gratification of their own vain and insatiable desires, they divide with the poor the produce of all their improvements. They are led by an invisible hand to make nearly the same distribution of the necessaries of life which would have been made had the earth been divided into

equal portions among all its inhabitants; and thus, without intending it, without knowing it, advance the interest of the society, and afford means to the multiplication of the species. When Providence divided the earth among a few lordly masters, it neither forgot nor abandoned those who seemed to have been left out in the partition. These last too enjoy their share of all that it produces.

The invisible hand postulate in Smith, thus, speaks to the likelihood that individuals pursuing their self-interest within the institutional framework that typically characterizes commercial societies generates a complex but unintended social order that aligns their individual interests with the general interests.

Adam Smith articulated a view of the economy that stressed the limits to human generosity, rationality, and knowledge; the importance of formal rules and social norms; and the potential of the invisible hand to lead individuals pursuing their self-interest in commercial settings to behave in socially beneficial ways. The six Nobel Laureates in Economics featured in this volume share these characteristic views of mainline economics, recognize their distinction from the mainstream of the discipline, and argue for continued work within the mainline tradition.

## Six Nobel Lectures in the Mainline Tradition

The Sveriges Riksbank Prize in Economic Sciences in Memory of Alfred Nobel (Nobel Prize in Economics) has been awarded annually since 1969 to scholars who have made significant contributions to the field. Nobel Prize addresses are typically opportunities for the laureates to summarize their work and reflect on their scholarly contributions. They are, however, also opportunities to comment on the state of the economics profession and to offer advice to current and future economists.

It should be noted that while we include only six addresses here, we do not mean to suggest that the other Nobel Laureates in Economics (seventy-six to date at the printing of this volume) have rejected Adam Smith's ideas or have not been influenced by Smith's arguments. We argue, instead, that the six Nobel Laureates in Economics featured here are the ones who most consistently embrace and seek to advance the insights found in Adam Smith. These six addresses also offer serious critiques of the mainstream of the discipline and make an appeal to a return to the mainline.

In chapter 1, "The Pretense of Knowledge," Friedrich August von Hayek discusses his disappointment with the economics profession over its failure to guide public policy in a direction that would have avoided the economic problems of the 1970s as well as as his disappointment with those economists who are more concerned with appearing scientific than actually being scientific.

Hayek, along with Gunnar Myrdal, won the Nobel Prize in Economics in 1974 for "their pioneering work in the theory of money and economic fluctuations and for their penetrating analysis of the interdependence of economic, social and institutional phenomena."[7] The Nobel Committee also highlighted Hayek's work on comparative economic systems, specifically noting his contributions to the inherent problems with central planning and market socialism, and the ability of different economic systems to access, interpret, and utilize decentralized knowledge to solve collective problems.

Rather than using his Nobel address to celebrate his own work or influence, as was by then and would continue to be the typical subject matter of Nobel addresses, Hayek used his address to criticize the economics profession. As Hayek (see page 25) states, "We have indeed at the moment little cause for pride: as a profession we have made a mess of things." He cautions that while economists are often asked to design policies, they must recognize the limits of central planning and interventionism as well as the unintended consequences of tinkering with how people engage in commercial and social activity.

In fact, Hayek chided economists for their hubris. The economist's hubris, Hayek explained, is manifested in a "pretense of knowledge," a pretense that economists can and do know what it is actually impossible for us to know in an effort to imitate and appear on par with the physical sciences. But, given the complexity of the subject matter, the economist can at best attain "true but imperfect knowledge," which might leave "much indetermined and unpredictable" (see page 32). And, economists should acknowledge as much when advising on public policy rather than pretending to have access to an "exact knowledge which is likely to be false" (ibid.). Moreover, as Hayek concludes, "If man is not to do more harm than good in his efforts to improve the social order, he will have to learn that . . . he cannot acquire the full knowledge which would make mastery of the events possible." Ultimately, Hayek argues, economists should remain humble when weighing in on public policy discussions. "The recognition of the insuperable limits to his knowledge," Hayek states, "ought indeed to teach the student of society a lesson of humility which should guard him against becoming an accomplice in men's fatal striving to control society."

In chapter 2, "The Constitution of Economic Policy," James M. Buchanan emphasizes the importance of methodological symmetry when studying both markets and politics, and highlights his intellectual indebtedness to Wicksell.

Buchanan won the Nobel Prize in Economics in 1986 for "his development of the contractual and constitutional bases for the theory of economic and political decision-making."[8] The Nobel Committee recognized Buchanan's contributions to the development of the fields of public choice economics and constitutional political economy, specifically noting his utilization of the tools of economics to examine the political process and his emphasis on the importance of the rules of the game in determining the success or failure of political action.

Buchanan used his Nobel lecture to remind economists that individuals in politics, just as in markets, act purposively, pursue their own interests, and engage in exchange in order to secure the (political) goods and services for themselves or others. As such, economists would do well to heed the guidance of Wicksell. "Stripped to its essentials," Buchanan (see page 44) asserts, "Wicksell's message was clear, elementary, and self-evident. Economists should cease proffering policy advice as if they were employed by a benevolent despot, and they should look to the structure within which political decisions are made."

The nature of the institutions that govern political decision-making and the difference between political and market institutions matter a great deal to Buchanan. For Buchanan, the differences we observe between politics and markets (which we can think of as two games we chose to play) have more to do with the different rules governing action within the two games and less to do with any differences in the players who are attracted to those games. As Buchanan (see page 50) asserts, "The relevant difference between markets and politics does not lie in the kinds of values/interest that persons pursue, but in the conditions under which they pursue their various interests."

Buchanan believes that a focus on the rules of the political process, the processes by which citizens can alter these rules, and the likely consequences of any policy proposal, given the existing or likely institutional environment in which it will be implemented, rather than advocacy of specific policies and interventions, should become the central focus of the political economist. Like Hayek, then, Buchanan (see page 58) argues for a more humble role for the political economist: "Positively, this role involves analysis of the working properties of alternative sets of constraining rules. . . . Normatively, the task for the constitutional political economist is to assist individuals, as citizens who ultimately control their own social order, in their continuing search for those rules of the political game that will best serve their purposes, whatever these might be."

In chapter 3, "The Institutional Structure of Production," Ronald H. Coase discusses the importance of industrial organization theory as well as the role of institutions in shaping social activity.

Coase won the Nobel Prize in Economics in 1991 for "his discovery and clarification of the significance of transaction costs and property rights for the institutional structure and functioning of the economy."[9] Specifically, the Nobel Committee highlighted Coase's introduction of a focus on the costs associated with engaging in exchange and managing organizations into economic analysis as well as his success in explaining the institutional structure of the economy.

Coase, in his Nobel lecture, described modern economics as an attempt to fill in the gaps in Adam Smith's system and to make certain principles in Adam Smith's analysis more exact. As Coase explained (see page 64), "A principal theme of *The Wealth of Nations* was that government regulation or centralized planning were not necessary to make an economic system function in an orderly way. The economy could be coordinated by a system of prices (the 'invisible hand') and, furthermore, with beneficial results. A major task of economists since the publication of *The Wealth of Nations* . . . has been to formalize this proposition of Adam Smith." Coase noted that his contributions, in particular, sought to explain the existence and size of firms by explicitly introducing transaction costs into economics, which in many ways was just an extension of Smith's implicit use of transaction costs when discussing how certain "hindrances to commerce" might exist and could be overcome by the use of money. Additionally, Coase notes that he hoped that his research would highlight the importance of examining legal institutions for economic analysis.

Throughout his address, Coase emphasizes the role of institutions in shaping social activity. Although understanding economic systems and the likely effects of public policy necessitates a focus on institutions, Coase argues that institutions have long been ignored by contemporary economists. There is, Coase (see page 66) explains, a "neglect of the market or more specifically the institutional arrangements which govern the process of exchange. As these institutional arrangements determine to a large extent what is produced, what we have is a very incomplete theory." This neglect, according to Coase, occurred because of the increasing formalization and abstraction of the discipline. "What is studied," Coase (ibid.) laments, "is a system which lives in the minds of economists but not earth.... The firm and the market appear by name but they lack any substance." Coase meant for his research to be a corrective to this trend and describes his work as bringing institutional analysis back into the discipline by contributing to the understanding of the various ways in which individuals overcome transaction costs (through firms, legal structures, and so on). "In fact," Coase (see page 70) argues, "a large part of what we think of as economic activity is designed to accomplish what high transaction costs would otherwise prevent or to reduce transaction costs so that individuals can freely negotiate and we can take of advantage of that diffused knowledge of which Hayek has told us."

Douglass C. North, in chapter 4, "Economic Performance Through Time," argues that neoclassical economics, which neglects the importance of institutions and time, is ill-suited to study economic history and development.

North, along with Robert W. Fogel, won the Nobel Prize in Economics in 1993 for "having renewed research in economic history by applying economic theory and quantitative methods in order to explain economic and institutional change."[10] The Nobel Committee highlighted North's role in pioneering New Institutional Economics and, in particular, his explication of the role of institutions in shaping economic processes as well as his key insights regarding the process of institutional change.

North explained in his address that "neoclassical theory is simply an inappropriate tool to analyze and prescribe policies that will induce development" (see page 81). While the study of economic performance through time must acknowledge that time matters and must account for the role of institutions, neoclassical theory assumes "(i) that institutions don't matter and (ii) that time does not matter" (see page 82). "When applied to economic history and development," North (ibid.) explained, neoclassical theory "focused on technological development and more recently human-capital investment but ignored the incentive structure embodied in institutions that determined the extent of societal investment in those factors."

North, however, advances an approach to studying economic history and development that modifies neoclassical theory to include institutions and to explicitly account for the passage of time. Institutions, North (see page 83) explains, "are the humanly devised constraints that structure human interaction." These include formal constraints (like laws), informal constraints (like social norms), and the mechanisms through which these constraints are enforced. According to North, the institutions "define the incentive structure of societies" (ibid.) as well as explain the "organizations that come into existence" (see page 86). And, it is the interactions between the rules of the game (the institutions) and the players of the game (the organizations) that lead to the "institutional evolution of an economy" (ibid.). Institutional change occurs when the players perceive that they could do better under different rules.

In chapter 5, "Constructivist and Ecological Rationality in Economics," Vernon L. Smith emphasizes the shortcomings of the standard socioeconomic science model of rationality, the limits of constructivism, and the importance of emergent phenomena like norms, traditions, and morality in understanding how social order comes about through the interaction of individuals.

Smith won the Nobel Prize in Economics in 2002, along with Daniel Kahneman, for "having established laboratory experiments as a tool in empirical economic analysis, especially in the study of alternative market mechanisms."[11] The Nobel Committee also recognized Smith's role in developing multiple experimental methods as well as setting standards for examining economic questions in the lab.

In his Nobel address, Smith distinguishes between two types of rational social orders: constructivist rationality and ecological rationality. According to Smith (see page 108), constructivist rationality (what Hayek called constructivism) "uses reason to deliberately create rules of action, and create human socioeconomic institutions that yield outcomes deemed preferable, given particular circumstances, to those produced by alternative arrangements." Contrastingly, ecological rationality (which appreciates emergent order) "uses reason—rational reconstruction— to examine the behavior of individuals based on their experience and folk knowledge, who are 'naive' in their ability to apply constructivist tools to the decisions they make; to understand the emergent order in human cultures; to discover the possible intelligence embodied in the rules, norms, and institutions of our cultural and biological heritage that are created from human interactions but not by deliberate human design" (see pages 110–11).

While we should be proud of the achievements of constructivism, as Smith points out, most institutions and decision-making are guided by ecological rationality rather than constructivist rationality. Most people follow rules that might be tacit. Most people engage in social practices that they might not be able to explain. Understanding this rule following and norm performance is critical to understanding the existence, emergence, and evolution of social order. According to Smith (ibid.), recognizing the importance of the "undesigned ecological system that emerges out of cultural and biological evolutionary processes" is "the intellectual heritage of the Scottish philosophers [including Adam Smith], who described and interpreted the social and economic order they observed." Economic experiments, Smith explains, allow us to explore both how constructed orders are likely to perform as well as the functioning of the "undesigned ecological system."

In chapter 6, "Beyond Markets and States: Polycentric Governance of Complex Economic Systems," Elinor C. Ostrom argues for social science research that appreciates the complexity of polycentric self-governance systems in order to more fully understand how complex human beings live within a variety of institutional arrangements to satisfy their individual goals and work together or fail to work together to solve collective problems.

Ostrom won the Nobel Prize in Economics in 2009, along with Oliver E. Williamson, for "her analysis of economic governance, especially the commons."[12] Specifically, the Nobel Committee highlighted Ostrom's use of fieldwork to study real-world collective action problems, like governing common-pool resources, as well as her efforts to explain how groups overcome those challenges and establish effective governance mechanisms.

Ostrom was dissatisfied with the use of simple constructions that were traditionally used by social scientists. Fortunately, Ostrom (see page 193) explains, "scholars are slowly shifting from positing simple systems to using more complex frameworks, theories, and models to understand the diversity of puzzles and problems facing humans interacting in contemporary societies." She highlights her work on common-pool resources and the ways in which communities find ways to govern, use, and conserve these resources despite clear ownership and exclusion rights. Adopting traditional distinctions between public and private goods, she explains, would not have been adequate for understanding the collective solutions that emerged to deal with this challenge. Through extensive fieldwork and case studies (such as examining forests, fisheries, and water rights management, as well as policing services) throughout the world, however, she discovered a set of design principles for successful common-pool resource management. Such principles include establishing boundaries, appropriation and provision rules, collective choice arrangements regarding rights and rules, monitoring, graduated sanctions, conflict resolution, and nested governance systems.

Ostrom's investigation of these collective efforts to overcome community challenges and her appreciation of the commonalities between successful collective solutions to these problems taught her critical lessons for conducting public policy analysis. One key lesson regards the difficulty of monitoring and the importance of trust in group settings. Another is related to the inadequacy of using simple models to make sense of complex phenomena. And, an additional key lesson speaks to the error of advocating one-size-fits-all solutions to similar but distinct social problems. However, "the most important lesson for public policy analysis derived from the intellectual journey I have outlined here," Ostrom (see page 237) concludes, "is that humans have a more complex motivational structure and more capability to solve social dilemmas than posited in earlier rational-choice theory. . . . Extensive empirical research leads me to argue that instead, a core goal of public policy should be to facilitate the development of institutions that bring out the best in humans."

# Notes

1.   Boettke developed his concept of mainline economics from Kenneth Boulding, who also used the term. Boulding (1971) argued that Adam Smith was a part of the "extended present," that not all of his insights had been incorporated into present-day theories, and so he still has something to teach contemporary readers and researchers. See also Boettke et al. (2014).

2.   Though, at least four of the six authors here (Hayek, Buchanan, Coase, and Smith) have attempted rather deep historical interpretations of Adam Smith and the Scottish Enlightenment as part of their projects. Additionally, North and Ostrom have at least reflected on their connections to Smith.

3.   Smith ([1776] 1981: 16) states, "The labour too which is necessary to produce any one complete manufacture, is almost always divided among a great number of hands. How many different trades are employed in each branch of the linen and woollen manufactures, from the growers of the flax and the wool, to the bleachers and smoothers of the linen, or to the dyers and dressers of the cloth!" And,

> Observe the accommodation of the most common artificer or day-labourer in a civilized and thriving country, and you will perceive that the number of people of whose industry a part, though but a small part, has been employed in procuring him this accommodation, exceeds all computation. The woollen coat, for example, which covers the day-labourer, as coarse and rough as it may appear, is the produce of the joint labour of a great multitude of workmen. The shepherd, the sorter of the wool, the wool-comber or carder, the dyer, the scribbler, the spinner, the weaver, the fuller, the dresser, with many others, must all join their different arts in order to complete even this homely production. How many merchants and carriers, besides, must have been employed in transporting the materials from some of those workmen to others who often live in a very distant part of the country! How much commerce and navigation in particular, how many ship-builders, sailors, sail-makers, rope-makers, must have been employed in order to bring together the different drugs made use of by the dyer, which often come from the remotest corners of the world! What a variety of labour too is necessary in order to produce the tools of the meanest of those workmen! To say nothing of such complicated machines as the ship of the sailor, the mill of the fuller, or even the loom of the weaver, let us consider only what a variety of labour is requisite in order to form that very simple machine, the shears with which the shepherd clips the wool. The miner, the builder of the furnace for smelting the ore, the feller of the timber, the burner of the charcoal to be made use of in the smelting-house, the brick-maker, the brick-layer, the workmen who attend the furnace, the mill-wright, the forger, the smith, must all of them join their different arts in order to produce them. . . . if we examine, I say, all these things, and consider what a variety of labour is employed about each of them, we shall be sensible that without the assistance and co-operation of many thousands, the very meanest person in a civilized country could not be provided, even according to, what we very falsely

imagine, the easy and simple manner in which he is commonly accommodated. (22–23)

Similarly, Leonard E. Read (1958) explored the complicated process of manufacturing another abundant and inexpensive product, the pencil.

4.    According to Smith ([1759] 1982: 213), "The care of the health, of the fortune, of the rank and reputation of the individual, the objects upon which his comfort and happiness in this life are supposed principally to depend, is considered as the proper business of that virtue which is commonly called prudence."

5.    See also Smith's ([1776] 1981: 788) discussion of established churches and religious competition. He argued that competition in religion would lead to more religiosity in society, as preachers would be incentivized to be more effective. As Smith (ibid.: 788) wrote, "The teachers of the doctrine which contains this instruction, in the same manner as other teachers, may either depend altogether for their subsistence upon the voluntary contribution of their hearers; or they may derive it from some other fund to which the law of their country may entitle them; such as a landed estate, a tythe or land tax, an established salary or stipend. Their exertion, their zeal and industry, are likely to be much greater in the former situation than in the latter."

6.    Smith pairs this with a warning against insisting that businesses allow social aims to trump commercial goals. According to Smith ([1776] 1981: 456), "I have never known much good done by those who affected to trade for the public good." Additionally, Smith (ibid.) writes, "The statesman, who should attempt to direct private people in what manner they ought to employ their capitals, would not only load himself with a most unnecessary attention, but assume an authority which could safely be trusted, not only to no single person, but to no council or senate whatever, and which would nowhere be so dangerous as in the hands of a man who had folly and presumption enough to fancy himself fit to exercise it."

7.    "The Prize in Economics 1974—Press Release," *Nobelprize.org,* accessed March 9, 2016, http://www.nobelprize.org/nobel_prizes/economic-sciences/laureates /1974/press.html.

8.    "The Prize in Economics 1986—Press Release," *Nobelprize.org,* accessed March 10, 2016, http://www.nobelprize.org/nobel_prizes/economic-sciences/laureates /1986/press.html.

9.    "The Prize in Economics 1991—Press Release," *Nobelprize.org,* March 10, 2016.    http://www.nobelprize.org/nobel_prizes/economic-sciences/laureates/1991 /press.html.

10.    "The Prize in Economics 1993—Press Release," *Nobelprize.org,* accessed March 10, 2016, http://www.nobelprize.org/nobel_prizes/economic-sciences/laureates /1993/press.html.

11.    "The Sveriges Riksbank Prize in Economic Sciences in Memory of Alfred Nobel 2002," *Nobelprize.org,* accessed March 2, 2016, http://www.nobelprize.org/nobel _prizes/economic-sciences/laureates/2002/.

12.    "The Sveriges Riksbank Prize in Economic Sciences in Memory of Alfred Nobel 2009," *Nobelprize.org,* accessed March 10, 2016, http://www.nobelprize.org/nobel _prizes/economic-sciences/laureates/2009/.

# References

**Boettke, Peter J.** 2012. *Living Economics: Yesterday, Today, and Tomorrow.* Oakland, CA: The Independent Institute.

**Boettke, Peter J., Christopher J. Coyne, and Peter T. Leeson.** 2014. "Earw(h)ig: I Can't Hear You Because Your Ideas Are Old." *Cambridge Journal of Economics* 38: 531–44.

**Boulding, Kenneth E.** 1971. "After Samuelson, Who Needs Adam Smith?" *History of Political Economy*, 3(2): 225–237.

**Lavoie, Don.** 2015. *Rivalry and Central Planning: The Socialist Calculation Debate Reconsidered.* Arlington, VA: Mercatus Center. (Orig. pub. 1985.)

———. 2016. *National Economic Planning: What Is Left?* Arlington, VA: Mercatus Center. (Orig. pub. 1985.)

**Read, Leonard E.** 1958. *I, Pencil: My Family Tree as Told to Leonard E. Read.* Irvington-on-Hudson, NY: The Foundation for Economic Education.

**Smith, Adam.** 1981. *An Inquiry into the Nature and Causes of the Wealth of Nations.* Vols. 1 and 2. Edited by R. H. Campbell and A. S. Skinner. Indianapolis, IN: Liberty Fund. (Orig. pub. 1776.)

———. 1982. *The Theory of Moral Sentiments.* Edited by D. D. Raphael and A. L. Macfie. Indianapolis, IN: Liberty Fund. (Orig. pub. 1759.)

# CHAPTER 1

✵

# F. A. HAYEK

Friedrich August von Hayek won the Sveriges Riksbank Prize in Economic Sciences in Memory of Alfred Nobel in 1974, along with Gunnar Myrdal, for "their pioneering work in the theory of money and economic fluctuations and for their penetrating analysis of the interdependence of economic, social and institutional phenomena." The Nobel Committee recognized Hayek for his profound and original contributions to economic theory, citing in particular his work on business cycles and the effects of monetary and credit policy. In his efforts to provide a more detailed analysis of the monetary mechanisms that give rise to business cycles, it credited Hayek with not only predicting the possibility of a major economic crisis before the economic collapse of 1929 but also connecting those mechanisms to the prevailing discussion of monetary phenomena in the postwar period. The Nobel Committee noted, "Hayek's analysis of the functional efficiency of different economic systems is one of his most significant contributions to economic research," highlighting his work on the problems of central planning and the ineffectiveness of market socialism to make use of the dispersed knowledge possessed by individuals in the market. It further honored Hayek for extending "his field of study to embrace such elements as the legal framework of economic systems and issues concerning the way individuals, organizations, and various social systems function."

# THE PRETENSE of KNOWLEDGE

## F. A. HAYEK

The particular occasion of this lecture, combined with the chief practical problem which economists have to face today, have made the choice of its topic almost inevitable. On the one hand the still recent establishment of the Nobel Memorial Prize in Economic Science marks a significant step in the process by which, in the opinion of the general public, economics has been conceded some of the dignity and prestige of the physical sciences. On the other hand, the economists are at this moment called upon to say how to extricate the free world from the serious threat of accelerating inflation which, it must be admitted, has been brought about by policies which the majority of economists recommended and even urged governments to pursue. We have indeed at the moment little cause for pride: as a profession we have made a mess of things.

It seems to me that this failure of the economists to guide policy more successfully is closely connected with their propensity to imitate as closely as possible the procedures of the brilliantly successful physical sciences—an attempt which in our field may lead to outright error. It is an approach which has come to be described as the "scientistic" attitude—an attitude which, as I defined it some thirty years ago, "is decidedly unscientific in the true sense of the word, since it involves a mechanical and uncritical application of habits of thought to fields different from those in which they have been formed."[1] I want today to begin by explaining how some of the gravest errors of recent economic policy are a direct consequence of this scientistic error.

The theory which has been guiding monetary and financial policy during the last thirty years, and which I contend is largely the product of such a mistaken conception of the proper scientific procedure, consists in the assertion that there exists a simple positive correlation between total employment and the size of the aggregate demand for goods and services; it leads to the belief that we can permanently assure full employment by maintaining total money expenditure at an appropriate level. Among the various theories advanced to account for extensive unemployment, this is probably the only one in support of which strong quantitative evidence can be adduced. I nevertheless regard it as fundamentally false, and to act upon it, as we now experience, as very harmful.

This brings me to the crucial issue. Unlike the position that exists in the physical sciences, in economics and other disciplines that deal with essentially complex phenomena, the aspects of the events to be accounted for about which we can get quantitative data are necessarily limited and may not include the important ones. While in the physical sciences it is generally assumed, probably with good reason, that any important factor which determines the observed events will itself be directly observable and measurable, in the study of such complex phenomena as the market, which depend on the actions of many individuals, all the circumstances which will determine the outcome of a process, for reasons which I shall explain later, will hardly ever be fully known or measurable. And while in the physical sciences the investigator will be able to measure what, on the basis of a *prima facie* theory, he thinks important, in the social sciences often that is treated as important which happens to be accessible to measurement. This is sometimes carried to the point where it is demanded that our theories must be formulated in such terms that they refer only to measurable magnitudes.

It can hardly be denied that such a demand quite arbitrarily limits the facts which are to be admitted as possible causes of the events which occur in the real world. This view, which is often quite naively accepted as required by scientific procedure, has some rather paradoxical consequences. We know, of course, with regard to the market and similar social structures, a great many facts which we cannot measure and on which indeed we have only some very imprecise and general information. And because the effects of these facts in any particular instance cannot be confirmed by quantitative evidence, they are simply disregarded by those sworn to admit only what they regard as scientific evidence: they thereupon happily proceed on the fiction that the factors which they can measure are the only ones that are relevant.

The correlation between aggregate demand and total employment, for instance, may only be approximate, but as it is the *only* one on which we have quantitative data, it is accepted as the only causal connection that counts. On this standard there may thus well exist better "scientific" evidence for a false theory, which will be accepted because it is more "scientific," than for a valid explanation, which is rejected because there is no sufficient quantitative evidence for it.

Let me illustrate this by a brief sketch of what I regard as the chief actual cause of extensive unemployment—an account which will also explain why such unemployment cannot be lastingly cured by the inflationary policies recommended by the now fashionable theory. This correct explanation appears to me to be the existence of discrepancies between the distribution of demand among the different goods and services and the allocation of labor and other resources among the production of those outputs. We possess a fairly good "qualitative" knowledge of the forces by which a correspondence between demand and supply in the different sectors of the economic system is brought about, of the conditions under which it will be achieved, and of the factors likely to prevent such an adjustment. The separate steps in the account of this process rely on facts of everyday experience, and few who take the trouble to follow the argument will question the validity of the factual assumptions, or the logical correctness of the conclusions drawn from them. We have indeed good reason to believe that unemployment indicates that the structure of relative prices and wages has been distorted (usually by monopolistic or governmental price fixing), and that to restore equality between the demand and the supply of labor in all sectors changes of relative prices and some transfers of labor will be necessary.

But when we are asked for quantitative evidence for the particular structure of prices and wages that would be required in order to assure a smooth continuous sale of the products and services offered, we must admit that we have no such information. We know, in other words, the general conditions in which what we call, somewhat misleadingly, an equilibrium will establish itself: but we never know what the particular prices or wages are which would exist if the market were to bring about such an equilibrium. We can merely say what the conditions are in which we can expect the market to establish prices and wages at which demand will equal supply. But we can never produce statistical information which would show how much the prevailing prices and wages *deviate* from those which would secure a continuous sale of the current supply of labor. Though this account of the causes of unemployment is an empirical theory, in the sense that it might be proved false, e.g. if, with a constant money supply, a general increase of wages did not lead to unemployment, it is certainly not the kind of theory which we could use to obtain specific numerical predictions concerning the rates of wages, or the distribution of labor, to be expected.

Why should we, however, in economics, have to plead ignorance of the sort of facts on which, in the case of a physical theory, a scientist would certainly be expected to give precise information? It is probably not surprising that those impressed by the example of the physical sciences should find this position very unsatisfactory and should insist on the standards of proof which they find there. The reason for this state of affairs is the fact, to which I have already briefly referred, that the social sciences, like much of biology but unlike most fields of the physical sciences, have to deal with structures of *essential* complexity, i.e. with structures whose characteristic properties can be exhibited only by models made up of relatively large numbers of variables. Competition, for instance, is a process which will produce certain results only if it proceeds among a fairly large number of acting persons.

In some fields, particularly where problems of a similar kind arise in the physical sciences, the difficulties can be overcome by using, instead of specific information about the individual elements, data about the relative frequency, or the probability, of the occurrence of the various distinctive properties of the elements. But this is true only where we have to deal with what has been called by Dr. Warren Weaver (formerly of the Rockefeller Foundation), with a distinction which ought to be much more widely understood, "phenomena of unorganized complexity," in contrast to those "phenomena of organized complexity" with which we have to deal in the social sciences.[2] Organized complexity here means that the character of the structures showing it depends not only on the properties of the individual elements of which they are composed, and the relative frequency with which they occur, but also on the manner in which the individual elements are connected with each other. In the explanation of the working of such structures we can for this reason not replace the information about the individual elements by statistical information, but require full information about each element if from our theory we are to derive specific predictions about individual events. Without such specific information about the individual elements we shall be confined to what on another occasion I have called mere pattern predictions—predictions of some of the general attributes of the structures that will form themselves, but not containing specific statements about the individual elements of which the structures will be made up.[3]

This is particularly true of our theories accounting for the determination of the systems of relative prices and wages that will form themselves on a well-functioning market. Into the determination of these prices and wages there will enter the effects of particular information possessed by every one of the participants in the market process—a sum of facts which in their totality cannot be known to the scientific observer, or to any other single brain. It is indeed the source of the superiority of the market order, and the reason why, when it is not suppressed by the powers of government, it regularly displaces other types of order, that in the resulting allocation of resources more of the knowledge of particular facts will be utilized which exists only dispersed among uncounted persons, than any one person can possess. But because we, the observing scientists, can thus never know all the determinants of such an order, and in consequence also cannot know at which particular structure of prices and wages demand would everywhere equal supply, we also cannot measure the deviations from that order; nor can we statistically test our theory that it is the deviations from that "equilibrium" system of prices and wages which make it impossible to sell some of the products and services at the prices at which they are offered.

Before I continue with my immediate concern, the effects of all this on the employment policies currently pursued, allow me to define more specifically the inherent limitations of our numerical knowledge which are so often overlooked. I want to do this to avoid giving the impression that I generally reject the mathematical method in economics. I regard it in fact as the great advantage of the mathematical technique that it allows us to describe, by means of algebraic equations, the general character of a pattern even where we are ignorant of the numerical values which will determine its particular manifestation. We could scarcely have achieved that comprehensive picture of the mutual interdependencies of the different events in a market without this algebraic technique. It has led to the illusion, however, that we can use this technique for the determination and prediction of the numerical values of those magnitudes; and this has led to a vain search for quantitative or numerical constants. This happened in spite of the fact that the modern founders of mathematical economics had no such illusions. It is true that their systems of equations describing the pattern of a market equilibrium are so framed that *if* we were able to fill in all the blanks of the abstract formulae, i.e., *if* we knew all the parameters of these equations, we could calculate the prices and quantities of all commodities and services sold. But, as Vilfredo Pareto, one of the founders of this theory, clearly stated, its purpose cannot be "to arrive at a numerical calculation of prices," because, as he said, it would be "absurd" to assume that we could ascertain all the data.[4] Indeed, the chief point was already seen by those remarkable anticipators of modern economics, the Spanish schoolmen of the sixteenth century, who emphasized that what they called *pretium mathematicum*, the mathematical price, depended on so many particular circumstances that it could never be known to man but was known only to God.[5] I sometimes wish that our mathematical economists would take this to heart. I must confess that I still doubt whether their search for measurable magnitudes has made significant contributions to our *theoretical* understanding of economic phenomena—as distinct from their value as a description of particular situations. Nor am I prepared to accept the excuse that this branch of research is still very young: Sir William Petty, the founder of economet-rics, was after all a somewhat senior colleague of Sir Isaac Newton in the Royal Society!

There may be few instances in which the superstition that only mea-surable magnitudes can be important has done positive harm in the economic field: but the present inflation and employment problems are a very serious one. Its effect has been that what is probably the true cause of extensive unemployment has been disregarded by the scien-tistically minded majority of economists, because its operation could not be confirmed by directly observable relations between measurable magnitudes, and that an almost exclusive concentration on quantita-tively measurable surface phenomena has produced a policy which has made matters worse.

It has, of course, to be readily admitted that the kind of theory which I regard as the true explanation of unemployment is a theory of somewhat limited content because it allows us to make only very gen-eral predictions of the *kind* of events which we must expect in a given situation. But the effects on policy of the more ambitious constructions have not been very fortunate and I confess that I prefer true but imper-fect knowledge, even if it leaves much indetermined and unpredictable, to a pretense of exact knowledge that is likely to be false. The credit which the apparent conformity with recognized scientific standards can gain for seemingly simple but false theories may, as the present instance shows, have grave consequences.

In fact, in the case discussed, the very measures which the dominant "macro-economic" theory has recommended as a remedy for unem-ployment, namely the increase of aggregate demand, have become a cause of a very extensive misallocation of resources which is likely to make later large-scale unemployment inevitable. The continuous injection of additional amounts of money at points of the economic system where it creates a temporary demand which must cease when the increase of the quantity of money stops or slows down, together with the expectation of a continuing rise of prices, draws labor and other resources into employments which can last only so long as the increase of the quantity of money continues at the same rate—or perhaps even only so long as it continues to accelerate at a given rate. What this policy has produced is not so much a level of employment that could not have been brought about in other ways, as a distribution of employment which cannot be indefinitely maintained and which after some time can be maintained only by a rate of inflation which would rapidly lead to a disorganization of all economic activity. The fact is that by a mistaken theoretical view we have been led into a precarious position in which we cannot prevent substantial unemployment from reappearing; not because, as this view is sometimes misrepresented, this unemployment is deliberately brought about as a means to combat inflation, but because it is now bound to occur as a deeply regrettable but inescapable consequence of the mistaken policies of the past as soon as inflation ceases to accelerate.

I must, however, now leave these problems of immediate practical importance which I have introduced chiefly as an illustration of the momentous consequences that may follow from errors concerning abstract problems of the philosophy of science. There is as much reason to be apprehensive about the long run dangers created in a much wider field by the uncritical acceptance of assertions which have the *appearance* of being scientific as there is with regard to the problems I have just discussed. What I mainly wanted to bring out by the topical illustration is that certainly in my field, but I believe also generally in the sciences of man, what looks superficially like the most scientific procedure is often the most unscientific, and, beyond this, that in these fields there are definite limits to what we can expect science to achieve. This means that to entrust to science—or to deliberate control according to scientific principles—more than the scientific method can achieve may have deplorable effects. The progress of the natural sciences in modern times has of course so much exceeded all expectations that any suggestion that there may be some limits to it is bound to arouse suspicion. Especially all those will resist such an insight who have hoped that our increasing power of prediction and control, generally regarded as the characteristic result of scientific advance, applied to the processes of society, would soon enable us to mold society entirely to our liking. It is indeed true that, in contrast to the exhilaration which the discoveries of the physical sciences tend to produce, the insights which we gain from the study of society more often have a dampening effect on our aspirations; and it is perhaps not surprising that the more impetuous younger members of our profession are not always prepared to accept this. Yet the confidence in the unlimited power of science is only too often based on a false belief that the scientific method consists in the application of a ready-made technique, or in imitating the form rather than the substance of scientific procedure, as if one needed only to follow some cooking recipes to solve all social problems. It sometimes almost seems as if the techniques of science were more easily learnt than the thinking that shows us what the problems are and how to approach them.

The conflict between what in its present mood the public expects science to achieve in satisfaction of popular hopes and what is really in its power is a serious matter because, even if the true scientists should all recognize the limitations of what they can do in the field of human affairs, so long as the public expects more there will always be some who will pretend, and perhaps honestly believe, that they can do more to meet popular demands than is really in their power. It is often difficult enough for the expert, and certainly in many instances impossible for the layman, to distinguish between legitimate and illegitimate claims advanced in the name of science. The enormous publicity recently given by the media to a report pronouncing in the name of science on *The Limits to Growth*, and the silence of the same media about the devastating criticism this report has received from the competent experts[6] must make one feel somewhat apprehensive about the use to which the prestige of science can be put. But it is by no means only in the field of economics that far-reaching claims are made on behalf of a more scientific direction of all human activities and the desirability of replacing spontaneous processes by "conscious human control." If I am not mistaken, psychology, psychiatry and some branches of sociology, not to speak about the so-called philosophy of history, are even more affected by what I have called the scientistic prejudice, and by specious claims of what science can achieve.[7]

If we are to safeguard the reputation of science, and to prevent the arrogation of knowledge based on a superficial similarity of procedure with that of the physical sciences, much effort will have to be directed toward debunking such arrogations, some of which have by now become the vested interests of established university departments. We cannot be grateful enough to such modern philosophers of science as Sir Karl Popper for giving us a test by which we can distinguish between what we may accept as scientific and what not—a test which I am sure some doctrines now widely accepted as scientific would not pass. There are some special problems, however, in connection with those essentially complex phenomena of which social structures are so important an instance, which make me wish to restate in conclusion in more general terms the reasons why in these fields not only are there only absolute obstacles to the prediction of specific events, but why to act as if we possessed scientific knowledge enabling us to transcend them may itself become a serious obstacle to the advance of the human intellect.

The chief point we must remember is that the great and rapid advance of the physical sciences took place in fields where it proved that explanation and prediction could be based on laws which accounted for the observed phenomena as functions of comparatively few variables—either particular facts or relative frequencies of events. This may even be the ultimate reason why we single out these realms as "physical" in contrast to those more highly organized structures which I have here called essentially complex phenomena. There is no reason why the position must be the same in the latter as in the former fields. The difficulties which we encounter in the latter are not, as one might at first suspect, difficulties about formulating theories for the explanation of the observed events—although they cause also special difficulties about testing proposed explanations and therefore about eliminating bad theories. They are due to the chief problem which arises when we apply our theories to any particular situation in the real world. A theory of essentially complex phenomena must refer to a large number of particular facts; and to derive a prediction from it, or to test it, we have to ascertain all these particular facts. Once we succeeded in this there should be no particular difficulty about deriving testable predictions—with the help of modern computers it should be easy enough to insert these data into the appropriate blanks of the theoretical formulae and to derive a prediction. The real difficulty, to the solution of which science has little to contribute, and which is sometimes indeed insoluble, consists in the ascertainment of the particular facts.

A simple example will show the nature of this difficulty. Consider some ball game played by a few people of approximately equal skill. If we knew a few particular facts in addition to our general knowledge of the ability of the individual players, such as their state of attention, their perceptions and the state of their hearts, lungs, muscles, etc. at each moment of the game, we could probably predict the outcome. Indeed, if we were familiar both with the game and the teams we should probably have a fairly shrewd idea on what the outcome will depend. But we shall of course not be able to ascertain those facts and in consequence the result of the game will be outside the range of the scientifically predictable, however well we may know what effects particular events would have on the result of the game. This does not mean that we can make no predictions at all about the course of such a game. If we know the rules of the different games we shall, in watching one, very soon know which game is being played and what kinds of actions we can expect and what kind not. But our capacity to predict will be confined to such general characteristics of the events to be expected and not include the capacity of predicting particular individual events.

This corresponds to what I have called earlier the mere pattern predictions to which we are increasingly confined as we penetrate from the realm in which relatively simple laws prevail into the range of phenomena where organized complexity rules. As we advance we find more and more frequently that we can in fact ascertain only some but not all the particular circumstances which determine the outcome of a given process; and in consequence we are able to predict only some but not all the properties of the result we have to expect. Often all that we shall be able to predict will be some abstract characteristic of the pattern that will appear—relations between kinds of elements about which individually we know very little. Yet, as I am anxious to repeat, we will still achieve predictions which can be falsified and which therefore are of empirical significance.

Of course, compared with the precise predictions we have learnt to expect in the physical sciences, this sort of mere pattern predictions is a second best with which one does not like to have to be content. Yet the danger of which I want to warn is precisely the belief that in order to have a claim to be accepted as scientific it is necessary to achieve more. This way lies charlatanism and worse. To act on the belief that we possess the knowledge and the power which enable us to shape the processes of society entirely to our liking, knowledge which in fact we do *not* possess, is likely to make us do much harm. In the physical sciences there may be little objection to trying to do the impossible; one might even feel that one ought not to discourage the over-confident because their experiments may after all produce some new insights. But in the social field the erroneous belief that the exercise of some power would have beneficial consequences is likely to lead to a new power to coerce other men being conferred on some authority. Even if such power is not in itself bad, its exercise is likely to impede the functioning of those spontaneous ordering forces by which, without understanding them, man is in fact so largely assisted in the pursuit of his aims. We are only beginning to understand on how subtle a communication system the functioning of an advanced industrial society is based—a communications system which we call the market and which turns out to be a more efficient mechanism for digesting dispersed information than any that man has deliberately designed.

If man is not to do more harm than good in his efforts to improve the social order, he will have to learn that in this, as in all other fields where essential complexity of an organized kind prevails, he cannot acquire the full knowledge which would make mastery of the events possible. He will therefore have to use what knowledge he can achieve, not to shape the results as the craftsman shapes his handiwork, but rather to cultivate a growth by providing the appropriate environment, in the manner in which the gardener does this for his plants. There is danger in the exuberant feeling of ever growing power which the advance of the physical sciences has engendered and which tempts man to try, "dizzy with success," to use a characteristic phrase of early communism, to subject not only our natural but also our human environment to the control of a human will. The recognition of the insuperable limits to his knowledge ought indeed to teach the student of society a lesson of humility which should guard him against becoming an accomplice in men's fatal striving to control society—a striving which makes him not only a tyrant over his fellows, but which may well make him the destroyer of a civilization which no brain has designed but which has grown from the free efforts of millions of individuals.

## Notes

1. "Scientism and the Study of Society," *Economica*, vol. IX, no. 35, August 1942, reprinted in *The Counter-Revolution of Science*, Glencoe, Ill., 1952, p. 15 of this reprint.

2. Warren Weaver, "A Quarter Century in the Natural Sciences," *The Rockefeller Foundation Annual Report 1958*, chapter 1, "Science and Complexity."

3. See my essay "The Theory of Complex Phenomena" in *The Critical Approach to Science and Philosophy. Essays in Honor of K. R. Popper,* ed. M. Bunge, New York 1964, and reprinted (with additions) in my *Studies in Philosophy, Politics and Economics*, London and Chicago 1967.

4. V. Pareto, *Manuel d'economie politique*, 2nd. ed., Paris 1927, pp. 223–4.

5. See, e.g., Luis Molina, *De iustitia et iure*, Cologne 1596–1600, tom. II, disp. 347, no. 3, and particularly Johannes de Lugo, *Disputationum de lustitia et iure tomus secundus*, Lyon 1642, disp. 26, sect. 4, no. 40.

6. See *The Limits to Growth: A Report of the Club of Rome's Project on the Predicament of Mankind*, New York 1972; for a systematic examination of this by a competent economist cf. Wilfred Beckerman, *In Defence of Economic Growth*, London 1974, and, for a list of earlier criticisms by experts, Gottfried Haberler, *Economic Growth and Stability*, Los Angeles 1974, who rightly calls their effect "devastating."

7. I have given some illustrations of these tendencies in other fields in my inaugural lecture as Visiting Professor at the University of Salzburg, *Die Irrtumer des Konstruktivismus und die Grundlagen legitimer Kritik gesellschaftlicher Gebilde*, Munich 1970, now re-issued for the Walter Eucken Institute, at Freiburg i.Brg. by J. C. B. Mohr, Tubingen 1975.

# CHAPTER 2

✳

# JAMES M. BUCHANAN

James M. Buchanan won the Sveriges Riksbank Prize in Economic Sciences in Memory of Alfred Nobel in 1986 for "his development of the contractual and constitutional bases for the theory of economic and political decision-making." He was recognized by the Nobel Committee for his leading role in the development of public choice theory, which applied economic analysis to political decision-making. Filling this lacuna in traditional economic analysis, Buchanan revealed the important role that "the rules of the game" (i.e., constitutional rules) play in determining political outcomes. He explored not only how rules succeed or fail in aligning the incentives of political decision makers to act in accordance with socially desirable outcomes but also how the voluntary adoption of these rules can be instituted. "Buchanan's foremost achievement," the Nobel Committee noted, "is that he has consistently and tenaciously emphasized the significance of fundamental rules and applied the concept of the political system as an exchange process for the achievement of mutual advantages." It further acknowledged that "developments over the last few decades have confirmed Buchanan's realistic view of the scope of economic policy and the importance of continuously reconsidering fundamental rules of the game, while retaining stable rules."

# THE CONSTITUTION *of* ECONOMIC POLICY

## JAMES M. BUCHANAN

---

## I. Introduction

The science of public finance should always keep . . . political
conditions clearly in mind. Instead of expecting guidance from
a doctrine of taxation that is based on the political philosophy of by-gone ages, it should instead endeavor to unlock the
mysteries of the spirit of progress and development.

—WICKSELL, P. 87[1]

On this of all occasions I should be remiss if I failed to acknowledge the influence of that great Swede, Knut Wicksell, on my
own work, an influence without which I should not be making this
presentation. Many of my contributions, and especially those in political economy and fiscal theory, might be described as varied reiterations,
elaborations, and extensions of Wicksellian themes; this paper is no
exception.

One of the most exciting intellectual moments of my career was
my 1948 discovery of Wicksell's unknown and untranslated dissertation, *Finanztheoretische Untersuchungen* (1896), buried in the dusty stacks

of Chicago's old Harper Library. Only the immediate postdissertation leisure of an academic novice allowed for the browsing that produced my own dramatic example of learning by serendipity. Wicksell's new principle of justice in taxation gave me a tremendous surge of self-confidence. Wicksell, who was an established figure in the history of economic ideas, challenged the orthodoxy of public finance theory along lines that were congenial with my own developing stream of critical consciousness. From that moment in Chicago, I took on the determination to make Wicksell's contribution known to a wider audience, and I commenced immediately a translation effort that took some time, and considerable help from Elizabeth Henderson, before final publication.

Stripped to its essentials, Wicksell's message was clear, elementary, and self-evident. Economists should cease proffering policy advice as if they were employed by a benevolent despot, and they should look to the structure within which political decisions are made. Armed with Wicksell, I, too, could dare to challenge the still-dominant orthodoxy in public finance and welfare economics. In a preliminary paper (1949), I called upon my fellow economists to postulate some model of the state, of politics, before proceeding to analyze the effects of alternative policy measures. I urged economists to look at the "constitution of economic policy," to examine the rules, the constraints within which political agents act. Like Wicksell, my purpose was ultimately normative rather than antiseptically scientific. I sought to make economic sense out of the relationship between the individual and the state before proceeding to advance policy nostrums.

Wicksell deserves the designation as the most important precursor of modern public choice theory because we find, in his 1896 dissertation, all three of the constitutive elements that provide the foundations of this theory: methodological individualism, *homo economicus*, and politics-as-exchange. I shall discuss these elements of analytical structure in the sections that follow. In Section V, I integrate these elements in a theory of economic policy. This theory is consistent with, builds upon, and systematically extends the traditionally accepted principles of Western liberal societies. The implied approach to institutional-constitutional reform continues, however, to be stubbornly resisted almost a century after Wicksell's seminal efforts. The individual's relation to the state, is, of course, the central subject matter of political philosophy. Any effort by economists to shed light on this relationship must be placed within this more comprehensive realm of discourse; a summary effort is contained in Section VI.

## II. Methodological Individualism

> If utility is zero for each individual member of the community, the total utility for the community cannot be other than zero.
>
> —WICKSELL, P. 77

The economist rarely examines the presuppositions of the models with which he works. The economist simply commences with individuals as evaluating, choosing, and acting units. Regardless of the possible complexity of the processes or institutional structures from which outcomes emerge, the economist focuses on individual choices. In application to market or private-sector interactions, this procedure is seldom challenged. Individuals, as buyers and sellers of ordinary (legally tradable) goods and services are presumed able to choose in accordance with their own preferences, whatever these may be, and the economist does not feel himself obliged to inquire deeply into the content of these preferences (the arguments in individuals' utility functions). Individuals themselves are the sources of evaluation, and the economist's task is to offer an explanation-understanding of the process through which these unexamined preferences are ultimately translated into a complex outcome pattern.

The eighteenth-century discovery that, in an institutional framework that facilitates voluntary exchanges among individuals, this process generates results that might be evaluated positively, produced "economics," as an independent academic discipline or science. The relationship between the positively valued results of market processes and the institutional characteristics of these processes themselves emerged as a source of ambiguity when "the market" came to be interpreted functionally, as if something called "the economy" existed for the purpose of value maximization. Efficiency in the allocation of resources came to be defined independently of the processes through which individual choices are exercised.

Given this subtle shift toward a teleological interpretation of the economic process, it is not surprising that politics, or governmental process, was similarly interpreted. Furthermore, a teleological interpretation of politics had been, for centuries, the dominating thrust of political theory and political philosophy. The interpretations of "the economy" and "the polity" seemed, therefore, to be mutually compatible in the absence of inquiry into the fundamental difference in the point of evaluation. There was a failure to recognize that individuals who choose and act in the market generate outcomes that, under the specified constraints, can be judged to be value maximizing for participating individuals, *without* the necessity of introducing an external evaluative criterion. The nature of the process itself insures that individual values are maximized. This "value-maximization" perspective cannot be extended from the market to politics since the latter does not directly embody the incentive compatible structure of the former. There is no political counterpart to Adam Smith's invisible hand. It is not, therefore, surprising that the attempt by Wicksell and other continental European scholars to extend economic theory to the operation of the public sector remained undeveloped for so many years.

An economic theory that remains essentially individualistic need not have become trapped in such a methodological straitjacket. If the maximization exercise is restricted to explanation-understanding of the individual who makes choices, and without extension to the economy as an aggregation, there is no difficulty at all in analyzing individual choice behavior under differing institutional settings, and in predicting how these varying settings will influence the outcomes of the interaction processes. The individual who chooses between apples and oranges remains the same person who chooses between the levers marked "Candidate A" and "Candidate B" in the polling booth. Clearly, the differing institutional structures may, themselves, affect choice behavior. Much of modern public choice theory explains these relationships. But my point here is the more basic one to the effect that the choice behavior of the individual is equally subject to the application of analysis in all choice environments. Comparative analysis should allow for predictions of possible differences in the characteristics of the results that emerge from market and political structures of interaction. These predictions, as well as the analysis from which they are generated, are totally devoid of normative content.

## III. *Homo Economicus*

... [N]either the executive nor the legislative body, and even less the deciding majority in the latter, are in reality ... what the ruling theory tells us they should be. They are not pure organs of the community with no thought other than to promote the common weal.

> ... [M]embers of the representative body are, in the over-
> whelming majority of cases, precisely as interested in the general
> welfare as are their constituents, neither more nor less.
>
> —WICKSELL, PP. 86, 87

This analysis can yield a limited set of potentially falsifiable hypotheses without prior specification of the arguments in individual utility functions. If, however, predictions are sought concerning the effects of shifts in constraints on choice behavior, some identification and signing of these arguments must be made. With this step, more extensive falsifiable propositions may be advanced. For example, if both apples and oranges are positively valued "goods," then, if the price of apples falls relative to that of oranges, more apples will be purchased relative to oranges; if income is a positively valued "good," and, then, if the marginal rate of tax on income source $A$ increases relative to that on income source $B$, more effort at earning income will be shifted to source $B$; if charitable giving is a positively valued "good," then, if charitable gifts are made tax deductible, more giving will be predicted to occur; if pecuniary rents are positively valued, then, if a political agent's discretionary power to distribute rents increases, individuals hoping to secure these rents will invest more resources in attempts to influence the agent's decisions. Note that the identification and signing of the arguments in the utility functions takes us a considerable way toward operationalization without prior specification of the relative weights of the separate arguments. There is no need to assign net wealth or net income a dominating motivational influence on behavior in order to produce a fully operational economic theory of choice behavior, in market or political interaction.

In any extension of the model of individual rational behavior to politics, this difference between the identification and signing of arguments on the one hand and the weighting of these arguments on the other deserves further attention. Many critics of the "economic theory of politics" base their criticisms on the presumption that such theory necessarily embodies the hypothesis of net wealth maximization, an hypothesis that they observe to be falsified in many situations. Overly zealous users of this theory may have sometimes offered grounds for such misinterpretation on the part of critics. The minimal critical assumption for the explanatory power of the economic theory of politics is only that identifiable economic self-interest (for example, net wealth, income, social position) is a positively valued "good" to the individual who chooses. This assumption does not place economic interest in a dominating position and it surely does not imply imputing evil or malicious motives to political actors; in this respect the theory remains on all fours with the motivational structure of the standard economic theory of market behavior. The differences in the predicted results stemming from market and political interaction stem from differences in the structures of these two institutional settings rather than from any switch in the motives of persons as they move between institutional roles.

## IV. Politics as Exchange

> It would seem to be a blatant injustice if someone should be forced to contribute toward the costs of some activity which does not further his interests or may even be diametrically opposed to them. —WICKSELL, P. 89

Individuals choose, and as they do so, identifiable economic interest is one of the "goods" that they value positively, whether behavior takes place in markets or in politics. But markets are institutions of *exchange*; persons enter markets to exchange one thing for another. They do not enter markets to further some supra-exchange or supra-individualistic result. Markets are not motivationally functional; there is no conscious sense on the part of individual choosers that some preferred aggregate outcome, some overall "allocation" or "distribution," will emerge from the process.

The extension of this exchange conceptualization to politics counters the classical prejudice that persons participate in politics through some common search for the good, the true, and the beautiful, with these ideals being defined independently of the values of the participants as these might or might not be expressed by behavior. Politics, in this vision of political philosophy, is instrumental to the furtherance of these larger goals.

Wicksell, who is followed in this respect by modern public choice theorists, would have none of this. The relevant difference between markets and politics does not lie in the kinds of values/interest that persons pursue, but in the conditions under which they pursue their various interests. Politics is a structure of complex exchange among individuals, a structure within which persons seek to secure collectively their own privately defined objectives that cannot be efficiently secured through simple market exchanges. In the absence of individual interest, there is no interest. In the market, individuals exchange apples for oranges; in politics, individuals exchange agreed-on shares in contributions toward the costs of that which is commonly desired, from the services of the local fire station to that of the judge.

This ultimately voluntary basis for political agreement also counters the emphasis on politics as power that characterizes much modern analysis. The observed presence of coercive elements in the activity of the state seems difficult to reconcile with the model of voluntary exchange among individuals. We may, however, ask: Coercion to what purpose? Why must individuals subject themselves to the coercion inherent in collective action? The answer is evident. Individuals acquiesce in the coercion of the state, of politics, only if the ultimate constitutional "exchange" furthers their interests. Without some model of exchange, no coercion of the individual by the state is consistent with the individualistic value norm upon which a liberal social order is grounded.

## V. The Constitution of Economic Policy

... [W]hether the benefits of the proposed activity to the individual citizens would be greater than its cost to them, no one can judge this better than the individuals themselves.

—WICKSELL, P. 79

The exchange conceptualization of politics is important in the derivation of a normative theory of economic policy. Improvement in the workings of politics is measured in terms of the satisfaction of that which is desired by individuals, whatever this may be, rather than in terms of moving closer to some externally defined, supra-individualistic ideal. That which is desired by individuals may, of course, be common for many persons, and, indeed, the difference between market exchange and political exchange lies in the sharing of objectives in the latter. The idealized agreement on the objectives of politics does not, however, allow for any supersession of individual evaluation. Agreement itself emerges, again conceptually, from the revealed choice behavior of individuals. Commonly shared agreement must be carefully distinguished from any externally defined definition or description of that "good" upon which persons "should agree."

The restrictive implications for a normative theory of economic policy are severe. There is no criterion through which policy may be directly evaluated. An indirect evaluation may be based on some measure of the degree to which the political process facilitates the translation of expressed individual preferences into observed political outcomes. The focus of evaluative attention becomes the process itself, as contrasted with end-state or outcome patterns. "Improvement" must, therefore, be sought in reforms in process, in institutional change that will allow the operation of politics to mirror more accurately that set of results that are preferred by those who participate. One way of stating the difference between the Wicksellian approach and that which is still orthodoxy in normative economics is to say that the *constitution* of policy rather than policy itself becomes the relevant object for reform. A simple game analogy illustrates the difference here. The Wicksellian approach concentrates on reform in the rules, which may be in the potential interest of *all* players, as opposed to improvement in strategies of play for particular players within defined or existing rules.

In the standard theory of choice in markets, there is little or no concern with the constitution of the choice environment. We simply presume that the individual is able to implement his preferences; if he wants to purchase an orange, we presume that he can do so. There is no institutional barrier between the revealed expression of preference and direct satisfaction. Breakdown or failure in the market emerges, not in the translation of individual preferences into outcomes, but in the possible presentation of some choosers with alternatives that do not correspond to those faced by others in the exchange nexus. "Efficiency" in market interaction is insured if the participants are faced with the same choice options.

In political exchange, there is no decentralized process that allows "efficiency" to be evaluated deontologically, akin to the evaluation of a market. Individuals cannot, by the nature of the goods that are collectively "purchased" in politics, adjust their own behavior to common terms of trade. The political analogue to decentralized trading among individuals must be that feature common over all exchanges, which is *agreement* among the individuals who participate. The unanimity rule for collective choice is the political analog to freedom of exchange of partitionable goods in markets.

It is possible, therefore, to evaluate politics independently of results only by ascertaining the degree of correspondence between the rules of reaching decisions and the unique rule that would guarantee "efficiency," that of unanimity or agreement among all participants. If, then, "efficiency" is acknowledged to be the desired criterion, again as interpreted here, normative improvement in process is measured by movement toward the unanimity requirement. It is perhaps useful to note, at this point, that Wicksell's own characterization of his proposals in terms of "justice" rather than "efficiency" suggests the precise correspondence of these two norms in the context of voluntary exchange.

Politics as observed remains, of course, far from the idealized collective-cooperative exchange that the unanimity rule would implement. The political equivalent to transactions cost makes the pursuit of idealized "efficiency" seem even more out of the bounds of reason than the analogous pursuit in markets. But barriers to realization of the ideal do not imply rejection of the benchmark definition of the ideal itself. Instead, such barriers are themselves incorporated into a generalized "calculus of consent."

Wicksell himself did not go beyond advocacy of reform in legislative decision structures. He proposed a required linking of spending and financing decisions, and he proposed that a quasi-unanimity rule be introduced for noncommitted outlays. Wicksell did not consciously extend his analysis to constitutional choice, to the choice of the rules within which ordinary politics is to be allowed to operate. His suggested reforms were, of course, constitutional, since they were aimed to improve the process of decision-making. But his evaluative criterion was restricted to the matching of individual preferences with political outcomes in particularized decisions, rather than over any sequence.

It is perhaps worth noting that Wicksell himself did not look upon his suggested procedural reforms as restrictive. By introducing greater flexibility into the tax-share structure, Wicksell predicted the potential approval of spending programs that would continue to be rejected under rigid taxing arrangements. Critics have, however, interpreted the Wicksellian unanimity constraint to be restrictive, and especially as compared to the extended activity observed in ordinary politics. This restrictive interpretation was perhaps partially responsible for the continued failure of political economists to recognize his seminal extension of the efficiency norm to the political sector. Such restrictiveness is very substantially reduced, and, in the limit, may be altogether eliminated, when the unanimity criterion is shifted one stage upward, to the level of potential agreement on constitutional rules within which ordinary politics is to be allowed to operate. In this framework, an individual may rationally prefer a rule that will, on particular occasions, operate to produce results that are opposed to his own interests. The individual will do so if he predicts that, on balance over the whole sequence of "plays," his own interests will be more effectively served than by the more restrictive application of the Wicksellian requirement in-period. The in-period Wicksellian criterion remains valid as a measure of the particularized efficiency of the single decision examined. But the in-period violation of the criterion does not imply the inefficiency of the rule so long as the latter is itself selected by a constitutional rule of unanimity.[2]

As noted, the shift of the Wicksellian criterion to the constitutional stage of choice among rules also serves to facilitate agreement, and, in the limiting case, may remove altogether potential conflicts among separate individual and group interests. To the extent that the individual reckons that a constitutional rule will remain applicable over a long sequence of periods, with many in-period choices to be made, he is necessarily placed behind a partial "veil of uncertainty" concerning the effects of any rule on his own predicted interests. Choice among rules will, therefore, tend to be based on generalizable criteria of fairness, making agreement more likely to occur than when separable interests are more easily identifiable.

The political economist who operates from within the Wicksellian research program, as modified, and who seeks to offer normative advice must, of necessity, concentrate on the process or structure within which political decisions are observed to be made. Existing constitutions, or structures of rules, are the subject of critical scrutiny. The conjectural question becomes: Could these rules have emerged from agreement by participants in an authentic constitutional convention? Even here, the normative advice that is possible must be severely circumscribed. There is no external set of norms that provides a basis for criticism. But the potential economist may, cautiously, suggest changes in procedures, in rules, that may come to command general assent. Any suggested change must be offered only in the provisional sense, and, importantly, it must be accompanied by a responsible recognition of political reality. Those rules and rules changes worthy of consideration are those that are predicted to be workable within the politics inhabited by ordinary men and women, and not those that are appropriate only for idealized, omniscient, and benevolent beings. Policy options must remain within the realm of the feasible, and the interests of political agents must be recognized as constraints on the possible.

## VI. Constitutionalism and Contractarianism

> The ultimate goal . . . is equality before the law, greatest possible liberty, and the economic well-being and peaceful cooperation of all people. —Wicksell, p. 88

As the basic Wicksellian construction is shifted to the choice among rules or constitutions and as a veil of uncertainty is utilized to facilitate the potential bridging of the difference between identifiable and general interest, the research program in political economy merges into that of contractarian political philosophy, both in its classical and modern variations. In particular, my own approach has affinities with the familiar construction of John Rawls (1971), who utilizes the veil of ignorance along with the fairness criterion to derive principles of justice that emerge from a conceptual agreement at a stage prior to the selection of a political constitution.

Because of his failure to shift his own analytical construction to the level of constitutional choice, Wicksell was confined to evaluation of the political process in generating current allocative decisions. He was unable, as he quite explicitly acknowledged, to evaluate political action involving either prior commitments of the state, for example, the financing of interest on public debt, or fiscally implemented transfers of incomes and wealth among persons and groups. Distributional questions remain outside the Wicksellian evaluative exercise, and because they do so, we locate another source of the long-continued and curious neglect of the fundamental analytical contribution. With the shift to the constitutional stage of politics, however, this constraint is at least partially removed. Behind a sufficiently thick veil of uncertainty and/or ignorance, contractual agreement on rules that allow for some in-period fiscal transfers seems clearly to be possible.

The precise features of a constitutionally approved transfer structure cannot, of course, be derived independently because of the restriction of evaluative judgment to the process of constitutional agreement. In this respect, the application is fully analogous to Wicksell's unwillingness to lay down specific norms for tax sharing independently of the process of agreement. *Any* distribution of tax shares generating revenues sufficient to finance the relevant spending project passes Wicksell's test, provided only that it meets with general agreement. Analogously, *any* set of arrangements for implementing fiscal transfers, in-period, meets the constitutional stage Wicksellian test, provided only that it commands general agreement.

This basic indeterminacy is disturbing to political economists or philosophers who seek to be able to offer substantive advice, over and beyond the procedural limits suggested. The constructivist urge to assume a role as social engineer, to suggest policy reforms that "should" or "should not" be made, independently of any revelation of individuals' preferences through the political process, has simply proved too strong for many to resist. The scientific integrity dictated by consistent reliance on individualistic values has not been a mark of modern political economy.

The difficulty of maintaining such integrity is accentuated by the failure to distinguish explanatory and justificatory argument, a failure that has described the position of almost all critics of social contract theories of political order. We do not, of course, observe the process of reaching agreement on constitutional rules, and the origins of the rules that are in existence at any particular time and in any particular polity cannot satisfactorily be explained by the contractarian model. The purpose of the contractarian exercise is not explanatory in this sense. It is, by contrast, justificatory in that it offers a basis for normative evaluation. Could the observed rules that constrain the activity of ordinary politics have emerged from agreement in constitutional contract?

To the extent that this question can be affirmatively answered, we have established a legitimating linkage between the individual and the state. To the extent that the question prompts a negative response, we have a basis for normative criticism of the existing order, and a criterion for advancing proposals for constitutional reform.[3]

It is at this point, and this point only, that the political economist who seeks to remain within the normative constraints imposed by the individualistic canon may enter the ongoing dialogue on constitutional policy. The deficit-financing regimes in modern Western democratic polities offer the most dramatic example. It is almost impossible to construct a contractual calculus in which representatives of separate generations would agree to allow majorities in a single generation to finance currently enjoyed public consumption through the issue of public debt that insures the imposition of utility losses on later generations of taxpayers. The same conclusion applies to the implicit debt obligations that are reflected in many of the intergenerational transfer programs characteristic of the modern welfare state.

The whole contractarian exercise remains empty if the critical dependence of politically generated results upon the rules that constrain political action is denied. If end states are invariant over shifts in constitutional structure, there is no role for constitutional political economy. On the other hand, if institutions do indeed matter, the role is well defined. Positively, this role involves analysis of the working properties of alternative sets of constraining rules. In a game-theoretic analogy, this analysis is the search for solutions of games, as the latter are defined by sets of rules. Normatively, the task for the constitutional political economist is to assist individuals, as citizens who ultimately control their own social order, in their continuing search for those rules of the political game that will best serve their purposes, whatever these might be.

In 1987, the United States celebrates the bicentennial anniversary of the constitutional convention that provided the basic rules for the

American political order. This convention was one of the very few historical examples in which political rules were deliberately chosen. The vision of politics that informed the thinking of James Madison was not dissimilar, in its essentials, from that which informed Knut Wicksell's less comprehensive, but more focused, analysis of taxation and spending. Both rejected any organic conception of the state as superior in wisdom to the individuals who are its members. Both sought to bring all available scientific analysis to bear in helping to resolve the continuing question of social order: How can we live together in peace, prosperity, and harmony, while retaining our liberties as autonomous individuals who can, and must, create our own values?

## Notes

1. This and subsequent citations are from Knut Wicksell, "A New Principle of Just Taxation," included in R. A. Musgrave and A. T. Peacock (1958, pp. 72–118). The more inclusive work from which this translated essay is taken is Wicksell, *Finanztheoretische Untersuchungen* (1896).

2. In my own retrospective interpretation, the shift of the Wicksellian construction to the constitutional stage of choice was the most important contribution in *The Calculus of Consent* (1962), written jointly with Gordon Tullock.

3. A generalized argument for adopting the constitutionalist-contractarian perspective, in both positive and normative analysis, is developed in *The Reason of Rules* (1985), written jointly with Geoffrey Brennan.

## References

**Brennan, Geoffrey and Buchanan, James,** *The Reason of Rules*, Cambridge: Cambridge University Press, 1985.

**Buchanan, James M.,** "The Pure Theory of Public Finance: A Suggested Approach," *Journal of Political Economy*, December 1949, *57*, 496–505.

**Buchanan, James M., and Tullock, Gordon,** *The Calculus of Consent*, Ann Arbor: University of Michigan Press, 1962.

**Musgrave, R. A. and Peacock, A. T.,** *Classics in the Theory of Public Finance*, London: Macmillan, 1958.

**Rawls, John,** *A Theory of Justice*, Cambridge: Harvard University Press, 1971.

**Wicksell, Knut,** *Finanztheoretische Untersuchungen*, Jena: Gustav Fisher, 1896.

# CHAPTER 3

✸

# RONALD H. COASE

Ronald H. Coase was awarded the Sveriges Riksbank Prize in Economic Sciences in Memory of Alfred Nobel in 1991 for "his discovery and clarification of the significance of transaction costs and property rights for the institutional structure and functioning of the economy." By spearheading previously unrealized extensions of microeconomic theory, Coase demonstrated how costs associated with contracting and managing organizations explain not only the existence and varying characteristics of firms but also the role of property rights as "a basic component in analyses of the institutional structure of the economy." Coase's contributions were highly significant to the development of property rights economics and the field of law and economics and, at the time of the award, were credited by the Nobel Committee as "among the most dynamic forces behind research in economic science and jurisprudence."

# THE INSTITUTIONAL STRUCTURE
## *of* PRODUCTION

### RONALD H. COASE

In my long life I have known some great economists, but I have never counted myself among their number nor walked in their company. I have made no innovations in high theory. My contribution to economics has been to urge the inclusion in our analysis of features of the economic system so obvious that, like the postman in G. K. Chesterton's Father Brown tale, "The Invisible Man," they have tended to be overlooked. Nonetheless, once included in the analysis, they will, as I believe, bring about a complete change in the structure of economic theory, at least in what is called price theory or microeconomics. What I have done is to show the importance for the working of the economic system of what may be termed the institutional structure of production. In this lecture I shall explain why, in my view, these features of the economic system were ignored and why their recognition will lead to a change in the way we analyze the working of the economic system and in the way we think about economic policy, changes which are already beginning to occur. I will also speak about the empirical work that needs to be done if this transformation in our approach is to increase our understanding. In speaking about this transformation, I do not wish to suggest that it is the result of my work alone. Oliver Williamson,

Harold Demsetz, and Steven Cheung, among others, have made out-standing contributions to the subject, and without their work and that of many others, I doubt whether the significance of my writings would have been recognized. While it has been a great advantage of the creation of the Prize in Economic Sciences in Memory of Alfred Nobel that, by drawing attention to the significance of particular fields of economics, it encourages further research in them, the highlighting of the work of a few scholars, or, in my case, one scholar, tends to obscure the importance of the contributions of other able scholars whose researches have been crucial to the development of the field.

I will be speaking of that part of economics which has come to be called industrial organization, but to understand its present state, it is necessary to say something about the development of economics in general. During the two centuries since the publication of *The Wealth of Nations*, the main activity of economists, it seems to me, has been to fill the gaps in Adam Smith's system, to correct his errors, and to make his analysis vastly more exact. A principal theme of *The Wealth of Nations* was that government regulation or centralized planning were not necessary to make an economic system function in an orderly way. The economy could be coordinated by a system of prices (the "invisible hand") and, furthermore, with beneficial results. A major task of economists since the publication of *The Wealth of Nations*, as Harold Demsetz (1988 p. 145) has explained, has been to formalize this proposition of Adam Smith. The given factors are technology and the tastes of consumers, and individuals, who follow their own interest, are governed in their choices by a system of prices. Economists have uncovered the conditions necessary if Adam Smith's results are to be achieved and where, in the real world, such conditions do not appear to be found, they have proposed changes which are designed to bring them about. It is what one finds in the textbooks. Harold Demsetz has said rightly that what this theory analyzes is a system of extreme decentralization. It has been a great intellectual achievement, and it throws light on many aspects of the economic system. But it has not been by any means all gain. The concentration on the determination of prices has led to a narrowing of focus which has had as a result the neglect of other aspects of the economic system. Sometimes, indeed, it seems as though economists conceive of their subject as being concerned only with the pricing system and anything outside this is considered as no part of their business. Thus, my old chief and wonderful human being, Lionel Robbins, wrote, in *The Nature and Significance of Economic Science*, about the "glaring deficiencies" of the old treatment of the theory of production with its discussion of peasant proprietorships and industrial forms: "It suggests that from the point of view of the economist 'organisation' is a matter of internal industrial (or agricultural) arrangement—if not internal to the firm, at any rate internal to 'the' industry. At the same time it tends to leave out completely the governing factor of all productive organisation—the relationship of prices and cost . . ." (Robbins, 1932 p. 70). What this comes down to is that, in Robbins's view, an economist does not interest himself in the internal arrangements within organizations but only in what happens on the market, the purchase of factors of production, and the sale of the goods that these factors produce. What happens in between the purchase of the factors of production and the sale of the goods that are produced by these factors is largely ignored. I do not know how far economists today share Robbins's attitude but it is undeniable that microeconomics is largely a study of the determination of prices and output; indeed, this part of economics is often called price theory.

This neglect of other aspects of the system has been made easier by another feature of modern economic theory—the growing abstraction of the analysis, which does not seem to call for a detailed knowledge of the actual economic system or, at any rate, has managed to proceed without it. Bengt Holmstrom and Jean Tirole (1989) writing on "The

Theory of the Firm" in the recently published *Handbook of Industrial Organization*, conclude at the end of their article of 63 pages that "the evidence/theory ratio . . . is currently very low in this field." Sam Peltzman (1991) has written a scathing review of the *Handbook* in which he points out how much of the discussion in it is theory without any empirical basis. What is studied is a system which lives in the minds of economists but not on earth. I have called the result "blackboard economics." The firm and the market appear by name but they lack any substance. The firm in mainstream economic theory has often been described as a "black box." And so it is. This is very extraordinary given that most resources in a modern economic system are employed within firms, with how these resources are used dependent on administrative decisions and not directly on the operation of a market. Consequently, the efficiency of the economic system depends to a very considerable extent on how these organizations conduct their affairs, particularly, of course, the modern corporation. Even more surprising, given their interest in the pricing system, is the neglect of the market or more specifically the institutional arrangements which govern the process of exchange. As these institutional arrangements determine to a large extent what is produced, what we have is a very incomplete theory. All this is beginning to change, and in this process I am glad to have played my part. The value of including such institutional factors in the corpus of mainstream economics is made clear by recent events in Eastern Europe. These ex-communist countries are advised to move to a market economy, and their leaders wish to do so, but without the appropriate institutions no market economy of any significance is possible. If we knew more about our own economy, we would be in a better position to advise them.

What I endeavored to do in the two articles cited by the Royal Swedish Academy of Sciences was to attempt to fill these gaps or more exactly to indicate the direction in which we should move if they are ultimately to be filled. Let me start with "The Nature of the Firm." I went as a student to the London School of Economics in 1929 to study for a Bachelor of Commerce degree, specializing in the Industry group, supposedly designed for people who wished to become works managers, a choice of occupation for which I was singularly ill-suited. However, in 1931 I had a great stroke of luck. Arnold Plant was appointed Professor of Commerce in 1930. He was a wonderful teacher. I began to attend his seminar in 1931, some five months before I took the final examinations. It was a revelation. He quoted Sir Arthur Salter: "The normal economic system works itself." And he explained how a competitive economic system coordinated by prices would lead to the production of goods and services which consumers valued most highly. Before being exposed to Plant's teaching, my notions on how the economy worked were extremely woolly. After Plant's seminar I had a coherent view of the economic system. He introduced me to Adam Smith's "invisible hand." As I had taken the first year of university work while still at high school, I managed to complete the requirements for a degree in two years. However, University regulations required three years of residence before a degree could be granted. I had therefore a year to spare. I then had another stroke of luck. I was awarded a Cassel travelling scholarship by the University of London. I decided to spend the year in the United States, this being treated as a year's residence at the London School of Economics, the regulations being somewhat loosely interpreted.

I decided to study vertical and lateral integration of industry in the United States. Plant had described in his lectures the different ways in which various industries were organized, but we seemed to lack any theory which would explain these differences. I set out to find it. There was also another puzzle which, in my mind, needed to be solved and which seemed to be related to my main project. The view of the pricing system as a coordinating mechanism was clearly right, but there were aspects of the argument which troubled me. Plant was opposed to all schemes, then very fashionable during the Great Depression, for the coordination of industrial production by some form of planning. Competition, according to Plant, acting through a system of prices, would do all the coordination necessary. And yet we had a factor of production, management, whose function was to coordinate. Why was it needed if the pricing system provided all the coordination necessary? The same problem presented itself to me at that time in another guise. The Russian Revolution had taken place only 14 years earlier. We knew then very little about how planning would actually be carried out in a communist system. Lenin had said that the economic system in Russia would be run as one big factory. However, many economists in the West maintained that this was an impossibility. And yet there were factories in the West, and some of them were extremely large. How did one reconcile the views expressed by economists on the role of the pricing system and the impossibility of successful central economic planning with the existence of management and of these apparently planned societies, firms, operating within our own economy?[1]

I found the answer by the summer of 1932. It was to realize that there were costs of using the pricing mechanism. What the prices are have to be discovered. There are negotiations to be undertaken, contracts have to be drawn up, inspections have to be made, arrangements have to be made to settle disputes, and so on. These costs have come to be known as transaction costs. Their existence implies that methods of coordination alternative to the market, which are themselves costly and in various ways imperfect, may nonetheless be preferable to relying on the pricing mechanism, the only method of coordination normally analyzed by economists. It was the avoidance of the costs of carrying out transactions through the market that could explain the existence of the firm in which the allocation of factors came about as a result of administrative decisions (and I thought it did). In my 1937 article I argued that in a competitive system there would be an optimum of planning since a firm, that little planned society, could only continue to exist if it performed its coordination function at a lower cost than would be incurred if it were achieved by means of market transactions and also at a lower cost than this same function could be performed by another firm. To have an efficient economic system it is necessary not only to have markets but also areas of planning within organizations of the appropriate size. What this mix should be we find as a result of competition. This is what I said in my article of 1937. However, as we know from a letter I wrote in 1932 which has been preserved, all the essentials of this argument had been presented in a lecture I gave in Dundee at the beginning of October, 1932 (see Williamson and Winter, 1991 pp. 34–5). I was then 21 years of age, and the sun never ceased to shine. I could never have imagined that these ideas would become some 60 years later a major justification for the award of a Nobel Prize. And it is a strange experience to be praised in my eighties for work I did in my twenties.

There is no doubt that the recognition by economists of the importance of the role of the firm in the functioning of the economy will prompt them to investigate its activities more closely. The work of Oliver Williamson and others has led to a greater understanding of the factors which govern what a firm does and how it does it. And we can also hope to learn much more in future from the studies of the activities of firms which have recently been initiated by the Center for Economic Studies of the Bureau of the Census of the United States. But it would be wrong to think that the most important consequence for economics of the publication of "The Nature of the Firm" has been to direct attention to the importance of the firm in our modern economy, a result which, in my view, would have come about in any case. What I think will be considered in the future to have been the important contribution of this article is the explicit introduction of transaction costs into economic analysis. I argued in "The Nature of the Firm" that the existence of transaction costs leads to the emergence of the firm. But the effects are pervasive in the economy. Businessmen in deciding on their ways of doing business and on what to produce have to take into account transaction costs. If the costs of making an exchange are greater than the gains which that exchange would bring, that exchange would not take place and the greater production that would flow from specialization would not be realized. In this way transaction costs affect not only contractual arrangements, but also what goods and services are produced. Not to include transaction costs in the theory leaves many aspects of the working of the economic system unexplained, including the emergence of the firm, but much else besides. In fact, a large part of what we think of as economic activity is designed to accomplish what high transaction costs would otherwise prevent or to reduce transaction costs so that individuals can freely negotiate and we can take advantage of that diffused knowledge of which Hayek has told us.

I know of only one part of economics in which transaction costs have been used to explain a major feature of the economic system, and that relates to the evolution and use of money. Adam Smith pointed out the hindrances to commerce that would arise in an economic system in which there was a division of labor but in which all exchange had to take the form of barter. No one would be able to buy anything unless he possessed something that the producer wanted. This difficulty, he explained, could be overcome by the use of money. A person wishing to buy something in a barter system has to find someone who has this product for sale but who also wants some of the goods possessed by the potential buyer. Similarly, a person wishing to sell something has to find someone who both wants what he has to offer and also possesses something that the potential seller wants. Exchange in a barter system requires what W. S. Jevons called "this double coincidence." Clearly the search for partners in exchange with suitable qualifications is likely to be very costly and will prevent many potentially beneficial exchanges from taking place. The benefit brought about by the use of money consists of a reduction in transaction costs. The use of money also reduces transaction costs by facilitating the drawing up of contracts as well as by reducing the quantity of goods that need to be held for purposes of exchange. However, the nature of the benefits secured by the use of money seems to have faded into the background so far as economists are concerned, and it does not seem to have been noticed that there are other features of the economic system which exist because of the need to mitigate transaction costs.

I now turn to that other article cited by the Swedish Academy, "The Problem of Social Cost," published some 30 years ago. I will not say much here about its influence on legal scholarship, which has been immense, but will mainly consider its influence on economics, which has not been immense, although I believe that in time it will be. It is my view that the approach used in that article will ultimately transform the structure of microeconomics—and I will explain why. I should add that in writing this article I had no such general aim in mind. I thought that I was exposing the weaknesses of Pigou's analysis of the divergence between private and social products, an analysis generally accepted by economists, and that was all. It was only later, and in part as a result of conversations with Steven Cheung in the 1960s that I came to see the general significance for economic theory of what I had written in that article and also to see more clearly what questions needed to be further investigated.

Pigou's conclusion and that of most economists using standard economic theory was (and perhaps still is) that some kind of government action (usually the imposition of taxes) was required to restrain those whose actions had harmful effects on others (often termed negative externalities). What I showed in that article, as I thought, was that in a regime of zero transaction costs, an assumption of standard economic theory, negotiations between the parties would lead to those arrangements being made which would maximize wealth and this irrespective of the initial assignment of rights. This is the infamous Coase theorem, named and formulated by George Stigler, although it is based on work of mine. Stigler argues that the Coase theorem follows from the standard assumptions of economic theory. Its logic cannot be questioned, only its domain (Stigler, 1989 pp. 631–3). I do not disagree with Stigler. However, I tend to regard the Coase theorem as a stepping stone on the way to an analysis of an economy with positive transaction costs. The significance to me of the Coase Theorem is that it undermines the Pigovian system. Since standard economic theory assumes transaction costs to be zero, the Coase theorem demonstrates that the Pigovian solutions are unnecessary in these circumstances. Of course, it does not imply, when transaction costs are positive, that government actions (such as government operation, regulation, or taxation, including subsidies) could not produce a better result than relying on negotiations between individuals in the market. Whether this would be so could be discovered not by studying imaginary governments but what real governments actually do. My conclusion: let us study the world of positive transaction costs.

If we move from a regime of zero transaction costs to one of positive transaction costs, what becomes immediately clear is the crucial importance of the legal system in this new world. I explained in "The Problem of Social Cost" that what are traded on the market are not, as is often supposed by economists, physical entities, but the rights to perform certain actions, and the rights which individuals possess are established by the legal system. While we can imagine in the hypothetical world of zero transaction costs that the parties to an exchange would negotiate to change any provision of the law which prevents them from taking whatever steps are required to increase the value of production, in the real world of positive transaction costs, such a procedure would be extremely costly and would make unprofitable, even where it was allowed, a great deal of such contracting around the law. Because of this, the rights which individuals possess, with their duties and privileges, will be, to a large extent, what the law determines. As a result, the legal system will have a profound effect on the working of the economic system and may in certain respects be said to control it. It is obviously desirable that these rights should be assigned to those who can use them most productively and with incentives that lead them to do so and that, to discover (and maintain) such a distribution of rights, the costs of their transference should be low, through clarity in the law and by making the legal requirements for such transfers less onerous. Since this can come about only if there is an appropriate system of property rights (and they are enforced), it is easy to understand why so many academic lawyers (at least in the United States) have found so attractive the task of uncovering the character of such a property-rights system and why the subject of "law and economics" has flourished in American law schools. Indeed, work is going forward at such a pace that I do not consider it overoptimistic to believe that the main outlines of the subject will be drawn within five or ten years.

Until quite recently, most economists seem to have been unaware of this relationship between the economic and legal systems except in the most general way. Stock and produce exchanges are often used by economists as examples of perfect or near-perfect competition. But these exchanges regulate in great detail the activities of traders (and this quite apart from any public regulation there may be). What can be traded, when it can be traded, the terms of settlement, and so on are all laid down by the authorities of the exchange. There is, in effect, a private law. Without such rules and regulations, the speedy conclusion of trades would not be possible. Of course, when trading takes place outside exchanges (and this is almost all trading) and where the dealers are scattered in space and have very divergent interests, as in retailing and wholesaling, such a private law would be difficult to establish, and their activities will be regulated by the laws of the State. It makes little sense for economists to discuss the process of exchange without specifying the institutional setting within which the trading takes place, since this affects the incentives to produce and the costs of transacting. I think this is now beginning to be recognized and has been made crystal-clear by what is going on in Eastern Europe today. The time has surely gone in which economists could analyze in great detail two individuals exchanging nuts for berries on the edge of the forest and then feel that their analysis of the process of exchange was complete, illuminating though this analysis may be in certain respects. The process of contracting needs to be studied in a real-world setting. We would then learn of the problems that are encountered and of how they are overcome, and we would certainly become aware of the richness of the institutional alternatives between which we have to choose.

Oliver Williamson has ascribed the nonuse or limited use of my thesis in "The Nature of the Firm" to the fact that it has not been made "operational," by which he means that the concept of transaction costs has not been incorporated into a general theory. I think this is correct. There have been two reasons for this. First, incorporating transaction costs into standard economic theory, which has been based on the assumption that they are zero, would be very difficult, and economists who, like most scientists, as Thomas Kuhn has told us, are extremely conservative in their methods, have not been inclined to attempt it. Second, Williamson has also pointed out that although I was correct in making the choice between organization within the firm or through the market the centerpiece of my analysis, I did not indicate what the factors were that determined the outcome of this choice and thus made it difficult for others to build on what is often described as a "fundamental insight." This also is true. But the interrelationships which govern the mix of market and hierarchy, to use Williamson's terms, are extremely complex, and in our present state of ignorance it will not be easy to discover what these factors are. What we need is more empirical work. In a paper written for a conference of the National Bureau of Economic Research, I explained why I thought this was so. This is what I said: "An inspired theoretician might do as well without such empirical work, but my own feeling is that the inspiration is most likely to come through the stimulus provided by the patterns, puzzles, and anomalies revealed by the systematic gathering of data, particularly when the prime need is to break our existing habits of thought (Coase, 1988 p. 71). This statement was made in 1970. I still think that in essentials it is true today. Although much interesting and important research was done in the 1970s and 1980s and we certainly know much more than we did in 1970, there is little doubt that a great deal more empirical work is needed. However, I have come to the conclusion that the main obstacle faced by researchers in industrial organization is the lack of available data on contracts and the activities of firms. I have therefore decided to do something about it.

Believing that there is a great deal of data on contracts and the activities of firms in the United States available in government departments and agencies in Washington, DC, and that this information is largely unknown to economists, I organized a conference at the University of Chicago Law School in the summer of 1990 at which government officials presented papers in which they described what data was available and how to get access to it and also reported on some of the research being carried out within their departments. The audience consisted of academic economists. It was, as a colleague remarked, a case of supply meeting demand. The proceedings of this conference will be published in a special issue of the *Journal of Law and Economics*.

Another development with which I am associated is the establishment of the Center for the Study of Contracts and the Structure of Enterprise at the Business School of the University of Pittsburgh. This Center will make large-scale collections of business contracts and will prepare databases which will be made available to all researchers, whatever their institution. Nor should we forget the work now getting started at the Center for Economic Studies of the Bureau of the Census. This greater availability of data and the encouragement given to all researchers working on the institutional structure of production by the award to me of the Nobel Prize should result in a reduction in that elegant but sterile theorizing so commonly found in the economics literature on industrial organization and should lead to studies which increase our understanding of how the real economic system works.

My remarks have sometimes been interpreted as implying that I am hostile to the mathematization of economic theory. This is untrue. Indeed, once we begin to uncover the real factors affecting the performance of the economic system, the complicated interrelations between them will clearly necessitate a mathematical treatment, as in the natural sciences, and economists like myself, who write in prose, will take their bow. May this period soon come.

I am very much aware that many economists whom I respect and admire will not agree with the opinions I have expressed, and some may even be offended by them. But a scholar must be content with the knowledge that what is false in what he says will soon be exposed and, as for what is true, he can count on ultimately seeing it accepted, if only he lives long enough.

## Notes

1. A fuller account of these events will be found in Oliver E. Williamson and Sidney G. Winter (1991 pp. 34–47).

# References

Coase, R. H. *The Firm, The Market, and the Law*, Chicago: University of Chicago Press, 1988.

Demsetz, Harold. *Ownership, Control, and the Firm*, Vol. I, Oxford: Blackwell, 1988.

Holmstrom, Bengt, and Jean Tirole. "The Theory of the Firm," in Richard Schmalensee and Robert D. Willig, eds., *Handbook of Industrial Organization*, Amsterdam: North-Holland, 1989, pp. 61–128.

Peltzman, Sam. "The Handbook of Industrial Organization: A Review Article," *Journal of Political Economy*, February 1991, *99*, 201–17.

Robbins, Lionel. *The Nature and Significance of Economic Science*, London: Macmillan, 1932.

Stigler, George J. "Two Notes on the Coase Theorem," *Yale Law Journal*, December 1989, *99*, 631–3.

Williamson, Oliver E., and Sidney G. Winter, eds. *The Nature of the Firm, Origins, Evolution, and Development*, Oxford: Oxford University Press, 1991.

# CHAPTER 4

❂

# DOUGLASS C. NORTH

Douglass C. North was awarded the Sveriges Riksbank Prize in Economic Sciences in Memory of Alfred Nobel in 1993, along with historian Robert W. Fogel, for "having renewed research in economic history by applying economic theory and quantitative methods in order to explain economic and institutional change." Both scholars were credited with making significant advances to the field of modern economic history in integrating economics, sociology, statistics, and history to achieve a greater depth in "knowledge and understanding within fundamental areas of research, as to how, why and when economic change occurs." Beyond North's contributions to developing explanatory models of American economic development, the Nobel Committee also recognized North for his work on the preconditions and process of institutional transition arising from the realization by individuals of changes in the relative costs and benefits of alternative institutional arrangements. His work was cited for highlighting the problem of relying exclusively on neoclassical models of economic growth and for emphasizing that "economic, political, and social factors must be taken into account if we are to understand the development of those institutions that have played a role for economic growth, and how these institutions have been affected by ideological and noneconomic factors." The Nobel Committee honored North for being "an inspirer, a produced of ideas, who identifies new problems and shows how economists can solve the old ones more effectively."

# ECONOMIC PERFORMANCE
## *through* TIME

### DOUGLASS C. NORTH

---

## I

Economic history is about the performance of economies through time. The objective of research in the field is not only to shed new light on the economic past, but also to contribute to economic theory by providing an analytical framework that will enable us to understand economic change. A theory of economic dynamics comparable in precision to general equilibrium theory would be the ideal tool of analysis. In the absence of such a theory we can describe the characteristics of past economies, examine the performance of economies at various times, and engage in comparative static analysis; but missing is an analytical understanding of the way economies evolve through time.

A theory of economic dynamics is also crucial for the field of economic development. There is no mystery why the field of development has failed to develop during the five decades since the end of World War II. Neoclassical theory is simply an inappropriate tool to analyze and prescribe policies that will induce development. It is concerned with the operation of markets, not with how markets develop. How can one prescribe policies when one doesn't understand how economies develop? The very methods employed by neoclassical economists have dictated the subject matter and militated against such a development. That theory in the pristine form that gave it mathematical precision and elegance modeled a frictionless and static world. When applied to economic history and development it focused on technological development and more recently human-capital investment but ignored the incentive structure embodied in institutions that determined the extent of societal investment in those factors. In the analysis of economic performance through time it contained two erroneous assumptions: (i) that institutions do not matter and (ii) that time does not matter.

This essay is about institutions and time. It does not provide a theory of economic dynamics comparable to general equilibrium theory. We do not have such a theory.[1] Rather it provides the initial scaffolding of an analytical framework capable of increasing our understanding of the historical evolution of economies and a necessarily crude guide to policy in the ongoing task of improving the economic performance of economies. The analytical framework is a modification of neoclassical theory. What it retains is the fundamental assumption of scarcity and hence competition and the analytical tools of microeconomic theory. What it modifies is the rationality assumption. What it adds is the dimension of time.

Institutions form the incentive structure of a society, and the political and economic institutions, in consequence, are the underlying determinants of economic performance. Time as it relates to economic and societal change is the dimension in which the learning process of human beings shapes the way institutions evolve. That is, the beliefs that individuals, groups, and societies hold which determine choices are a consequence of learning through time—not just the span of an individual's life or of a generation of a society, but the learning embodied in individuals, groups, and societies that is cumulative through time and passed on intergenerationally by the culture of a society.

The next two sections of this essay summarize the work I, and others, have done on the nature of institutions and the way they affect economic performance (Section II) and then characterize the nature of institutional change (Section III).[2] The remaining four sections describe a cognitive-science approach to human learning (Section IV); provide an institutional/cognitive approach to economic history (Section V); indicate the implications of this approach for improving our understanding of the past (Section VI); and finally suggest implications for current development policies (Section VII).

## II

Institutions are the humanly devised constraints that structure human interaction. They are made up of formal constraints (e.g., rules, laws, constitutions), informal constraints (e.g., norms of behavior, conventions, self-imposed codes of conduct), and their enforcement characteristics. Together they define the incentive structure of societies and specifically economies.

Institutions and the technology employed determine the transaction and transformation costs that add up to the costs of production. It was Ronald Coase (1960) who made the crucial connection between institutions, transaction costs, and neoclassical theory. The neoclassical result of efficient markets only obtains when it is costless to transact. Only under the conditions of costless bargaining will the actors reach the solution that maximizes aggregate income regardless of the institutional arrangements. When it is costly to transact, then institutions matter. And it is costly to transact. John J. Wallis and North (1986) demonstrated in an empirical study that 45 percent of U.S. GNP was devoted to the transaction sector in 1970. Efficient markets are created in the real world when competition is strong enough via arbitrage and efficient information feedback to approximate the Coase zero-transaction-cost conditions and the parties can realize the gains from trade inherent in the neoclassical argument.

But the informational and institutional requirements necessary to achieve such efficient markets are stringent. Players must not only have objectives, but know the correct way to achieve them. But how do the players know the correct way to achieve their objectives? The instrumental rationality answer is that, even though the actors may initially have diverse and erroneous models, the informational feedback process and arbitraging actors will correct initially incorrect models, punish deviant behavior, and lead surviving players to correct models.

An even more stringent implicit requirement of the discipline-of-the-competitive-market model is that, when there are significant transaction costs, the consequent institutions of the market will be designed to induce the actors to acquire the essential information that will lead them to correct their models. The implication is not only that institutions are designed to achieve efficient outcomes, but that they can be ignored in economic analysis because they play no independent role in economic performance.

These are stringent requirements that are realized only very exceptionally. Individuals typically act on incomplete information and with subjectively derived models that are frequently erroneous; the information feedback is typically insufficient to correct these subjective models. Institutions are not necessarily or even usually created to be socially efficient; rather they, or at least the formal rules, are created to serve the interests of those with the bargaining power to create new rules. In a world of zero transaction costs, bargaining strength does not affect the efficiency of outcomes; but in a world of positive transaction costs it does.

It is exceptional to find economic markets that approximate the conditions necessary for efficiency. It is impossible to find political markets that do. The reason is straightforward. Transaction costs are the costs of specifying what is being exchanged and of enforcing the consequent agreements. In economic markets what is being specified (measured) is the valuable attributes—the physical and property-rights dimensions—of goods and services or the performance of agents. While measurement can frequently be costly, there are some standard criteria: the physical dimensions have objective characteristics (size, weight, color, etc.), and the property-rights dimensions are defined in legal terms. Competition also plays a critical role in reducing enforcement costs. The judicial system provides coercive enforcement. Still, economic markets in the past and present are typically imperfect and beset by high transaction costs.

Measuring and enforcing agreements in political markets is far more difficult. What is being exchanged (between constituents and legislators in a democracy) is promises for votes. The voter has little incentive to become informed because the likelihood that one's vote matters is infinitesimal; further, the complexity of the issues produces genuine uncertainty. Enforcement of political agreements is beset by difficulties. Competition is far less effective than in economic markets. For a variety of simple, easy-to-measure, and important-to-constituent-well-being policies, constituents may be well informed, but beyond such straightforward policy issues ideological stereotyping takes over and (as I shall argue below in Section IV) shapes the consequent performance of economies.[3] It is the polity that defines and enforces property rights, and in consequence it is not surprising that efficient economic markets are so exceptional.

## III

It is the interaction between institutions and organizations that shapes the institutional evolution of an economy. If institutions are the rules of the game, organizations and their entrepreneurs are the players.

Organizations are made up of groups of individuals bound together by some common purpose to achieve certain objectives. Organizations include political bodies (e.g., political parties, the Senate, a city council, regulatory bodies), economic bodies (e.g., firms, trade unions, family farms, cooperatives), social bodies (e.g., churches, clubs, athletic associations), and educational bodies (e.g., schools, universities, vocational training centers).

The organizations that come into existence will reflect the opportunities provided by the institutional matrix. That is, if the institutional framework rewards piracy then piratical organizations will come into existence; and if the institutional framework rewards productive activities then organizations—firms—will come into existence to engage in productive activities.

Economic change is a ubiquitous, ongoing, incremental process that is a consequence of the choices individual actors and entrepreneurs of organizations are making every day. While the vast majority of these decisions are routine (Richard Nelson and Sidney G. Winter, 1982), some involve altering existing "contracts" between individuals and organizations. Sometimes that recontracting can be accomplished within the existing structure of property rights and political rules; but sometimes new contracting forms require an alteration in the rules. Equally, norms of behavior that guide exchanges will gradually be modified or wither away. In both instances, institutions are being altered.

Modifications occur because individuals perceive that they could do better by restructuring exchanges (political or economic). The source of the changed perceptions may be exogenous to the economy—for instance a change in the price or quality of a competitive product in another economy that alters perceptions of entrepreneurs in the given economy about profitable opportunities. But the most fundamental long-run source of change is learning by individuals and entrepreneurs of organizations.

While idle curiosity will result in learning, the rate of learning will reflect the intensity of competition among organizations. Competition, reflecting ubiquitous scarcity, induces organizations to engage in learning to survive. The degree of competition can and does vary. The greater the degree of monopoly power, the lower is the incentive to learn.

The speed of economic change is a function of the rate of learning, but the direction of that change is a function of the expected payoffs to acquiring different kinds of knowledge. The mental models that the players develop shape perceptions about the payoffs.

## IV

It is necessary to dismantle the rationality assumption underlying economic theory in order to approach constructively the nature of human learning. History demonstrates that ideas, ideologies, myths, dogmas, and prejudices matter; and an understanding of the way they evolve is necessary for further progress in developing a framework to understand societal change. The rational-choice framework assumes that individuals know what is in their self-interest and act accordingly. That may be correct for individuals making choices in the highly developed markets of modern economies,[4] but it is patently false in making choices under conditions of uncertainty—the conditions that have characterized the political and economic choices that shaped (and continue to shape) historical change.

Herbert Simon (1986 pp. S210–11) has stated the issues succinctly:

If . . . we accept the proposition that both the knowledge and the computational power of the decisionmaker are severely limited, then we must distinguish between the real world and the actor's perception of it and reasoning about it. That is to say we must construct a theory (and test it empirically) of the process of decision. Our theory must include not only the reasoning processes but also the processes that generated the actor's subjective representation of the decision problem, his or her frame.

The analytical framework we must build must originate in an understanding of how human learning takes place. We have a way to go before we can construct such a theory, but cognitive science has made immense strides in recent years—enough strides to suggest a tentative approach that can help us understand decision-making under uncertainty.[5]

Learning entails developing a structure by which to interpret the varied signals received by the senses. The initial architecture of the structure is genetic, but the subsequent scaffolding is a result of the experiences of the individual. The experiences can be classified into two kinds—those from the physical environment and those from the sociocultural linguistic environment. The structures consist of categories—classifications that gradually evolve from earliest childhood to organize our perceptions and keep track of our memory of analytic results and experiences. Building on these classifications, we form mental models to explain and interpret the environment—typically in ways relevant to some goal. Both the categories and the mental models will evolve, reflecting the feedback derived from new experiences: feedback that sometimes strengthens our initial categories and models or may lead to modifications—in short, learning. Thus the mental models may be continually redefined with new experiences, including contact with others' ideas.

At this juncture the learning process of human beings diverges from that of other animals (such as the sea slug—a favorite research subject of cognitive scientists) and particularly diverges from the computer analogy that dominated early studies of artificial intelligence. The mind appears to order and reorder the mental models from their special-purpose origins to successively more abstract forms so that they become available to process other information. The term used by Andy Clark and Annette Karmiloff-Smith (1993) is "representational redescription." The capacity to generalize from the particular to the general and to use analogy is a part of this redescription process. It is this capacity that is the source not only of creative thinking, but also of the ideologies and belief systems that underlie the choices humans make.[6]

A common cultural heritage provides a means of reducing the divergence in the mental models that people in a society have and constitutes the means for the intergenerational transfer of unifying perceptions. In pre-modern societies cultural learning provided a means of internal communication; it also provided shared explanations for phenomena outside the immediate experiences of the members of society in the form of religions, myths, and dogmas. Such belief structures are not, however, confined to primitive societies, but are an essential part of modern societies as well.

Belief structures get transformed into societal and economic structures by institutions—both formal rules and informal norms of behavior. The relationship between mental models and institutions is an intimate one. Mental models are the internal representations that individual cognitive systems create to interpret the environment; institutions are the external (to the mind) mechanisms individuals create to structure and order the environment.

# V

There is no guarantee that the beliefs and institutions that evolve through time will produce economic growth. Let me pose the issue that time presents us by a brief institutional/cognitive story of long-run economic/political change.

As tribes evolved in different physical environments, they developed different languages and, with different experiences, different mental models to explain the world around them. The languages and mental models formed the informal constraints that defined the institutional framework of the tribe and were passed down intergenerationally as customs, taboos, and myths that provided cultural continuity.[7]

With growing specialization and division of labor, the tribes evolved into polities and economies; the diversity of experience and learning produced increasingly different societies and civilizations with different degrees of success in solving the fundamental economic problems of scarcity. The reason is that as the complexity of the environment increased as human beings became increasingly interdependent, more complex institutional structures were necessary to capture the potential gains from trade. Such evolution requires that the society develop institutions that will permit anonymous, impersonal exchange across time and space. To the extent that the culture and local experiences had produced diverse institutions and belief systems with respect to the gains from such cooperation, the likelihood of creating the necessary institutions to capture the gains from trade of more complex contracting varied. In fact, most societies throughout history got "stuck" in an institutional matrix that did not evolve into the impersonal exchange essential to capturing the productivity gains that came from the specialization and division of labor that have produced the wealth of nations.

The key to the foregoing story is the kind of learning that the individuals in a society acquired through time. Time in this context entails not only current experiences and learning, but also the cumulative experience of past generations that is embodied in culture. Collective learning—a term used by Friedrich A. Hayek—consists of those experiences that have passed the slow test of time and are embodied in our language, institutions, technology, and ways of doing things. It is "the transmission in time of our accumulated stock of knowledge" (Hayek, 1960 p. 27). It is culture that provides the key to path dependence—a term used to describe the powerful influence of the past on the present and future. The current learning of any generation takes place within the context of the perceptions derived from collective learning. Learning then is an incremental process filtered by the culture of a society which determines the perceived payoffs, but there is no guarantee that the cumulative past experience of a society will necessarily fit them to solve new problems. Societies that get "stuck" embody belief systems and institutions that fail to confront and solve new problems of societal complexity.

We need to understand a great deal more about the cumulative learning of a society. The learning process appears to be a function of (i) the way in which a given belief structure filters the information derived from experiences and (ii) the different experiences confronting individuals and societies at different times. The perceived rate of return (private) may be high to military technology (in medieval Europe), to the pursuit and refinement of religious dogma (Rome during and after Constantine), or to the research for an accurate chronometer to determine longitude at sea (for which a substantial reward was offered during the Age of Exploration).

The incentives to acquire pure knowledge, the essential underpinning of modern economic growth, are affected by monetary rewards and punishments; they are also fundamentally influenced by a society's tolerance of creative developments, as a long list of creative individuals from Galileo to Darwin could attest. While there is a substantial literature on the origins and development of science, very little of it deals with the links between institutional structure, belief systems, and the incentives and disincentives to acquire pure knowledge. A major factor in the development of Western Europe was the gradual perception of the utility of research in pure science.

Incentives embodied in belief systems as expressed in institutions determine economic performance through time, and however we wish to define economic performance the historical record is clear. Throughout most of history and for most societies in the past and present, economic performance has been anything but satisfactory. Human beings have, by trial and error, learned how to make economies perform better; but not only has this learning taken ten millennia (since the first economic revolution), it has still escaped the grasp of almost half of the world's population. Moreover the radical improvement in economic performance, even when narrowly defined as material wellbeing, is a modem phenomenon of the last few centuries and confined until the last few decades to a small part of the world. Explaining the pace and direction of economic change throughout history presents a major puzzle.

Let us represent the human experience to date as a 24-hour clock in which the beginning consists of the time (apparently in Africa between 4 and 5 million years ago) when humans became separate from other primates. Then the beginning of so-called civilization occurs with the development of agriculture and permanent settlement in about 8000 B.C. in the Fertile Crescent—in the last three or four minutes of the clock. For the other 23 hours and 56 or 57 minutes, humans remained hunters and gatherers, and while population grew, it did so at a very slow pace.

Now if we make a new 24-hour clock for the time of civilization— the 10,000 years from development of agriculture to the present—the pace of change appears to be very slow for the first 12 hours, although our archeological knowledge is very limited. Historical demographers speculate that the rate of population growth may have doubled as compared to the previous era but still was very slow. The pace of change accelerates in the past 5,000 years with the rise and then decline of economies and civilizations. Population may have grown from about 300 million at the time of Christ to about 800 million by 1750—a substantial acceleration as compared to earlier rates of growth. The last 250 years—just 35 minutes on our new 24-hour clock—are the era of modern economic growth, accompanied by a population explosion that now puts world population in excess of 5 billion.

If we focus now on the last 250 years, we see that growth was largely restricted to Western Europe and the overseas extensions of Britain for 200 of those 250 years.

Not only has the pace varied over the ages; the change has not been unidirectional. That is not simply a consequence of the decline of individual civilizations; there have been periods of apparent secular stagnation—the most recent being the long hiatus between the end of the Roman Empire in the West and the revival of Western Europe approximately 500 years later.

## VI

What can an institutional/cognitive approach contribute to improving our understanding of the economic past? First of all it should make sense out of the very uneven pattern of economic performance described in the previous section. There is nothing automatic about the evolving of conditions that will permit low-cost transacting in the impersonal markets that are essential to productive economies. Game theory characterizes the issue. Individuals will usually find it worthwhile cooperating with others in exchange when the play is repeated, when they possess complete information about the other players' past performance, and when there are small numbers of players. Cooperation is difficult to sustain when the game is not repeated (or there is an endgame), when information about the other players is lacking, and when there are large numbers of players. Creating the institutions that will alter the benefit/cost ratios in favor of cooperation in impersonal exchange is a complex process, because it not only entails the creation of economic institutions, but requires that they be undergirded by appropriate political institutions.

We are just beginning to explore the nature of this historical process. The remarkable development of Western Europe from relative backwardness in the 10th century to world economic hegemony by the 18th century is a story of a gradually evolving belief system in the context of competition among fragmented political/economic units producing economic institutions and political structure that produced modern economic growth.[8] And even within Western Europe there were successes (the Netherlands and England) and failures (Spain and Portugal) reflecting diverse external environmental experiences.[9]

Second, institutional/cognitive analysis should explain path dependence, one of the remarkable regularities of history. Why do economies once on a path of growth or stagnation tend to persist? Pioneering work on this subject is beginning to give us insights into the sources of path dependence (Brian Arthur, 1989; Paul David, 1985). But there is much that we still do not know. The rationality assumption of neoclassical theory would suggest that political entrepreneurs of stagnating economies could simply alter the rules and change the direction of failed economies. It is not that rulers have been unaware of poor performance. Rather, the difficulty of turning economies around is a function of the nature of political markets and, underlying that, the belief systems of the actors. The long decline of Spain, for example, from the glories of the Hapsburg Empire of the 16th century to its sorry state under Francisco Franco in the 20th century was characterized by endless self appraisals and frequently bizarre proposed solutions.[10]

Third, this approach will contribute to our understanding of the complex interplay between institutions, technology, and demography in the overall process of economic change. A complete theory of economic performance would entail such an integrated approach to economic history. We certainly have not put all the pieces together yet. For example, Robert Fogel's path-breaking work on demographic theory[11] and its historical implications for reevaluating past economic performance have yet to be integrated fully with institutional analysis. The same is true for technological change. The important contributions of Nathan Rosenberg (1976) and Joel Mokyr (1990) exploring the impetus for and consequences of technological change have ongoing implications which need to be integrated with institutional analysis. An essay by Wallis and North (1994) is a beginning at integrating technological and institutional analysis. But a major task of economic history is to integrate these separate strands of research.

## VII

We cannot account for the rise and decline of the Soviet Union and world communism with the tools of neoclassical analysis, but we should with an institutional/cognitive approach to contemporary problems of development. To do so—and to provide an analytical framework to understand economic change—we must take into account the following implications of this approach:

1. It is the admixture of formal rules, informal norms, and enforcement characteristics that shapes economic performance. While

the rules may be changed overnight, the informal norms usually change only gradually. Since it is the norms that provide "legitimacy" to a set of rules, revolutionary change is never as revolutionary as its supporters desire, and performance will be different than anticipated. And economies that adopt the formal rules of another economy will have very different performance characteristics than the first economy because of different informal norms and enforcement. The implication is that transferring the formal political and economic rules of successful Western market economies to third-world and Eastern European economies is not a sufficient condition for good economic performance. Privatization is not a panacea for solving poor economic performance.

2. Polities significantly shape economic performance because they define and enforce the economic rules. Therefore an essential part of development policy is the creation of polities that will create and enforce efficient property rights. However, we know very little about how to create such polities because the new political economy (the new institutional economics applied to politics) has been largely focused on the United States and developed polities. A pressing research need is to model third-world and Eastern European polities. However the foregoing analysis does have some implications: (a) Political institutions will be stable only if undergirded by organizations with a stake in their perpetuation. (b) Both institutions and belief systems must change for successful reform since it is the mental models of the actors that will shape choices. (c) Developing norms of behavior that will support and legitimize new rules is a lengthy process, and in the absence of such reinforcing mechanisms polities will tend to be unstable. (d) While economic growth can occur in the short run with autocratic regimes, long-run eco-

nomic growth entails the development of the rule of law. (e) Informal constraints (norms, conventions, and codes of conduct) favorable to growth can sometimes produce economic growth even with unstable or adverse political rules. The key is the degree to which such adverse rules are enforced.

3. It is adaptive rather than allocative efficiency which is the key to long-run growth. Successful political/economic systems have evolved flexible institutional structures that can survive the shocks and changes that are a part of successful evolution. But these systems have been a product of long gestation. We do not know how to create adaptive efficiency in the short run.

We have just set out on the long road to achieving an understanding of economic performance through time. The ongoing research embodying new hypotheses confronting historical evidence will not only create an analytical framework enabling us to understand economic change through time; in the process it will enrich economic theory, enabling it to deal effectively with a wide range of contemporary issues currently beyond its ken. The promise is there. The recognition of that promise by the Nobel Committee should be the essential spur to move us on down that road.

## Notes

1. In fact such a theory is unlikely. I refer the reader to Frank Hahn's prediction about the future of economic theory (Hahn, 1991).

2. These two sections briefly summarize material contained in North (1990a).

3. See the author's "A Transaction Cost Theory of Politics" for a transaction-cost approach to the relative inefficiency of political markets (North, 1990b).

4. However, see the anomalies even here in the studies by Amos Tversky and Daniel Kahneman (1986) and others (Robin M. Hogarth and Melvin W. Reder, 1986).

5. See John H. Holland et al. (1986) for an excellent introduction to the cognitive-science literature.

6. Ideologies are shared frameworks of mental models that groups of individuals possess that provide both an interpretation of the environment and a prescription as to how that environment should be ordered.

7. Ronald Heiner (1983), in a path-breaking article, not only made the connection between the mental capacities of humans and the external environment, but suggested the implications for arresting economic progress.

8. See North and Robert P. Thomas (1973), E. L. Jones (1981), and Nathan Rosenberg and L. E. Birdzell (1986) for accounts of this growth.

9. See part III of North (1990a) for a brief discussion of the contrasting paths of the Netherlands and England on the one hand and Spain on the other.

10. DeVries (1976 p. 28) has a description of the bizarre remedies proposed by a royal commission to reverse Spain's decline.

11. See Fogel's (1994) accompanying Nobel lecture.

# References

**Arthur, Brian.** "Competing Technologies, Increasing Returns, and Lock-In by Historical Events." *Economic Journal*, March 1989, *99*(394), pp. 116–31.

**Clark, Andy, and Annette Karmiloff-Smith.** "The Cognizer's Innards: A Psychological and Philosophical Perspective on the Development of Thought." *Mind and Language*, 1993, *8*(4), pp. 487–519.

**Coase, Ronald.** "The Problem of Social Cost." *Journal of Law and Economics*, October 1960, *3*(1), pp. 1–44.

**David, Paul A.** "Clio and the Economics of QWERTY." *American Economic Review*, May 1985 (*Paper and Proceedings*), *75*(2), pp. 332–37.

**DeVries, Jan.** *The economy of Europe in an age of crises, 1600–1750.* Cambridge: Cambridge University Press, 1976.

**Fogel, Robert W.** "Economic Growth, Population Theory, and Physiology: The Bearing of Long-Term Processes on the Making of Economic Policy." *American Economic Review*, June 1994, *84*(3), pp. 369–95.

**Hahn, Frank.** "The Next Hundred Years." *Economic Journal*, January 1991, *101*(404), pp. 47–50.

**Hayek, Friedrich A.** *The constitution of liberty.* Chicago: University of Chicago Press, 1960.

**Hogarth, Robin M., and Melvin W. Reder, eds.** *Rational choice: The contrast between economics and psychology.* Chicago: University of Chicago Press, 1986.

**Heiner, Ronald.** "The Origin of Predictable Behavior." *American Economic Review*, September 1983, *73*(4), pp. 560–95.

**Holland, John H., Keith J. Holyoak, Richard E. Nisbett, and Paul R. Thagard.** *Induction: Processes of inference, learning, and discovery.* Cambridge, MA: MIT Press, 1986.

**Jones, E. L.** *The European miracle.* Cambridge: Cambridge University Press, 1981.

**Mokyr, Joel.** *The lever of riches.* New York: Oxford University Press, 1990.

**Nelson, Richard, and Sidney G. Winter.** *An evolutionary theory of economic change.* Cambridge, MA: Harvard University Press, 1982.

**North, Douglass C.** *Institutions, institutional change, and economic performance.* New York: Cambridge University Press, 1990a.

————. "A Transactions Cost Theory of Politics." *Journal of Theoretical Politics*, October 1990b, *2*(4), pp. 355–67.

**North, Douglass C., and Robert P. Thomas.** *The rise of the Western World: A new economic history*. Cambridge: Cambridge University Press, 1973.

**Rosenberg, Nathan.** *Perspectives on technology*. Cambridge: Cambridge University Press, 1976.

**Rosenberg, Nathan, and L. E. Birdzell.** *How the West grew rich: The economic transformation of the industrial world*. New York: Basic Books, 1986.

**Simon, Herbert.** "Rationality in Psychology and Economics," in Robin M. Hogarth and Melvin W. Reder, eds., *Rational choice: The contrast between economics and psychology*. Chicago: University of Chicago Press, 1986, pp. 25–40.

**Tversky, Amos, and Daniel Kahneman.** "Rational Choice and the Framing of Decisions," in Robin M. Hogarth and Melvin W. Reder, eds., *Rational choice: The contrast between economics and psychology*. Chicago: University of Chicago Press, 1986, pp. 67–94.

**Wallis, John J., and Douglass C. North.** "Measuring the Transaction Sector in the American Economy," in Stanley L. Engerman and Robert E. Gallman, eds., *Long-term factors in American economic growth*. Chicago: University of Chicago Press, 1986, pp. 95–148.

————. "Institutional Change and Technical Change in American Economic Growth: A Transactions Costs Approach." *Journal of Institutional and Theoretical Economics*, 1994 (forthcoming).

# CHAPTER 5

✸

# VERNON L. SMITH

Vernon L. Smith was awarded the Sveriges Riksbank Prize in Economic Sciences in Memory of Alfred Nobel in 2002, together with social psychologist Daniel Kahneman, for "having established laboratory experiments as a tool in empirical economic analysis, especially in the study of alternative market mechanisms." The Nobel Committee recognized Smith for his significant contributions to the field of experimental economics and for establishing reliable laboratory standards at a time when economics was considered to be a nonexperimental science. It also credited Smith for being crucial in instituting experiments as an important tool in empirical economic analysis and creating replicas of markets in a laboratory setting. His research focused on demonstrating "the importance of alternative market institutions" and testing alternative market designs. His methods for laboratory experiments, according to the Nobel Committee, greatly contributed to the understanding of economic psychology and economic behavior.

# CONSTRUCTIVIST *and* ECOLOGICAL RATIONALITY *in* ECONOMICS

## VERNON L. SMITH

---

When we leave our closet, and engage in the common affairs of life, [reason's] conclusions seem to vanish, like the phantoms of the night on the appearance of the morning; and 'tis difficult for us to retain even that conviction, which we had attained with difficulty. . . .

—DAVID HUME, 1739, 1985, p. 507.

. . . we must constantly adjust our lives, our thoughts and our emotions, in order to live simultaneously within different kinds of orders according to different rules. If we were to apply the unmodified, uncurbed rules [of caring intervention to do visible "good"] of the . . . small band or troop, or . . . our families . . . to the [extended order of cooperation through markets], as our instincts and sentimental yearnings often make us wish to do, *we would destroy it.* Yet if we were to always apply the [competitive] rules of the extended order to our more intimate groupings, *we would crush them.*

—FRIEDRICH A. HAYEK, 1988, p. 18; ITALICS ARE HIS,
BRACKETED REDUCTIONS ARE MINE.

We have become accustomed to the idea that a natural system like the human body or an ecosystem regulates itself. To explain

> the regulation, we look for feedback loops rather than a central planning and directing body. But somehow our intuitions about self-regulation do not carry over to the artificial systems of human society. [Thus] . . . the . . . disbelief always expressed by [my] architecture students [about] . . . medieval cities as marvelously patterned systems that had mostly just "grown" in response to myriads of individual decisions. To my students a pattern implied a planner. . . . The idea that a city could acquire its pattern as "naturally" as a snowflake was foreign to them.
>
> —HERBERT ALEXANDER SIMON, 1981, 1996, p. 33.

Historically, a recurrent theme in economics is that the values to which people respond are not confined to those one would expect based on the narrowly defined canons of rationality. These roots go back to Adam Smith (1759, 1776), who examined the moral sympathies that characterize natural human sociality.[1] Contrary to vulgar impressions, in Smith's view, each individual defined and pursued his own interest in his own way, and individuals were mischaracterized by the metaphor, "economic man" (cf., Hayek, 1991, p. 120). This careless scholarship fails to recognize the key proposition articulated by the Scottish philosophers: to do good for others, does **not** require deliberate action to further the perceived interest of others. As Mandeville so succinctly put it, "The worst of all the multitude did something for the common good." (See Mandeville's poem, "The Grumbling Hive" or "Knaves Turned Honest," 1705; quoted in Hayek, 1991, p. 82.) Many contemporary scholars, and not only popular writers, have reversed Mandeville's proposition, and argued that the standard socioeconomic science model (SSSM) requires, justifies, and promotes selfish behavior.[2] On the contrary, because enforceable rights can never cover every margin of decision, opportunism in all relational contracting and exchange across time are costs, not benefits, in achieving long-term value from trade; an ideology of honesty[3] means that people play the game of "trade," rather than "steal," although crime may often pay the rational lawbreaker who always chooses dominant strategies. Nor does non-selfish behavior in ordinary market transactions prevent those transactions from promoting specialization and creating wealth.

Cultures that have evolved markets have enormously expanded resource specialization, created commensurate gains from exchange, and are wealthier than those that have not. This proposition says nothing about the necessity of human selfishness—the increased wealth of particular individuals can be used for consumption, investment, to pay taxes, for Macarthur Fellows, gifted to the symphony, the Smithsonian, or the poor.[4] Markets economize on the need for virtue, but do not eliminate it.

Research in economic psychology[5] has prominently reported examples where "fairness" considerations are said to contradict the rationality assumptions of the standard socioeconomic science model. But experimental economists have reported mixed results on rationality: people are often better (e.g., in two-person anonymous interactions), in agreement with (e.g., in flow supply and demand markets), or worse (e.g., in asset trading), in achieving gains for themselves and others than is predicted by rational analysis. Patterns in these contradictions and confirmations provide important clues to the implicit rules or norms that people may follow, and can motivate new theoretical hypotheses for examination in both the field and the laboratory. The pattern of results greatly modifies the prevailing, and I believe misguided, rational SSSM, and richly modernizes the unadulterated message of the Scottish philosophers.

## I. On Two Forms of Rationality

The organizing principle throughout this paper is the simultaneous existence of two rational orders. I shall try to make the case that both orders are distinguishing characteristics of what we are as social creatures; that both are essential to understanding and unifying a large body of experience from socioeconomic life and the experimental laboratory, and in charting relevant new directions for economic theory as well as experimental-empirical programs.

## A. Constructivist Rationality

The first concept of a rational order derives from the SSSM going back to the seventeenth century. The SSSM is an example of what Hayek has called constructivist rationality (or "constructivism"), which stems particularly from Descartes (also Bacon and Hobbes),[6] who believed and argued that all worthwhile social institutions were and should be created by conscious deductive processes of human reason.[7] In economics the SSSM leads to rational predictive models of decision that motivate research hypotheses that experimentalists have been testing in the laboratory since the mid-twentieth century. Although the test results tend to be confirming in impersonal market exchange, the results are famously and recalcitrantly mixed in "personal exchange," notably in a great variety of two-person extensive-form games where some half of the people attempt and frequently succeed when risking cooperation, even when anonymously paired.[8] These results have motivated constructivist extensions of game theory based on other-regarding, in addition to own-regarding, preferences (e.g., Gary E Bolton, 1991; Matthew Rabin, 1993), and on "learning"—the idea that the predictions of the SSSM might be approached over time by trial-and-error adaptation processes (Ido Erev and Alvin E. Roth, 1998; Camerer and Teck-Hua Ho, 1999).

An alternative and perhaps complementary explanation of some of these contradictions to theory is that people may use social-grown norms of trust and reciprocity[9] (including equity, meaning to each according to his justly earned dessert; i.e., equality of opportunity, not outcome) to achieve cooperative states superior to individually rational defection outcomes. We will report some experimental tests designed to separate competing preference and reciprocity theories of behavior in personal exchange. Although reciprocity seems to be a leader in the comparisons we summarize, its strength is not uniform across all tests, and much remains to be learned about the hidden recesses of meaning in human behavior and the circumstances in which cooperative or non-cooperative behavior is manifest.[10] Technically, the issue is how most productively to model agent "types" by extending game theory so that types are an integral part of its **predictive** content, rather than merely imported as an *ex post* technical explanation of experimental results. For example, moves can signal types, and effect decision, which explains why game form matters, and why payoffs available, but forgone, can effect outcomes. These elements must be part of the internal structure of the theory such that outcomes become predictions conditional on the elementary characteristics of players who read each other's intentions. If successful, many of the basic results in game theory would become special cases of the extended theory.

In market experiments—where cooperation can occur through the coordination function of prices produced by, but simultaneously resulting from, interaction with individual choice behavior—the results are more commonly in accord with standard competitive models that maximize group welfare. This professional victory is hollowed by the failure of standard theory to predict the "surprisingly"[11] weak conditions under which the results obtain.[12]

Thus, for tractability, Cartesian rationalism provisionally assumes or "requires" agents to possess complete payoff and other information—far more than could ever be given to one mind. In economics the resulting exercises are believed to sharpen economic thinking, as if–then parables. Yet, these assumptions are unlikely to approximate the level of ignorance that has conditioned either individual behavior, or our evolved institutions, as abstract norms or rules independent of particular parameters, which have survived as part of the world of experience.[13] The temptation is to ignore this reality because it is poorly understood, and does not yield to our familiar but inadequate modeling tools, and to proceed in the implicit belief that our parables capture what is most essential about what we observe. Having sharpened our understanding on Cartesian complete information parables we carry these tools into the world for application without all the necessary caveats that reflect the tractability constraints imposed by our bounded professional cognitive capacities as theorists.

In summary, constructivism uses reason to deliberately create rules of action, and create human socioeconomic institutions that yield outcomes deemed preferable, given particular circumstances, to those produced by alternative arrangements. Although constructivism is one of the crowning achievements of the human intellect, it is important to remain sensitive to the fact that human institutions and most decision-making is not guided primarily, if at all, by constructivism. Emergent arrangements, even if initially constructivist in form, must have survival properties that take account of opportunity costs and environmental challenges invisible to our modeling efforts.

## B. Limitations and Distractions of Constructivist Rationality

Since our theories and thought processes about social systems involve the conscious and deliberate use of reason, it is necessary to constantly remind ourselves that human activity is diffused and dominated by unconscious, autonomic, neuropsychological systems that enable people to function effectively without always calling upon the brain's scarcest resource—attentional and reasoning circuitry. This is an important economizing property of how the brain works. If it were otherwise, no one could get through the day under the burden of the self-conscious monitoring and planning of every trivial action in detail.[14] Also, no one can express in thoughts, let alone words, all that he or she knows, and does not know but might call upon, or need to discover, for some purposive action. Imagine the strain on the brain's resources if at the supermarket a shopper were required to explicitly evaluate his preferences for every combination of the tens of thousands of grocery items that are feasible for a given budget. Such mental processes are enormously opportunity-costly and implicitly our brain knows, if our conscious mind does not know, that we must avoid incurring opportunity costs that are not worth the benefit.[15] The challenge of any unfamiliar action or problem appears first to trigger a search by the brain to bring to the conscious mind what one knows that is related to the decision context. Context triggers autobiographic experiential memory, which explains why context surfaces as a nontrivial treatment, particularly in small group experiments. The brain (including the entire neurophysiological system) takes over directly in the case of familiar, mastered tasks, and plays the equivalent of lightening chess when the "expert" trades, plays Beethoven's Fifth piano concerto, or connects with a 95-mile/hour fastball—all without self-aware "thinking" by the mind.

We fail utterly to possess natural mechanisms for reminding ourselves of the brain's off-line activities and accomplishments. This important proposition has led Michael S. Gazzaniga (1998) to ask why the brain fools the mind into believing it is in control.[16] And to Hayek, who thoroughly understood this proposition, what was the "fatal conceit"? "The idea that the ability to acquire skills stems from reason."

The constructivist mind makes a fatal "error," blinding itself to understanding, as we are warned, "one should never suppose that our reason is in the higher critical position and that only those moral rules are valid that reason endorses" (Hayek, 1988, p. 21). But the anthropocentric ( -morphic) mind routinely makes this significant error.

Most of our operating knowledge[17] we do not remember learning. Natural language is the most prominent example, but also music and virtually everything that constitutes our developmental socialization. We learn the rules of a language and of efficient social intercourse, without explicit instruction, simply by exposure to family and extended family social networks (Jerome Kagan and Sharon Lamb, 1987; Alan Page Fiske, 1991; Kagan, 1994; Steven Pinker, 1994). That the brain is capable of off-line subconscious learning is shown by experiments with amnesiacs who are taught a new task. They learn to perform well, but memory of having learned the task escapes them (Barbara J. Knowlton et al., 1996).

## C. Ecological Rationality

These considerations lead to the second concept of a rational order, as an undesigned ecological system that emerges out of cultural and biological evolutionary[18] processes: homegrown principles of action, norms, traditions, and "morality."[19] Ecological rationality uses reason—rational reconstruction—to examine the behavior of individuals based on their experience and folk knowledge, who are "naive" in their ability to apply constructivist tools to the decisions they make; to understand the emergent order in human cultures; to discover the possible intelligence embodied in the rules, norms, and institutions of our cultural and biological heritage that are created from human interactions but not by deliberate human design. People follow rules without being able to articulate them, but they can be discovered. This is the intellectual heritage of the Scottish philosophers, who described and interpreted the social and economic order they observed.

An eighteenth-century precursor of Herbert Simon, David Hume was concerned with the limits of reason, the bounds on human understanding, and with scaling back the exaggerated claims of Cartesian constructivism. To Hume, rationality was phenomena that reason discovers in emergent institutions. Thus, "the rules of morality ... are not conclusions of [our] reason" (Hume, 1985, p. 235). Adam Smith developed the idea of emergent order for economics. Truth is discovered in the form of the intelligence embodied in rules and traditions that have formed, inscrutably, out of the ancient history of human social interactions. This is the antithesis of the anthropocentric belief that if an observed social mechanism is functional, somebody in the unrecorded past must have used reason consciously to create it to serve its perceived intended purposes.[20]

In experimental economics the eighteenth-century Scottish tradition is revealed in the observation of emergent order in numerous studies of existing market institutions such as the continuous double auction (CDA).[21] To paraphrase Adam Smith, people in these experiments are led to promote group welfare-enhancing social ends that are not part of their intention. This principle is supported by hundreds of experiments whose environments and institutions (sealed bid, posted offer, and others besides CDA) may exceed the capacity of formal game-theoretic analysis to articulate predictive models. But they do not exceed the functional capacity of collectives of incompletely informed human decision makers, whose autonomic mental algorithms coordinate behavior through the rules of the institution—social algorithms—to generate high levels of measured performance.

Acknowledging and investigating the workings of unseen processes are essential to the growth of our understanding of social phenomena, and enable us to probe beyond the anthropocentric limitations of constructivism.

Both kinds of rationality have influenced the design and interpretation of experiments in economics. Thus, if people in certain contexts make choices that contradict our formal theory of rationality, rather than conclude that they are irrational, some ask why, reexamine maintained hypotheses including all aspects of the experiments—procedures, payoffs, context, instructions, etc.—and inquire as to what new concepts and experimental designs can help us to better understand the behavior. What is the subjects' perception of the problem that they are trying to solve?

Finally, understanding decision requires knowledge beyond the traditional bounds of economics,[22] a challenge to which Hume and Smith were not strangers.[23] This is manifest in the recent studies of the neural correlates of strategic interaction (McCabe calls it neuroeconomics) using fMRI and other brain-imaging technologies. That research explores the neurocorrelates of intentions or "mind reading," and other hypotheses about information, choice, and own versus other payoffs in determining interactive behavior.

The above themes will be illustrated and discussed in a wide variety of examples drawn from economics, law, experimental economics, and psychology. I will begin with impersonal exchange through markets, drawing on the learning from experiments and field observations to illustrate how the contrast between constructive and ecological rationality informs learning from observation. Then I will examine personal exchange, particularly in the context of two-person extensive-form games, asking why constructivist models are of limited success in predicting behavior in single-play games, even when subjects are anonymously matched.

## II. Impersonal Exchange: The Extended Order
## of the Market

### A. How Are the Two Concepts of a Rational
### Order Related?

Constructivism takes as given the social structures generated by emergent institutions that we observe in the world, and proceeds to model it formally. An example would be the Dutch auction or its alleged isomorphic equivalent, the sealed-bid auction (William Vickrey, 1961; Paul Milgrom and Robert J. Weber, 1982). Constructivist models need not ask why or how an auction institution arose or what were the ecological conditions that created it, or why there are so many distinct auction institutions. In some cases it is the other way around. Thus, revenue equivalence theorems show that the standard auctions generate identical expected outcomes, which, if taken literally, leave no modeled economic reason for choosing between them.

More generally, using rational theory, one represents an observed socioeconomic situation with an abstract interactive game tree. Contrarily, the ecological concept of rationality asks from whence came the structure captured by the tree? Why this social practice, from which we can abstract a particular game, and not another? Were there other practices and associated game trees that lacked survival properties and were successfully invaded by what we observe? There is a sense in which ecological systems, whether cultural or biological, must necessarily be, or are in the process of becoming, rational: they serve the fitness needs of those who unintentionally created them through their interactions. Constructivist mental models are based on assumptions about behavior, structure, and the value-knowledge environment. These assumptions might be correct, incorrect, or irrelevant, and the models may or may not lead to rational action in the sense of serving well the needs of those to whom the models apply. As theorists the professional charge for which we are paid is to formulate and prove theorems. A theorem is a mapping from assumptions into testable or observable implications. The demands of tractability loom large in this exercise, and to get anything much in the way of results it is necessary to consider both the assumptions and their implications as variables. Few game theorists, building on the assumption that agents always choose dominant strategies, believed this to characterize the behavior of all agents in all situations. Hence, the near-universal justification of theory as an exercise in "understanding." But the temptation is to believe that our "castles in the sky" (as W. Brock would say) have direct meaning in our worlds of experience and proceed to impose them where it may not be ecologically rational to do so.

To understand what is—the tip of the knowledge iceberg—requires understanding of a great deal that is not. In the laboratory we can not only rationally reconstruct counterfactuals, as in economic history, but also use experiments to test and examine their properties. Let us look at two contemporary examples.

*1. Deregulating Airline Routes.* Airline route deregulation brought an unanticipated reorganization of the network, called the hub-and-spoke system. (See, e.g., George Donahue, 2002). This is an ecologically rational response, apparently anticipated by none of the constructivist arguments for deregulation, and predicted by no one. Nor could it have been uncovered, I submit, in 1978 by surveys of airline managers, or by marketing surveys of airline customers. Unknown to both managers and customers was the subsequently revealed decision preferences of customers who unknowingly favored frequency of daily departure and arrival times—a preference that had to be discovered through market experimentation. Nonstop service between secondary cities was simply not sustainable in a deregulated world of free choice. The only way to achieve efficiency, both the demand for frequency of service and profitable load factors, among secondary cities was for the flights to connect through hubs. Hence, the hypothesis that a rational ecological equilibrium emerged to dominate repeated constructivist attempts, by business entrants and start-ups, to satisfy an incompatible set of constraints provided by the microstructure of demand, profitability, and technology.

Might it have been otherwise if airport runway rights, or "slots," had been an integral part of the deregulation of airline routes, and the time-of-day spot pricing of slots had emerged to reflect hub congestion costs? (Stephen Rassenti et al., 1982). We do not know, but the effect of this hypothetical counterfactual on the viability of hub bypass could be assessed in laboratory experiments. As in all studies of what is not, the challenge is to estimate the parameters that would implement the appropriate economic environment.

*2. The California Energy Crisis.* A second, and very troubling, example is the circumstances leading to the California energy crisis. As in other regions of the country and the world, deregulation was effected as a planned transition with numerous political compromises. In California it took the form of deregulating wholesale markets and prices while continuing to regulate retail prices at fixed hourly rates over the daily and seasonal cycles in consumption. The utilities negotiated an increase in these average retail rates to meet the revenue requirements of capital investments that were "stranded" (i.e., were believed to be unable to recover their costs under competition). This preoccupation with the past, and with average revenue/cost thinking by regulators and regulated alike, ill-prepared the state for the consequences of having no dynamic mechanisms for prioritizing the end use consumption of power.

As expected, traditional volatility in the marginal cost of generated electricity was immediately translated into volatile intra-day wholesale prices. What was not expected was that a combination of low rainfall (reducing Pacific Northwest hydroelectric output), growth in demand, unseasonably hot weather, generators down on normal maintenance schedules, etc., caused the temporary normal daily peaking of prices to be greatly accentuated, and to be much more lasting than had occurred earlier in the Midwest and South. Events of small probability happen at about the expected frequency, and since there are many such events the unexpected is not that unlikely. Constructivist planning failed to provide for retail competition to experiment with programs allowing consumers to save money by enabling their lower priority uses of power to be interrupted in times of supply stress. Interruptible deliveries are a direct substitute for both energy supply and energy reserves, and are an essential means of assuring adequate capacity and reserves that cover all the various supply contingencies faced by the industry.

Because of the regulatory mandate that all demand must be served at a fixed price, the planning did not allow for the early introduction of demand responsive retail prices and technologies to enable peak consumption to be reduced. Instead of mechanism design we had fixed retail price "design" to generate average revenue that was supposed to cover average cost, and it failed. The regulatory thought process is as follows: the function of price is to provide revenue, and the function of revenue is to cover cost. But this is the antithesis of the market function of price. For neither management nor the regulators was it natural to think in terms of profiting from selling less power. Yet that was precisely the route by which the California distributors could have avoided the loss of an estimated $15 billion: every peak kilowatt-hour not sold at the average retail rate would have saved up to ten times that amount of energy cost. Static technology, and the utter fantasy that all load can always be served, was protected from innovation by the legally franchised local wires monopoly. An entrant could not seek to win customers by offering discounts for switching from peak to off-peak consumption, and, at the entrant's investment risk, installing the required control devices on end-use appliances. This legacy—long entrenched, and jealously sheltered by local franchised monopolies after deregulation—gave California dispatchers no alternative but to trap people in elevators and shut down high-end computer programming facilities at critical times of peak power shortage.

All power delivery systems are vulnerable to a combination of unfavorable events that will produce short supplies at peak demand. Constructivism alone, without competitive trial-and-error ecological experimentation with retail delivery technologies and consumer preferences, cannot design mechanisms that process all the distributed knowledge that individuals either possess or will discover, and that is relevant to finding an efficient mix of both demand and supply responsiveness.[24]

**Economic Systems Design.**[25] What can we learn from experiments about how demand responsiveness could impact energy shortages as in the California crisis? Rassenti et al. (2003) measure this impact by creating a market in which a modest and achievable 16 percent of peak retail demand can be interrupted voluntarily at discount prices by wholesale energy providers. In the experiments, demand cycles through four levels each "day" and is expressed in the wholesale market with two contrasting experimental treatments: (1) robot buyers who reveal all demand at the spot market clearing price; (2) four profit-motivated human buyers who are free to bid strategically in the market to obtain the lowest available prices. In each case bids to supply power are entered by five profit-motivated human suppliers. In the passive-demand treatment prices average much above the benchmark competitive equilibrium, and are very volatile. In the treatment with human buyers, prices approach the competitive equilibrium, and price volatility becomes miniscule. By empowering wholesale buyers, in addition to sellers, to bid strategically in their own interest, even though 84 percent of peak demand is "must serve," buyers are able to effectively discipline sellers and hold prices at competitive levels.[26]

This example illustrates the use of the laboratory in economic systems design. In these exercises we can test-bed alternative market auction rules and the effect of transmission constraints on generator supply behavior (Steven R. Backerman et al., 2001), vary the degree of market concentration, or "power" in a nonconvex environment (Michael J. Denton et al., 2001), compare the effect of more or less strategic demand responsiveness (Rassenti et al., 2003), study network and multiple market effects also in a nonconvex environment (Mark Olson et al., 2003), and test-bed markets to inform, but not finalize, market liberalization policy (Rassenti et al., 2002). For a survey of many examples, see McCabe et al. (1991).

The two types of rational order are both expressed in the experimental methodology developed for economic systems design. This branch of experimental economics uses the lab as a test bed to examine the performance of proposed new institutions, and modifies their rules and implementation features in the light of the test results. The proposed designs are initially constructivist, although most applications, such as the design of electricity markets or auctions for spectrum licenses, are far too complicated for formal analysis (Jeffrey Banks et al., 2003; Rassenti et al., 2003).

But when a design is modified in the light of test results, the modifications tested, modified again, retested, and so on, one is using the laboratory to effect an evolutionary adaptation as in the ecological concept of a rational order. If the final result is implemented in the field, it certainly undergoes further evolutionary change in the light of practice, and of operational forces not tested in the experiments because they were unknown, or beyond current laboratory technology.[27] In fact this evolutionary process is essential if institutions, as dynamic social tools, are to be adaptive and responsive to changing conditions. How can such flexibility be made part of their design? We do not know because no one can foresee what changes will be needed.

**Market Institutions and Performance.** Noncooperative or Cournot-Nash competitive equilibrium (CE) theory has conventionally offered two specifications concerning the preconditions for achieving a CE: (1) agents require complete, or "perfect," information on the equations defining the CE; also common knowledge—all must know that all know that all know that they have this information. In this way all agents have common expectations of a CE and their behavior must necessarily produce it; (2) another tradition, popularly articulated in textbooks, and showing, perhaps, more sensitivity for plausibility, has argued for a weaker requirement that agents need only be price-takers in the market.

The alleged "requirement" of complete, common, or perfect information is vacuous: I know of no predictive theorem stating that when agents have such information their behavior produces a CE, and in its absence their behavior fails to produce a CE. If such a theorem existed, it could help us to design the experiments that could test these dichotomous predictions. I suggest that the idea that agents need complete information is derived from introspective error: as theorists we need complete information to calculate the CE. But this is not a theory of how information or its absence causes agent behavior to yield or not a CE. It is simply an unmotivated statement declaring, without evidence, that every agent is a constructivist in exactly the same sense as are we as theorists. And the claim that it is "as if" agents had complete information helps not a whit to understand the wellsprings of behavior. What is missing are models of the process whereby agents go from their initial circumstances, and dispersed information, using the algorithms of the institution to update their status, and converge (or not) to the predicted equilibrium.[28]

As a theory the price-taking parable is also a nonstarter: who makes price if all agents take price as given? If it is the Walrasian auctioneer, why have such processes been found to be so inefficient? (Corrine Bronfman et al., 1996).

Hundreds of experiments in the past 40 years (Smith, 1962, 1982; Douglas D. Davis and Charles A. Holt, 1993, 1995; John H. Kagel and Roth, 1995; Plott, 2001) demonstrate that complete information is not necessary for a CE to form out of a self-ordering interaction between agent behavior and the rules of information exchange and contract in a variety of different institutions, but most prominently in the continuous bid/ask double auction (CDA).[29] That complete information also may not be sufficient for a CE is suggested (the samples are small) by comparisons showing that convergence is slowed or fails under complete information in certain environments (Smith, 1976, 1980).

An interesting contribution by Dhananjay K. Gode and Shyam Sunder (hereafter GS; see Shyam Sunder, 2003, and the references it contains) is to demonstrate that an important component of the emergent order observed in these market experiments derives from the institution, not merely the presumed rationality of the individuals. Efficiency is necessarily a joint product of the rules of the institution and the behavior of agents. What Sunder and his coauthors have shown is that in the double-auction market for a single commodity (we know not yet how far it can be generalized), efficiency is high even with "zero" intelligence robot agents, each of whom chooses bids (asks) completely at random from all those that will not impose a loss on the agent. Thus, agents who are not rational constructivist profit maximizers, and use no learning or updating algorithms, achieve most of the possible social gains from trade using this institution. Does this example illustrate in a small way those "super-individual structures within which individuals found great opportunities . . . [and that] . . . could take account of more factual circumstances than individuals could perceive, and in consequence . . . is in some respects superior to, or 'wiser' than, human reason . . ."? (Hayek, 1988, pp. 77, 75).

We do not know if the GS results generalize to multiple market settings as discussed in the next paragraph. Ross M. Miller (2002), however, has shown that in a very elementary two-market environment—intertemporally separated markets for the same commodity—the GS results are qualified. Complex price dynamics, including "bubbles," appear, and there is loss of efficiency, although the loss is not substantial. On average the decline is apparently from around 94 percent to 88 percent.

In multiple market trading in nonlinear interdependent demand environments, each individual's maximum willingness-to-pay for a unit of commodity A depends on the price of B, and vice versa, and in this more complex economy double auction, markets also converge to the vector of CE prices and trading volumes. A two-commodity example is reported in Smith (1986), based on nonlinear demand (CES payoff function) and linear supply functions found in Arlington Williams and Smith (1986); also see Williams et al. (2000). In these experiments, numerical tables based on the preference and cost information defining the general-equilibrium solution of four nonlinear equations in two prices and two quantities are dispersed among the undergraduate subjects. They buy and sell units of each of the two commodities in a series of trading periods. Prices and trading volume converge, after several trading periods, to the CE defined by the nonlinear equations. The subjects would not have a clue as to how to solve the equations mathematically. The experimenter applies the tools of constructivist reason to solve for the benchmark CE, but in repeat play this "solution" emerges from the spontaneous order created by the subjects trading under the rules of the double-auction market institution. Numerous other experiments with many simultaneous interdependent markets show similar patterns of convergence (Plott, 1988, 2001).

**The Iowa Electronic Market.** What evidence do we have that the laboratory efficiency properties of continuous double auction trading apply also in the field? One of the best sources of evidence, I believe, is found in the Iowa Electronic Market (IEM) used widely around the world (Robert Forsythe et al., 1992, 1999). These markets are used to study the efficacy of futures markets in aggregating widely dispersed information on the outcomes of political elections, or any well-defined extra-laboratory event, such as a change in the discount rate by the Fed. The "laboratory" is the Internet. The "subjects" are all who log on and buy an initial portfolio of claims on the final event outcomes; they consist of whomever logs in, and are not any kind of representative or "scientific" sample as in the polls with which they are paired. The institution is the open-book double auction.

In the IEM, traders make a market in shares representing pari-mutuel claims on the popular vote (or winner-take-all) outcome of an election, referendum, etc. For example, the first IEM was on the 1988 presidential election. Each person wanting to trade shares deposits a minimum sum, $35, with the IEM and receives a trading account containing $10 cash for buying additional shares, and ten elemental portfolios at $2.50 each, consisting of one share of each of the candidates—Bush, Dukakis, Jackson, and "rest-of-field." Trading occurs continuously in an open-book bid-ask market for several months, and everyone knows that the market will be called (trading suspended) in November on election day, when the dividend paid on each share is equal to the candidate's fraction of the popular vote times $2.50. Hence if the final two candidates and all others receive popular vote shares (53.2 percent, 45.4 percent, 1.4 percent), these proportions (times $2.50) represent the payoff to a trader for each share held. Consequently, at any time $t$, normalizing on

$1, the price of a share (divided by $2.50) reflects the market expectation of that candidate's share of the total vote. A price, $0.43, means the market predicts that the candidate will poll 43 percent of the vote. Other forms of contract that can be traded in some IEMs include winner-take-all, or number of seats in the House, and so on.

The IEM data set includes 49 markets, 41 worldwide elections, and 13 countries. Several results stand out: the closing market prices, produced by a nonrepresentative sample of traders, show lower average absolute forecasting error (1.5 percent) than the representative exit poll samples (1.9 percent); in the subset of 16 national elections, the market outperforms the polls in 9 of 15 cases; in the course of several months preceding the election outcome, the market predictions are consistently much less volatile than the polls; generally, larger and more active markets predict better than smaller, thinner markets; surveys of the market traders show that their shareholdings are biased in favor of the candidates they themselves prefer.

In view of this last result, why do markets outperform the polls? Forsythe et al. (1992) argue that it's their marginal trader hypothesis. Those who are active in price "setting," that is, in entering limit bids or asks, are found to be less subject to this bias, than those traders accepting (selling and buying "at market") the limit bids and asks. Polls record unmotivated, representative, average opinion. Markets record motivated marginal opinion that cannot be described as "representative." This analysis helps to provide a good mechanical, if not ultimate, understanding of how human interaction with the rules of a bid/ask CDA yield efficient predictions.[30]

We have seen that markets economize on information, understanding, the number of agents, and individual rationality. Can they also economize on the need for external intervention to protect particular interests, if all are empowered by the trading institution to act in their individual interests?

## B. Strategy-Proofness: Theory and Behavior

Preferences are private and unobservable, and institutions have to rely on the messages reported by agents, not their true preferences. This follows from the fact that no one mind has all the information known together by all those in the market. It is therefore possible for an agent to affect prices and outcomes in a market by strategically misreporting preferences. This prospect has motivated the literature seeking strategy-proof mechanisms: "An allocation mechanism is strategy-proof if every agent's utility-maximizing choice of what preferences to report depends only on his own preferences and not on his expectations concerning the preferences that other agents will report" (Mark Satterthwaite, 1987, p. 519). This requires each agent to have a dominant strategy to report true preferences, and has led to impossibility theorems establishing the nonexistence of such a mechanism under certain conditions.

In view of such negative theoretical results and the narrow conditions under which solutions have been investigated, it is important to ask what people actually do in experimental environments in which the experimenter induces preferences privately on individual subjects. We know what is impossible, but what is possible in more open-ended systems than are modeled by theory? Is it possible that when all are free to choose from a large space of strategies, ecologically rational strategies will emerge that immunize against strategic manipulation? Given that information is inherently dispersed, has society evolved institutions in which forms of behavior arise that result in practical if not universal solutions to the problem of strategy-proofness?

The double auction is a well-known example yielding CE in a wide range of economic environments including small numbers. Are there other examples, and if there are, what are the strategic behavioral mechanisms that people adopt to achieve strategy-proofness?

One example is the sealed-bid-offer auction: in each contract period the submitted bids are ordered from highest to lowest, the offers (asks) from lowest to highest, with the intersection (cross) determining the uniform clearing price and volume exchanged (see Timothy Cason and Friedman, 1993; Friedman, 1993; and Wilson, 1993). Also see Smith et al. (1982) for comparative studies of different versions of the sealed-bid-offer mechanism and the continuous double auction.

In experiments with stationary supply and demand, initially both buyers and sellers greatly underreveal their true individual willingness to buy or sell. Volume is very low (10–15 percent of optimal), the market is inefficient and each agent can see that at the initial clearing price they are leaving money on the table. In repeat play they increase revelation, but mostly of units near the last period's clearing price. As volume increases and the clearing price closes in on the CE, the realized inverse demand and supply become very flat near the true clearing price with many tied or nearly tied bids and asks that exceed the capacity of any single buyer or seller. At this steady state, and given this behavior, if anyone withholds purchases or sales she is denied an allocation as other more competitively traded units substitute for hers. This results in a "behavioral strategy-proof equilibrium." Such is the power of motivated, privately informed agents in trial-and-error repeat interaction.

These experimental results make it plain that the theoretical condition for a strategy-proof equilibrium—that each agent have a dominate strategy to reveal true willingness-to-pay or willingness-to-accept for all units, and not just units near the margin—is much too strong. The above description from blind two-sided auctions, however, also shows that there is a social cost to the achievement of a strategy-proof equilibrium: blind two-sided auctions converge more slowly to the competitive equilibrium than continuous double auctions, and upon converging, may not be quite as efficient if agents occasionally attempt manipulation, are disciplined, and return to the full exchange volume.

A second example is the uniform price double auction (UPDA), a real-time continuous feedback mechanism clearing all trades at a single price in each trading period. This is a "designer market" invented by experimentalists who asked, "Can we combine the continuous information feedback advantages of the double auction with the uniform price (zero within-period volatility) advantages of the sealed-bid-offer auction?" As we have seen above, with blind bidding several repeat interactions are required to reach optimality, with many lost trades in the process. Can we accelerate the price discovery process by continuously feeding back information on the tentative state of the market, and allowing bids (asks) to be adjusted within each period?

This institution is made possible by high-speed computer and communication technology. It comes in several flavors, or variations on the rules. In all versions at each time, $t \leq T =$ time market is "called" (closed), the tentative clearing price, $p_t$, is displayed, and each agent knows the acceptance state of all her bids (asks). This allows bids and asks to be adjusted in real time. See the chapter by McCabe et al. (1993, pp. 311–16) for a report of 49 UPDA experiments comparing these different versions with the continuous double auction. UPDA exhibits even more underrevelation of demand and supply than the blind two-sided auction discussed above, but efficiency tends to be much higher, especially in the first periods, and, in one form (endogenous close, open book, the "other side" rule with conditional time priority), exceeds that of the continuous double auction.

Experiments using UPDA in a randomly fluctuating supply and demand environment routinely exhibit efficiencies of 95–100 percent, sometimes with as little as 5–10 percent of the available surplus revealed. This is shown in Table 1 for summary data from UPDA experiment UP 43. Most agents enter bids (asks) equal to or near the clearing price as it is continuously displayed in real time. It is of course true, hypothetically, that if all agents reveal their true demand or supply with the exception of one intra-marginal buyer or seller, then that agent can manipulate the price to his or her advantage. But this parable is irrelevant. The relevant question is what behavior is manifest when every agent has the potential for manipulating the price. Without knowledge or understanding of the whole, and without design or intention, the participants use the rules at their disposal to achieve three properties observed by the experimenter: (1) high efficiency, (2) maximum individual profit given the behavior of all other agents, and (3) protection from manipulation by their protagonists.[31] This ecological result illustrates the perceptive insight of Hayek (1988, pp. 19–20). "Rules alone can unite an extended order. . . . Neither all ends pursued, nor all means used, are known or need be known to anybody, in order for them to be taken account of within a spontaneous order. Such an order forms of itself. . . ."

TABLE 1—SUMMARY OF RESULTS: UPDA EXPERIMENT UP 43; 5, 5

|   | Pe | Qe | Pr | Qr | Eff% | Rev% |
|---|---|---|---|---|---|---|
| 1 | 295 | 18 | 300 | 16 | 91% | 22% |
| 2 | 405 | 18 | 400 | 18 | 100% | 7% |
| 3 | 545 | 18 | 540 | 18 | 100% | 14% |
| 4 | 460 | 18 | 448 | 18 | 92% | 14% |
| 5 | 360 | 18 | 350 | 18 | 100% | 9% |
| 6 | 500 | 18 | 500 | 18 | 98% | 12% |
| 7 | 260 | 18 | 250 | 17 | 96% | 26% |
| 8 | 565 | 18 | 553 | 15 | 92% | 28% |
| 9 | 300 | 18 | 300 | 18 | 100% | 28% |
| 10 | 610 | 18 | 610 | 18 | 100% | 33% |
| 11 | 365 | 18 | 350 | 15 | 85% | 88% |
| 12 | 550 | 18 | 558 | 15 | 88% | 55% |
| 13 | 450 | 18 | 450 | 18 | 100% | 31% |
| 14 | 410 | 18 | 410 | 18 | 100% | 5% |
| 15 | 485 | 18 | 484 | 19 | 89% | 39% |
|   |   |   | $\mu = 17.3$ |   | 95% | 27% |
|   |   |   | $\sigma = 1.3$ |   | 5 | 21 |

*Notes:* (Pe, Qe) = equilibrium price and quantity. (Pr, Qr) = realized price and quantity. Eff% = efficiency, % max surplus. Rev% = % of surplus revealed.

## C. Gresham's Law: If It Isn't Cournot-Nash,
## Why Is It a Law?

In this section I have given many examples of institutions in which the CE theory of markets predicts their observed behavior. Do we have contrary examples? Yes. Gresham's Law: bad money drives out good. This "law," while sometimes claimed to be an observed phenomenon in countries all over the world, is not a Cournot-Nash equilibrium.[32] If currencies A and B are both available, A having an intrinsic worth while B is worthless fiat money, then the theory predicts that A will drive out B. This is because each agent believes other agents are rational, and will accept only A in exchange. Each agent will therefore avoid getting stuck with the inferior B by accepting only A, which becomes the dominant circulating medium of exchange, while B is "hoarded." Experiments have confirmed that if both types of money are initially available, subjects use only the superior currency (an interest-bearing consol) as a medium of exchange. But in treatments in which subjects first experience a history of using fiat money, it being the only medium of exchange available, and then the consol is introduced, subjects continue trading with the fiat money, hoarding the interest-bearing consol (Gabriele Camera et al., 2003). This is entirely rational if each agent believes others will accept the fiat money in exchange and this belief is supported by experience. Think of Gresham's Law as a belief equilibrium in which theory alone is unable to predict when it might occur (Ledyard, 1986).

Complementing these results, another experimental study shows that when fiat money is the only currency, it will be used even under the condition that it is abandoned and replaced with a new fiat money issue at the end of a finite horizon. In this study the real economy is found to suffer some loss in efficiency relative to the use of "backed" (commodity) money, but the economy does not collapse even in short horizon treatments. Collapse in real sector efficiency is observed only when a "government" sector prints fiat money to purchase real goods from the private sector. Moreover, additional experimental tests show that the collapse cannot be due to the resulting inflation, but to interference with the real price discovery of markets when some agents are able to crowd out private real purchases with printing press money[33] (Deck et al., 2001).

## D. Psychology and Markets

Psychologists and "behavioral economists" who study decision behavior almost uniformly report results contrary to rational theory (Robin Hogarth and Melvin Reder, 1987). It was not always so,[34] but the focus on "anomalies," beginning in the 1970s, converted the emerging discovery enterprise into a search for contradictions between reports of behavior and the caricatures[35] of mainstream theory that constitute much of its core. Psychologists, to their credit, have maintained an intensive program examining the behavioral nature of these contradictions to the classical model. For example, Sidney Siegel (1959) and Lawrence E. Fouraker and Siegel (1963) reported both confirmations and contradictions, and used the pattern to propose improved models. Similarly, in prospect theory Kahneman and Tversky (1979) have proposed modifications in both the utility and probability weighting functions of standard expected utility theory.[36] Research strategies that focus on the study of errors, however, can distort professional beliefs, to say nothing of popular representations, if the primary emphasis is on the failures, to the exclusion of the predictive successes, of the theory.[37]

# E. Psychology, Economics, and the Two Kinds of Rationality

Curiously, the image of economists and psychologists as protagonists obscures their underlying agreement on foundations. Both rely upon constructivism: (1) to the extent that markets are rational[38] or irrational,[39] this derives directly and only from the rationality or irrationality of agents;[40] (2) individual rationality is a self-aware, calculating process of maximization;[41] (3) predominantly both are reluctant to allow that naive, unsophisticated agents can achieve socially optimal ends without comprehension of the whole, as well as their individual parts, implemented by deliberate action (there is no "magic," and no room for the GS zero intelligence traders); (4) consequently, psychologists test the rationality of individual decisions largely by asking for subject responses to choice problems to discover how they "reason." Rather than challenge this constructivist view, economists, subject to the identical vision (how do agents consciously think?), are critical of the question-response survey methods used in cognitive psychology: the stakes are zero or too low,[42] and the subjects are too unsophisticated, inexperienced, or untrained to allow a serious researcher to find out how "real agents really think." Many psychologists appear to find irrationality everywhere, and many economists appear to see the findings as everywhere irrelevant. To these economists, how agents think indeed exhausts the core of empirical economics; psychologists merely "fail" to properly implement their investigation of this core.[43]

In point of fact, opinion surveys can provide important insights: sometimes survey findings can be tested more rigorously with reward-motivated choices in the laboratory or the field and are found to have predictive content (e.g., the asymmetry between losses and gains in wealth). Sometimes what people actually do completely contradicts what they say, and sometimes you cannot find out by asking because the agents themselves do not know what they will do or are doing. For example:

- Comparisons of risk preferences under low and high monetary stakes have shown that actual reward levels have a statistically significant effect on decision, but that the qualitative conclusions from hypothetical choice response surveys are not refuted by studies using very high stakes—the accumulated payoffs average three times subjects' normal monthly living expenses (Steven J. Kachelmeier and Mohamed Shehata, 1992; also see Hans P. Binswanger, 1980, for similar findings).

- Consider the double auction in classroom demonstration experiments: in debriefings afterwards students deny that there is any kind of quantitative model that could predict their market price and exchange volume, or that they were able to maximize their profits; but a participant with an envelope containing the predictions provided in advance, opens it showing that this consensus is false. The dispersed private value/cost information is aggregated into prices that are at the equilibrium and each agent is maximizing his or her profit given the behavior of all others. Here there is indeed a kind of "magic," but only, I think, in not being well understood or modeled at the game-theoretic level of individual choice.[44] Our bounded rationality as economic theorists is far more constraining on economic science, than the bounded rationality of privately informed agents is constraining on their ability to maximize the gains from exchange.

- In asset trading, participant survey responses reflect the disconnect between their information on fundamental value and their puzzling experience of a price bubble and crash generated on the long path to the rational expectations equilibrium (T. Schwartz and J. S. Ang, 1989).

- Opinion polls administered to the IEM traders show the same judgment biases that psychologists and political scientists find in public opinion polls, but these biases did not interfere with the market's ability to predict the popular vote outcomes (Forsythe et al., 1992).

- In preference reversal survey experiments subjects report many inconsistent choices: gamble A is preferred to B but a subject will sell A for less than B. Arbitraging the subjects' cash-motivated choices quickly reduces these inconsistencies (Yun Peng Chu and Ruey Ling Chu, 1990, p. 906), and it has been shown that the inconsistencies are unbiased random errors under some, but not all, conditions (James C. Cox and David M. Grether, 1996); also see Barry Soper and Gary Gigiolotti, 1993, where choice intransitivity is studied directly and the errors are found to be random.

- Kahneman et al. (1986; hereafter KKT) provide many examples in which respondents are asked to rate the fairness,[45] on a four-point scale, of elementary business actions in competitive environments. In one case a hardware store raises the price of snow shovels from $15 to $20 after a snowstorm. Eighty-two percent of the respondents consider this action either unfair or very unfair. Franciosi et al. (1995, pp. 939–40) substitute the words "acceptable" for "fair" and "unacceptable" for "unfair"[46] and add one additional sentence to this KKT example: "The store does this to prevent a stock out for its regular customers since another store has raised its price to $20." Now only 32 percent rate the action unfavorably. This exercise suggests the possible sensitivity of survey results to emotive words and/or perceived "justification" in terms of impersonal market forces.

Note that it is in private information environments, where the market is aggregating information far beyond the reach of what each individual knows, and is able to comprehend, that the solicited opinions are so far off the mark. The surveys yield no useful understanding because the subjects have none to relate. In the complete information asset market, subjects are aware of its fundamental value structure, and come to have common expectations through an experiential process of repetition; i.e., initial common information is not sufficient to induce common expectations.[47] They play myopically and their expressed bafflement ("prices rise without cause") reflects this myopia. These comments suggest that much insight might be obtained from the systematic study of the conditions under which survey results are robustly informative and the conditions where they are not.

## F. Fairness: An Experimental Market Test

In developing a descriptive theory[48] of the "reference transaction," KKT state that what is considered "fair" may change: "Terms of exchange that are initially seen as unfair may in time acquire the status of a reference transaction" (KKT, 1991, p. 203). This paves the way for the adaptation of "fairness beliefs" to changes in the competitive equilibrium. Although the competitive model is the one that has static predictive content, its prediction is silent as to how long it will take to respond to a change in parameters. KKT's arguments are not predictive, but they tell a story about why markets might be sluggish in responding to change. How good is their story?

Franciosi et al. (1995) state a preference model of optimal choice that allows for a utilitarian tradeoff between own consumption and "fairness." For example, the utility of two commodities $(x, z)$ is given by: $u(x, z) = z + ax - (b/2) x^2 - \alpha x[(\pi/\pi_0) - 1]$, in which the seller's profit, $\pi$, relative to a reference profit, $\pi_0$, appears as an "externality" in the buyer's utility function. The usual maximization subject to an income constraint yields the inverse demand equation: $p = a - bx - \alpha[(\pi/\pi_0) - 1]$. Thus, for $\alpha > 0$ any change in the environment that increases a firm's profit relative to the reference profit has an external effect that lowers the buyer's inverse demand for units $x$. If $\alpha = 0$, then we have the standard own-maximizing theory. Consequently, Franciosi et al. (1995) can test the hypothesis, never using the word "fairness," that if subject buyers have a utilitarian concern for profits not being increased relative to a baseline then after a change from the baseline this should alter the observed equilibrium relative to the standard predicted equilibrium with no external effect, $\alpha = 0$. In a posted offer market giving KKT their best shot (sellers cannot see each other's posted prices, and therefore cannot knowingly emulate or undercut each other's prices), Franciosi et al. (1995) find that when $\alpha = 0$ (implemented by either no disclosure, or by marginal cost-justifying disclosure) the market converges quickly to the new competitive equilibrium. When $\alpha > 0$ (implemented by profit $\pi$ and $\pi_0$ disclosure) prices converge more slowly, but precisely, to the new equilibrium. Hence, under conditions most favorable to a "fairness" effect, the response dynamics is changed, but not the equilibrium as predicted by the standard competitive model. The discipline of the market swamps all but a transient "fairness" effect. If, realistically, sellers can see each other's prices, I would predict a much smaller "fairness" effect, if any.

## III. Personal Social Exchange

One of the most intriguing discoveries of experimental economics is that (1) as we have seen, people invariably behave noncooperatively in small and large group "impersonal" market exchange institutions; (2) many (up to half in single play; over 90 percent in repeat play) cooperate in "personal" exchange (two-person extensive-form games); (3) yet in both economic environments all interactions are between anonymous players. In this section I shall attempt to summarize some of the most compelling evidence of cooperation in personal exchange—in the field as well as the laboratory—and review some of the test results designed to discriminate among the more prominent predictive hypotheses for modeling cooperative behavior. Whatever might be the most useful way to model and explain cooperation, unaided by market incentives, my working hypothesis throughout is that it is a product of an unknown mix of cultural and biological evolution, with the biology providing abstract function defining potential, and culture shaping the emergent forms that we observe. But to motivate the whole exercise in thought, I will begin with a discussion of some persistent cross-cultural social practices from business, law, anthropology, and American economic history.

How might a social rule (practice, norm) emerge, become a cultural fixture, and be widely emulated? I will use a parable to illustrate how a rule for "bargaining in good faith" might become established.

In bargaining over the exchange price between a buyer and seller, suppose the seller begins by announcing a selling price, the buyer responds with a lower buying price, the seller reduces his asking price, and so on. In this concessionary process it is considered bad form for the buyer (or seller), once having made a concession, to return to a lower (or higher) price. This violates a principle of "bargaining in good faith" (see Siegel and Fouraker, 1960, p. 20). How might this come about? One can suppose that those who fail to bargain in good faith would be less likely to be sought out by others for repeat transactions. Such behavior raises transactions cost by increasing the time it takes to complete a sale. Trading pairs would be expected to self-select, tending to isolate the more time-consuming bargainers, and it would take them longer to find those willing to tolerate the time cost of bargaining. Such practices—inherently economizing in this parable—might then become part of a cultural norm, powerful enough to be codified ultimately in contract law and in stock exchange rules. Proposition: in this manner collectives discover law in those rules that persist long enough to become entrenched practices. In this example the emergent rule reduces transaction cost, leaving open the classical question of how equilibrium can be characterized in bilateral bargaining.

## A. Spontaneous Order without the Law[49]

The early "lawgivers" did not make the law they "gave"; they studied social traditions and informal rules and gave voice to them, as God's, or natural, law.[50] The common lawyer, Sir Edward Coke, championed seventeenth-century social norms as law commanding higher authority than the king. Remarkably, these forces prevailed, paving the way for the rule of law in England.[51] Similarly, the cattlemen's associations, land clubs, and mining districts in the American West all fashioned their own rules for establishing property rights and enforcing them: the brand on the hindquarters of his calf was the cattlemen's indelible ownership signature on his property, enforced by gunmen hired through his cattle club;[52] squatter's rights were defended ably (possession is nine points of the law?) by the land clubs composed of those brave enough to settle wilderness lands in advance of veterans exercising their land script claims, and of settlers under the Homestead Act; mining claims were defined, established, and defended by the guns of the mining clubbers, whose rules were later to become part of public mining law (Terry L. Anderson and Peter J. Hill, 1975; John Umbeck, 1977). For over a century, the Maine lobstermen have established rights, used threats, then force, to defend exclusive individual lobster-fishing territories in the ocean (James Acheson, 1975). Eskimo polar bear hunting teams awarded the upper half of the bear's skin (prized for its long mane hairs used to line women's boots) to that person who first fixed his spear in the prey (Peter Freuchen, 1961). Extant hunter-gatherers have evolved sharing customs for the products of communal hunting and gathering. For example, the Ache of Eastern Paraguay share the volatile products of the hunt widely within the tribe, while the low variance products of gathering are shared only within the nuclear family (Hillard Kaplan and Kim Hill, 1985; Kristen Hawkes, 1991).

## B. Ellickson Out-Coases Coase

Using the rancher/farmer parable, Ronald H. Coase (1960) argued that if there were no costs of transacting, then theoretically efficiency could not depend on who was liable for damages to crops caused by stray animals. Legal liability gives the rancher an incentive to employ cost-efficient measures to control straying cattle. But if she were not liable, then in a world of zero transactions cost, victims would be led in their own interest to negotiate a settlement paying the rancher to undertake the same efficient control measures induced by legal liability. In so doing, trespass victims save the cost of crop damage, assumed to be more than the cost of cattle control—otherwise it is inefficient to control them. The externality is internalized by market negotiation incentives. Curiously, the Coase Theorem—that in the absence of transactions cost efficiency does not depend upon the locus of liability—was controversial. It was clearly intended as a kindly spoof of oversimplified theories that, in particular, ignored transactions cost.[53] The real problem, addressed brilliantly by Coase, was to deal with the question of efficient liability rules in a world of significant transactions cost. He then proceeded to use the transactions cost framework to examine the problem of social cost in a variety of legal precedents and cases.[54]

In the beginning Shasta County, California, was governed by "open range" law, meaning that in principle ranchers are not legally liable for damages resulting from their cattle accidentally trespassing on unfenced land. Then, in 1945 a California law authorized the Shasta County Board of Supervisors to substitute a "closed range" ordinance in subregions of the county. Dozens of conversions have occurred since this enabling law. Under a closed range law the rancher is strictly liable—even if not negligent—for damage caused by his livestock. Robert C. Ellickson (1991), out-Coased Coase by, in effect, asking,

"Given that this county applies the polar legal rules used in Coase's illustration, how do neighbors in Shasta County actually handle the problem of stray cattle?" The answer: "Neighbors in fact are strongly inclined to cooperate, but they achieve cooperative outcomes not by bargaining from legally established entitlements,[55] as the parable supposes, but rather developing and enforcing adaptive norms of neighborliness that trump formal legal arrangements. Although the route chosen is not the one that the parable anticipates, the end reached is exactly the one that Coase predicted: coordination to mutual advantage without supervision by the state"[56] (Ellickson, 1991, p. 4). Thus, Shasta County citizens, including judges, attorneys, and insurance adjustors, do not have full working knowledge of formal local trespass law.[57] Citizens notify owners and help catch the trespassing animal; use mental accounting (reciprocity) to settle debts, e.g., a rancher whose cattle have strayed may tell the victim to come down and take some hay, or if your goat eats my tomato plants, you offer to help me replant them; use negative gossip, complain to officials, submit informal claims for money (but not through a lawyer) to punish deviant neighbors; rarely use lawyers to seek monetary compensation; share the building of fences, most often by a rule of proportionality—you pay more if you have more animals than your neighbor; ignore fence law as irrelevant; and do not change fence obligations with the planting of crops. Finally, contrary to the Coasian parable, the main cost of trespass is not from crop damage, but from highway collisions that kill animals and damage property.

## C. Extensive Form Interactions between Anonymously Paired Individuals

Cooperation has also emerged in anonymous two-person extensive-form games in laboratory experiments. Although such behavior is contrary to rational prescriptions, it is not inconsistent with our examples of spontaneous order without externally imposed law.

Why do we study anonymous interactions in the laboratory? The model of nonrepeated game theory is about strangers without a history or a future (Robert W. Rosenthal, 1981), but anonymity has long been used in small group experiments to control for the unknown complexities of natural social intercourse (Siegel and Fouraker, 1960). It is well documented that face-to-face interaction swamps subtler procedural effects in yielding cooperative outcomes (Hoffman and Spitzer, 1985; Kagel and Roth, 1995). But more important, I believe it is this condition that provides the greatest scope for exploring the human instinct for social exchange, and how it is affected by context, reward, and procedural conditions that vary elements of social distance. Again, studying what is not helps us to understand what is.

## D. Perception and the Internal Order of the Mind: Why Context Matters

Two decision tasks, represented by the same abstract game tree, may lead to different responses because they occur in different contexts. Why? The answer may be found in the process by which we perceive the external world. Hayek (1952)[58] was a pioneer in developing a theory of perception, which anticipated recent contributions to the neuroscience of perception. It is natural for our minds to suppose that experience is formed from the receipt of sensory impulses that reflect unchanging attributes of external objects in the environment. Instead, Hayek proposed that our current perception results from a relationship between external impulses and our past experience of similar conditions. Categories formed in the mind are based on the relative frequency with which current and past perceptions coincide. Memory consists of external stimuli that have been modified by processing systems whose organization is conditioned by past experience[59] (Hayek, 1952, pp. 64, 165). There is a "constant dynamic interaction between perception and memory, which explains the . . . identity of processing and representational networks of the cortex that modern evidence indicates." "Although devoid of mathematical elaboration, Hayek's model clearly contains most of the elements of those later network models of associative memory . . ." (Joaquin M. Fuster, 1999, pp. 88–89).

Hayek's model captures the idea that, in the internal order of the mind, perception is self-organized: abstract function combines with experience to determine network connectivity and expansion.[60] Loss can occur either from lack of function or the stimulus of developmental experience. Block or distort sensory input, and function is impaired; impair function by brain lesions or inherited deficiency, and development is compromised.

This model is consistent with the hypothesis that the mind is organized by interactive modules (circuits) that are specialized for vision, for language learning, for socialization, and a host of other functions (see Leda Cosmides and John Tooby, 1992; Pinker, 1994). In this view, mind is the unconscious product of coevolution between the biological and cultural development of our brains that distinguished us from other primates. It was what made reason possible. Our folk predilection for believing in the "blank slate" concept of mind (Pinker, 2002) makes plain that this interpretation of mind is just as consonant with our direct experience as was once the idea that the earth is flat, or that witches had to be destroyed. In each case to escape from the folk perception requires the falsifying indirect evidence, based on reason, to become part of our "felt" experience. Constructivist rationality then becomes ecologically rational.

## E. Experimental Procedures

The experiments I will report will show how social context can be important in the interactive decision behavior we observe. This possibility follows from the autobiographical character of memory and the manner in which past encoded experience interacts with current sensory input in creating memory. I will be reporting the results of decision-making in single play, two-person, sequential-move game trees. Subject instructions do not use technical and role-suggestive words like "game," "play," "players," "opponent," and "partner" (except where variations on the instructions are used as systematic treatments to identify their effect);[61] rather, reference is made to the "decision tree," "decision maker 1" (DM1) or 2 (DM2), and "your counterpart," etc. The purpose is to provide a baseline context, which avoids emotive words that might trigger unintended meanings by the experimenter.[62] I do not mean that the baseline is "neutral," a concept that is not clearly definable, given that context effects can depend on autobiographical experience. The effect of instructional variation on decision is an empirical matter and any particular set of instructions must always be considered a treatment unless the observations are shown to be robust to changes in the instructions. All observations must be seen as a joint product of experimental procedures and the theoretical hypotheses, implemented by particular parameters that it is our intention to test. This is not unique to laboratory observations, but a characteristic also of field observations, and the whole of science (see Smith, 2002, for examples from physics, astronomy, and experimental economics). It is therefore important to understand how procedures as well as different parameterizations (games, payoffs) affect behavior.

Subjects are recruited in advance for an economics experiment. Upon arrival at the appointed time they register, receive a show-up fee, and are assigned to a private computer terminal in a large room with 40 stations. Commonly there are 11 other people, well spaced throughout the room, in the experiments reported below. After everyone has arrived, each person logs into the experiment, reads through the instructions for the experiment, responds to instructional questions, and learns that he or she is matched anonymously with another person in the room, whose identity will never be known, and vice versa. This does not mean that a subject knows nothing about their matched counterpart. For example, it may appear evident that he or she is another "like" person, such as an undergraduate, or an industry executive with whom one may feel more-or-less an in-group identity. Obviously, each person imports into the experiment a host of different past experiences and impressions that are likely to be associated with the current experiment.

## F. The Context of Decision:
## The Ultimatum Game Example

Consider the ultimatum game, a two-stage, two-person game with the following abstract form: for each pair the experimenter makes a fixed sum of money, $m$, available (e.g., $m$ will be 10 one-dollar bills, or 10 ten-dollar bills); Player 1 moves first offering $0 \leq x \leq m$ units of the money to Player 2, Player 1 retaining $m - x$; Player 2 then responds by either accepting the offer, in which case Player 1 is paid $m - x$, and Player 2 is paid $x$, or rejecting the offer, in which case each player receives nothing.

Below I report ultimatum results from four different instructional/procedural treatments (contexts) that have the same underlying abstract game structure. In each case imagine that you are Player 1. See Hoffman et al. (1994; hereafter HMSS) for instructional details, and for references to the literature and the origins of the ultimatum game.

***Divide $10.***—You and your counterpart have been provisionally allocated $10, and randomly assigned to positions. Your task as Player 1 is to divide the $10 by filling out a form that will then go to your counterpart who will accept or reject it.

***Contest Entitlement.***—The 12 people in the room each answer the same 10 questions on a general knowledge quiz. Your score is the number of questions answered correctly; ties are broken in favor of the person who first finished the quiz. The scores are ranked from 1 (highest) through 12 (lowest). Those ranked 1–6 are informed that they have ***earned*** the right to be Player 1; the other six will be Player 2.

***Exchange.***—Player 1 is a seller, and Player 2 is a buyer. A table lists the buyer and seller profit for each price $0, $1, $2, . . . , $10 charged by the seller, and the buyer chooses to buy or not buy. The profit of the seller is the price chosen; the profit of the buyer is ($10 − price). Each receives nothing if the buyer refuses to buy.

***Contest/Exchange.***—This treatment combines Contest with Exchange; i.e., the sellers and buyers in Exchange are selected by the contest scoring procedure. In one version the total amount is 10 one-dollar bills, and in the second it is 10 ten-dollar bills.

Whatever the context there is a game-theoretic concept of equilibrium (subgame perfect) that yields the same prediction in all four treatments (Reinhard Selten, 1975): Player 1 offers the minimum unit of account, $1 ($10) if $m = \$10$ ($100), and Player 2 accepts the offer. This follows from the assumption that each player is self-interested in the narrow sense of always choosing the largest of two immediate payoffs for herself; that this condition is common knowledge for the two players; and that Player 1 applies backward induction to the decision problem faced by Player 2, conditional on Player 1's offer. Thus Player

1 reasons that any positive payoff is better than zero for Player 2 and therefore, Player 1 need only offer $x = \$1$ ($10).

One difficulty with this analysis is that, depending on context, the interaction may be interpreted as a social exchange between the two anonymously matched players who in day-to-day experience read intentions into the actions of others (S. Baron-Cohen, 1995). Suppose the situation is perceived as a social contract as follows: if Player 2 has an entitlement to more than the minimum unit of account, then an offer of less than the perceived entitlement (say, only $1, or even $2–$3) may be rejected by some Players 2. Player 1, introspectively anticipating this possible mental state of Player 2, might then offer $4 or $5 to insure acceptance of his offer. Alternatively, Player 1 might enjoy (get utility from) giving money to his counterpart. The point is simply that there are alternative models to that of subgame perfection that predict choices in the ultimatum game, and these alternatives leave wide latitude for the possibility of context affecting the behavior of both players. Abstract game theory can embrace these alternatives through the artifice of "types"—utilities, or beliefs states such as trust, trustworthiness, reciprocation, etc. Ultimately the predictive success of such models depends on relating task descriptions defining context to autobiographical characteristics of individuals that are then identified by types that in turn determine behavior. The point that needs emphasis is that it is easy to go from types (traditionally utility or beliefs about states) to game-theoretic choice; the hard part is to relate types to characteristics of the individual's memory-sensory system. Given the directions of neuroscience and the learning from brain imaging, I do not think this is an impossible order.

Observe that in "Divide $10" the original $10 is allocated imprecisely to both players. Moreover, a common definition of the word "divide" (Webster) includes the separation of some divisible quantity into equal parts. Finally, random devices are recognized as a standard mechanism for "fair" (equal) treatment. Consequently, the instructions might be interpreted as suggesting that the experimenter is engaged in the "fair" treatment of the subjects cueing them to be "fair" to each other.

As an alternative, Contest deliberately introduces a pre-game procedure that requires Player 1 to "earn" the right to be the first mover. This may cue some incipient norm of just desserts based on the pre-game quiz.

In Exchange the ultimatum game is imbedded in the gains from exchange from a transaction between a buyer and a seller. In an exchange, both the buyer and the seller are made better off, and buyers in our culture may accept the right of a seller to move first by quoting a price.

Contest/Exchange combines the implicit property right norm of a seller with a mechanism for earning the property right.

Table 2 summarizes the results from two different studies of ultimatum game bargaining with stakes of either 10 one-dollar or 10 ten-dollar bills for each of N pairs of players, where N varies from 23 to 33 subject pairs.

1. Comparing Divide $10 with Divide $100 under the random entitlement we observe a trivial difference in the amount offered between

TABLE 2—MEAN PERCENTAGE OFFERED BY TREATMENT IN ULTIMATUM GAMES[a]

| | | $10 stakes | | | $100 stakes | | |
|---|---|---|---|---|---|---|---|
| Context | Measure | Divide $10 | Exchange | Exchange, strategic prompt | Divide $100 | Exchange | Exchange (graduate students)[c] |
| Random entitlement | Mean (percent) | 43.7 | 37.1 | 41.7 | 44.1 | NA | NA |
| | N | 24 | 24 | 24 | 27 | NA | NA |
| | (Percent rejected)[b] | (8.3) | (8.3) | (12.5) | (3.7) | NA | NA |
| Earned entitlement | Mean (percent) | 36.2 | 30.8 | 39.6 | NA | 27.8 | 28.8 |
| | N | 24 | 24 | 24 | NA | 23 | 33 |
| | (Percent rejected)[b] | (0) | (12.5) | (2.9) | NA | (21.7) | (21.2) |

[a] Data from Hoffman et al. (1994; 1996a). See the references for the statistical significance of pairwise comparisons as discussed in the text.
[b] Refers to percentage of the N pairs in which the second player rejects the offer of the first.
[c] The graduate students were visiting participants in an introductory workshop in experimental economics. These are new data not previously reported.

the low stakes (43.7 percent) and the tenfold increase in the stakes (44.4 percent). Also, there is no significant difference in the percentage rate at which offers are rejected, 8.3 percent, and 3.7 percent, respectively.

2. When Exchange is combined with an earned entitlement the increase in stakes lowers the offer percentage from 30.8 percent for $10 stakes to 27.8 percent for $100 stakes, but this difference is within the normal range of sampling error using different groups of subjects and is not significant. Surprisingly, however, this miniscule decline in the mean offer causes the rejection rate to go up from 12.5 percent to 21.7 percent. Three of four subject Players 1 offering $10 are rejected, and one offer of $30 is rejected in the game with $100 stakes. As has been shown in trust/punishment games, this behavior is associated with a strong human propensity to incur personal cost to punish those who are perceived as cheaters, even under strict anonymity.

3. We note that comparing the Divide $10/Random entitlement condition with the Exchange entitlement, the offer percentage declines from 43.7 percent to 37.1 percent, and comparing the former to the Earned entitlement the decline is from 43.7 percent to 36.2 percent, both reductions being statistically significant. Even more significant is the reduction from 43.7 percent to 30.8 percent when the Earned and Exchange entitlements are combined. Moreover, in all four of these comparisons the rejection rate is null or modest (0 to 12.5 percent).

4. The small proportion of the offers that were rejected, except when the stakes were $100 in the Earned/Exchange context and the mean offers declined to a low of 27.8 percent, indicates that Players 1 read their counterparts well, and as the context is altered, normally offer a sufficient amount to avoid being rejected. The one exception shows clearly that pushing the edge, even if it seems justified by the higher stakes, may invite an escalation of rejections.

These data indicate that context is important in the ultimatum game: the percentage offered varies by over a third as we move from the highest (44 percent) to the lowest (28 percent) measured effect. Also see Hoffman et al. (2000). Like variation is reported in cross-cultural experiments: a comparison of two hunter-gather and five modern cultures reveals variation from a high of 48 percent (Los Angeles subjects) to a low of 26 percent (Machiguenga subjects from Peru) (Joseph Henrich, 2000). These comparisons used care in attempting to control for instructional differences across different languages, but this is inherently problematic, given the nature of perception, in that one cannot be sure that the instructions, translations, payoffs, or the procedures for handling the subjects, control adequately for context across cultures. In each culture one needs to vary the instructions/procedures and observe the sampling distribution of outcomes, then compare the sample distributions across cultures.

These instructional treatment effects call into question the extent to which one can define what is meant by "unbiased" instructions. If results are robust with respect to instructional changes, this can only be established empirically. Without such studies no claims can be made concerning the relative "neutrality" of instructions. The main lesson is that, because of the nature of perception and memory, context should matter, and in the ultimatum game the variation of observed results with systematic instructional changes designed to alter context shows clearly that context can and does matter. Experimenters, subject to the same perception/ memory variations, are likely to disagree as to what is "neutral."

## G. Dictator Games with and without Gains from Exchange

The ultimatum game is converted into a dictator game by removing the right of the second mover to veto the offer of the first. Forsythe et al. (1994; hereafter FHSS) note that if the observed tendency toward equal split of the prize is due primarily to "fairness"—a social norm of just division—then it should be of little consequence if this right is eliminated. But if it is the prospect of rejection—however irrational—that tempers the amount offered by Player 1, then the outcomes should be materially affected by removing the right of rejection, which converts the ultimatum game into what is called the dictator game. Thus a significant reduction in the mean percent offered in the dictator game would be consistent with the second hypothesis, while no significant reduction would be consistent with the first. Comparing the results in Table 3, column 1 with those for Divide $10, Random entitlement in Table 2, we see that the mean dictator offer is only 23.3 percent compared with the mean ultimatum offer of 43.7 percent. FHSS conclude that fairness alone cannot account for behavior in the ultimatum game. This is correct, but, equally of interest, why are dictators giving away nearly a quarter of their endowment? This research puzzle was picked up by HMSS who conjectured that such generosity might be, at least in part, a consequence of the incompleteness of anonymity. In all the games prior to the HMSS study the members of each player pair were anonymous with respect to each other but not with respect to the experimenter who knew every person's decision. Hence, they introduced a "double blind" treatment category (two versions) in which the protocol made it transparent that no one, including the experimenter, could learn the decisions of any player. Data from the second version, Double Blind 2, are reported in Table 3. In this treatment mean dictator offers decline to only 10.5 percent. Consequently, context—in this case social connectedness or distance—has an important effect on dictator transfers.[63] These issues are explored more fully in Hoffman et al. (1996b), who vary social distance by varying the instructional and protocol parameters that define various versions of single- and double-

TABLE 3—DICTATOR GIVING: WITH AND WITHOUT GAINS FROM EXCHANGE AND
SOCIAL HISTORY

| Treatments | Standard dictator game giving | | Double blind[b] dictator giving under gains from exchange[c] | | | |
| | | | Baseline | | Social history | |
| Player role | Single Blind FHSS[a] | Double Blind 2 HMSS[b] | Sent (Player 1) | Returned (Player 2) | Sent (Player 1) | Returned (Player 2) |
|---|---|---|---|---|---|---|
| Mean percent given of total available | 23.3 | 10.5 | 51.6 | 27.2[d] | 53.6 | 35.5[d] |
| Mean percent given by top 50 percent givers | 38.3 | 21.0 | 74.4 | 49.4 | 82.7 | 55.8 |

[a] Data from Forsythe et al. (1994), replicated by Hoffman et al. (1996b).
[b] Data from Hoffman et al. (1994), Double Blind 2.
[c] Data from Berg et al. (1995). Their procedures are different, but are nearest to those of Double Blind 2 in HMSS.
[d] Since the sender amount is tripled, if the receivers return an average of 33.3 percent, then the average amount returned will equal (pay back) the amount sent.

blind dictator games. Also reported in Table 3 is the percent given by the top 50 percent of the most generous dictators: 38.3 percent for Single Blind and 21 percent for Double Blind.

Berg et al. (1995, hereafter BDM) modify the dictator game to introduce gains from "exchange."[64] Their investment trust two-stage-dictator game also uses the Double Blind 2 protocol: dictators in room A send any portion of their $10 (0 to $10) to their random counterpart in room B. People in both rooms know that if $x is sent by anyone, it is tripled, so that the counterpart receives $3x. Thus, the most generous offer, $10, yields a gain of $30. The counterpart can then respond by sending any part (0 to $3x) of the amount received back to his or her matched sender. Now an exchange with gains to both parties is possible, and BDM ask if this context is a significant treatment. Note that the analysis of the game is no different than the one-stage dictator game: by the principle of backward induction Player 1 can see that Player 2's interest is to keep all the money received, and therefore nothing should be sent. The fact that the sender's transfer will be tripled is irrelevant. But it is not irrelevant if both players see the interaction as an exchange based on trust by Player 1 and trustworthiness by Player 2.

In Table 3 sender Players 1 now give 51.6 percent when the transfer is tripled, compared with 23.3 percent when it is not. Furthermore, the top 50 percent of the givers send 74.4 percent of the money, up from 38.3 percent. This shows how the tripled pie shifts the distribution toward larger transfers by Players 1. But on average the senders do not quite break even: an average of 27.2 percent of the amount received by Players 2 is returned to Players 1 (break even would be 33.3 percent since $x$ is tripled). In the social history treatment the instructions and protocol are the same as described above except that the second treatment group is shown the distribution of amounts transferred and returned for the first group. Comparing the social history with the baseline mean percent given and returned reveals the effect of being exposed to the decision data of the first group. Social history does not cause a reduction in transfers, which actually increases marginally from 51.6 percent to 53.6 percent. The average percent returned increases from 27.2 percent to 35.5 percent, just above the break-even level.

These results are not explicable by the canons of traditional game theory that assumes self-interested (in the sense of always choosing larger payoffs) types. By introducing gains from the investment by Player 1, who can only benefit if Player 2 perceives the process as an exchange calling for payment for services rendered, dictator giving more than doubles. And the effect of social history does not precipitate a decline in investment nor in the return to Player 2—in fact both increase slightly. The same behaviors have been observed in chimpanzee and capuchin monkey communities (Frans B. M. deWaal, 1989, 1997). Should such trusting and trustworthy behaviors be diminished in human communities characterized by the maxim that "the rules of morality are not . . . conclusions of [our] reason?"

## H. Trust Games

Ultimatum and dictator games have been studied extensively, but are much too simple to allow an adequate understanding of some of the underlying behavior manifest in them. It is tempting to overinterpret them in terms of a mixed utility for own and other reward. The potential for greatly expanding what can be learned is illustrated in Table 3 where BDM extended the dictator game to a two-stage game with gains from voluntary exchange. We turn therefore to a somewhat richer class of two-person extensive-form trust games in which equilibrium play, cooperation, and the prospect of defection can be studied in a richer parameter space than the ultimatum game.[65]

Figure 1 is a typical "trust" game tree.[66] Play starts at the top of the tree, node $x_1$, with Player 1 who can move right, which stops the game yielding the upper payoff to Player 1, $10, and the lower payoff to Player 2, $10, or move down in which case Player 2 chooses a move at node $x_2$. If Player 2's move is right, Player 1 receives $15, and Player 2, $25. This is the cooperative (C) outcome. If, however, Player 2 moves down, the payoffs to 1 and 2 are, respectively, $0 and $40. This is the defection (D) outcome, in which Player 2 defects on Player 1's offer to cooperate. The subgame-perfect equilibrium (SPE) is $10 for each player. This follows because at node 1 Player 1 can apply backward induction by observing that if play reaches node $x_2$, Player 2's dominant choice is to defect. Seeing that this is the case, Player 1's dominant choice is to move right at the top of the tree, yielding the SPE outcome.

These game-theoretic assumptions are very strong. As we see from the above discussion, however, they have the dubious merit of allowing "unambiguous" predictions to be made about behavior.[67] We particularly want to note that if every player is exactly like every other player,

FIGURE 1. INVEST $10 TRUST GAME: FREQUENCY OF PLAY

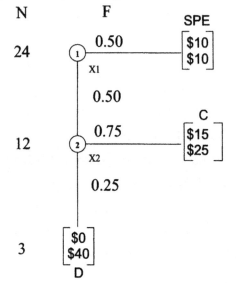

*Notes:* Abbreviations are as follows: N–number of subject pairs by node; F–frequency at which pairs move right or down; SPE–subgame-perfect equilibrium; C–cooperate; D–defect.

and is strictly self-interested, there is no room for "mind reading," or inferring intentions from actions, and no room for more sophisticated and subtle action in the self-interest.

To illustrate, suppose that you have been through the standard economics course in game theory and that you are in the position of Player 2 in Figure 1. Consequently, you expect Player 1 to move right at the top of the tree. He does not. He moves down, and it is your turn. Surely he did not move down because he prefers $0 to $10, or expects you to defect. He must think that you think that he wants you to choose C. Whatever else can he have in mind? Maybe he cannot do backward induction, or thinks you are not self-interested. So how are you going to respond? He is making it possible for you to increase your payoff by 150 percent, and his by 50 percent, compared with the SPE. He is not even asking for the larger share of the pie that his action has created! According to reciprocity theory, if you choose C, you will reciprocate his inferred intentions, and complete an exchange—exactly in the same way that you trade favors, services, and goods across time with your closer friends and associates in life (except for those who are victims of antisocial personality disorder, or sociopaths, and are unable to maintain social relations based on reciprocity),[68] also in the same way that you do not hesitate to leave a "tip" ("to insure promptness"?) for good service at a restaurant even in a foreign city. Without a conscious thought you often say, "I owe you one," in response to an acquaintance's favor. So you might choose C with hardly a thought, or, since he will never know your identity, upon closer reflection, you may think that it just makes no sense not to take the $40. Although you are not a clinical sociopath, here is an opportunity to cut a corner and no one can know. As Player 1 in Figure 1 are you certain that you would want to play SPE?[69]

In regard to this reciprocity analysis of the game, we should note that the game in Figure 1 is a much reduced-form version of the BDM game: think of Player 1 as sending $10, which becomes $30; Player 2 can either split the $30 equally with Player 1, giving the imputation C, or Player 2 can keep it all, yielding the D outcome. But there is another difference, one of context. In the experiment using Figure 1 the subjects play an abstract game, one that is not embedded in a BDM-type story about sending $10 upstairs, which becomes $30, and the receiver can either keep it all or split the gain made possible by the sender. But given the BDM outcomes reported above we should not be too surprised that some subject pairs might end at C.

The outcomes are shown in Figure 1 for 24 undergraduate subjects: 50 percent move down, and of these 75 percent "reciprocate."

**Why So Much Cooperation?** My coauthors and I have interpreted the outcome C as due to reciprocity. But there are other interpretations; e.g., that the subjects are game-theoretically unsophisticated or have nonselfish preferences. The effect of subjects on outcomes is an empirical matter, and is most important, but cannot be pursued here in depth. It is essential to programs concerned with extending game theory to "player types." Subject background diversity and resulting choice behavior can help inform the identification and classification of "types," whether reciprocators, sophisticates, or utilitarian (see McCabe and Smith, 2001; McCabe et al., 2001).

**Is It the Subjects? Undergraduates versus Graduates.** In the above trust game nearly half the Players 1 forgo the sure thing, SPE, and three-quarters of the responses are cooperative. We have often heard such results dismissed as a consequence of using naive subjects. (This dismissal has the logical implication that the original theoretical hypothesis is either not falsifiable or has no predictive content. See footnote 67.) McCabe and Smith (2000) examined this explanation using advanced graduate students from the population, a sample of whom participated in the $100 Exchange/Entitlement version of the ultimatum game reported in Table 2, showing almost identical results for graduate and undergraduate students. They used the trust game shown in Figure 1. For comparison, McCabe and Smith (2000) used the undergraduate data shown in Figure 2. In both groups 50 percent of Players 1 offer cooperation, while 75 percent of the undergraduate and 64 percent of the graduate student Players 2 reciprocate. However naive undergraduates are alleged to be, these tests suggest that graduate students with training in economic theory are capable of showing very similar behavior in this extensive-form game, and in the ultimatum game reported in Table 2.

**Is It Utility for Other?** Bolton (1991), Rabin (1993), Fehr and Schmidt (1999), and Bolton and Ockenfels (2000) have proposed useful preference models of decision that aim at accounting for behavior in a variety of experiments, most particularly ultimatum and dictator games.

FIGURE 2. INVEST $10 TRUST GAME COMPARING UNDERGRADUATES (U) AND GRADUATES (G)

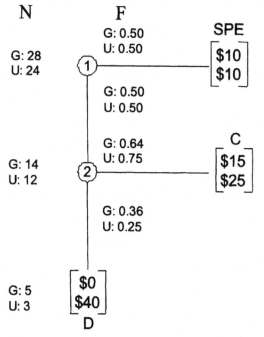

*Note:* For abbreviations, see Figure 1 notes.

The idea behind these models is that we can explain cooperation in bargaining games by saying that people have a taste for altruism or for "fair" outcomes (or a distaste for "unfair" outcomes), where fairness is understood as payoff equity, as in Franciosi et al. (1995). The hypothesis is that subjects seek to maximize these adjusted utilities. It is only the intrinsic properties of outcomes that are assumed to drive behavior; what alternatives the players faced at a previous decision node are irrelevant. This means that intentions, as reflected in the move choices, are assumed to be superfluous in the interactions between the parties. The former approach identifies utility types. The latter identifies types who signal intentions, who are into reading move signals, and risk misidentifying reciprocity versus defection types. The important testable distinctions are that the former are immune to instructional procedures and to path dependency—the opportunity costs of forgone options; this constitutes the core of the research program of my coauthors and me. This program leads naturally to an understanding of its own limitations as well as that of the utilitarian program, i.e., both types may be needed.

Other-regarding preference models are unable to account for our previous data demonstrating that procedures and context variables matter. In the ultimatum game data reported above where the context is varied from "Divide $10" to "Context/Exchange," ostensibly the utilities to the participants are the same under each ultimatum condition. However, behavior varies dramatically. These models also cannot explain the results reported above in the single versus double blind protocol in dictator games, and the dramatic change in dictator behavior in the BDM investment trust game. Clearly, the behavior is much more variable than is expected from outcome-based utility models.

An altruistic utility interpretation of cooperation can be invoked in trust games like that in Figure 1: Player 2 may move down because her utility for reward is increasing in both own and other payoff. Figure 3 is a trust game that enables us to distinguish subjects who cooperate from motivations of altruism, and those whose cooperation derives from reciprocity in an exchange. The game starts at the top, node $x_1$, with Player 1 who can move right, which stops the game yielding the upper payoff to Player 1, $7, and the lower payoff to Player 2, $14, or move down in which case Player 2 chooses a move at node $x_2$. If the move is right, each player gets $8. If Player 2 moves down, Player 1 can then move right at node $x_3$ yielding $10 for each, or down, yielding $12 for Player 1 and $6 for Player 2. The subgame-perfect equilibrium (SPE) is $8 for each player. This follows because at node $x_1$, Player 1 can apply backward induction by observing that if play reaches node $x_3$, Player 1 will want to move down. But Player 2, also using backward induction will see that at node $x_2$ he should

FIGURE 3. TRUST GAME WITH ALTRUISM: FREQUENCY OF PLAY

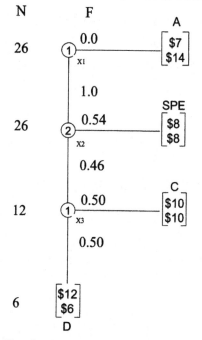

*Note:* For abbreviations, see Figure 1 notes.

move right. Since right at node $x_2$ yields a higher payoff to Player 1, at node $x_1$ Player 1 will conclude that he should move down. Hence, the SPE outcome would prevail by the logic of self-interested players who always choose dominant strategies, and apply the principle of backward induction.

If Player 1 has other-regarding preferences (altruism) and is willing to incur some cost to greatly increase the payoff to Player 2, Player 1 may move right at $x_1$. His payoff of $7 is only one-eighth smaller than his payoff at the SPE, and yields $14 for Player 2. Hence, at a cost of $1 to himself, Player 1 can increase his counterpart Player 2's payoff by $6. Player 1 need have only a modest preference for an increase in Player 2's welfare to induce him to move right because of the 6 to 1 return for the other player over the cost to Player 1.

At $x_2$, Player 2 may move down signaling to Player 1 that such a move enables both to profit (gains from exchange), provided that at $x_3$ Player 1 cooperates by reciprocating Player 2's favor. Alternatively at $x_3$ Player 1 can defect (D) on the offer to cooperate by choosing his dominate strategy, and move down.

The outcome frequencies for the trust game ($N = 26$ pairs) are entered directly on the tree in Figure 3. The first result—overwhelmingly decisively—is that no Player 1 chooses the A (altruistic) outcome; all choose to pass to Player 2 seeking a higher payoff for themselves, and being content to give Player 2 a smaller payoff than is achieved at A, depending upon the final outcome of the move sequence. Secondly, 46 percent offer to cooperate (down), and 50 percent reciprocate.

## I. Utility versus Exchange:
## Does Opportunity Cost Matter?

If reciprocity is perceived as an exchange in which each player gains relative to the default outcome (SPE), then the cooperative outcome must yield an increase in the size of the prize to be split between the two players (see McCabe et al., 2003). Also, Player 2 must believe that (i) Player 1 made a deliberate choice to make this outcome possible, and (ii) incurred an opportunity cost in doing so, i.e., gave up a smaller certain payoff risking a still smaller payoff if C is not attained. It then becomes credible to Player 2 that Player 1 did a favor for Player 2, and reasonably can expect reciprocal action in return. Notice that our argument is in the form of a constructivist theory that need not characterize the subjects' reasoning, even if it has predictive accuracy; i.e., constructive rationality may predict emergent ecologically rational outcomes, just as CE theory predicts market outcomes not part of the conscious intentions of the agents. McCabe et al. (2001), however, report fMRI brain-imaging data supporting the hypothesis that subjects who cooperate use the "mind reading" circuit modules in their brains (see Baron-Cohen, 1995). This circuitry is not activated in subjects who choose not to cooperate (SPE). In responding to postexperiment questions asking them to write their impressions of their decisions, subjects frequently report that the experiment is all about whether you can trust your counterpart. They do not refer to returning a favor, to reciprocity, an exchange, fairness, etc., suggesting that if their actions are driven by reciprocity motives, such are not part of a self-aware reasoning process.

Reciprocity reasoning motivated the alternative game trees shown in Figure 4 designed to test reciprocity against utility interpretations of choice. In Figure 4A, if Player 1 moves down at the top the potential prize increases from $40 to $50. Player 2 can defect at a cost to Player 1, and can clearly infer that Player 1 deliberately enabled the outcome to increase from ($20, $20) to ($25, $25). But in Figure 4B Player 2 can see that Player 1 was presented with no voluntary choice to move down. Consequently, Player 1 incurred no opportunity cost to enable Player 2 to achieve C. Player 1 did nothing intentionally for Player 2, and according

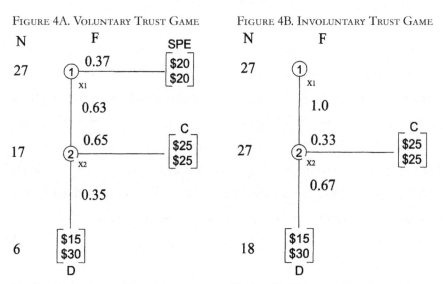

FIGURE 4A. VOLUNTARY TRUST GAME    FIGURE 4B. INVOLUNTARY TRUST GAME

*Note:* For abbreviations, see Figure 1 notes.    *Note:* For abbreviations, see Figure 1 notes.

to reciprocity reasoning, Player 2 incurred no implied debt that needed to be repaid. Player 2 can thus move down with impunity. Consequently, reciprocity theory predicts a greater frequency of right moves by Player 2 in Figure 4A than in Figure 4B. Since only outcomes matter, both own- and other-regarding utility theories predict no difference in Player 2's choices between Figures 4A and 4B. In fact, as shown by the frequency data on the trees, a third of the Players 2 on the right play C, whereas nearly twice that many choose C in the left game.

Intentions have also been found to matter in a study of ultimatum bargaining: "... we show that identical offers in an ultimatum game trigger vastly different rejection rates depending on the other offers available to the proposer" (Armin Falk et al., 1999, p. 2).

## J. Extensive- versus Normal-Form Games

A fundamental principle of game theory is that rational behavior is invariant to the form—extensive or normal—of the game. Behavior in the extensive and normal forms has been compared by Andrew Schotter et al. (1994), Amnon Rapoport (1997), and McCabe et al. (2000). All three reject the invariance principle, but in the first study the rationality principles they proposed to explain the invariance either failed to predict the differences, "or they were not what we expected" (Schotter et al., 1994, pp. 446–47). Rapoport provides two versions of the "Battle-of-the-Sexes" game to show how order-of-play information in the extensive form allows players to better coordinate their actions. McCabe et al. (2000) argue that the important principle that allows better coordination "derives from the human capacity to read another person's thoughts or intentions by placing themselves in the position and information state of the other person" (p. 4404). This "mind reading" to detect intentions underlies reciprocity. We summarize here the findings of McCabe et al. (2000) for the trimmed version of the game they study, which is the game we have depicted in Figure 3.

In the extensive form of the game in Figure 3, Player 2 sees the move of Player 1 before Player 2 chooses to move. In this form of the game, intentions can be clearly communicated along the lines storied above. In the normal (or strategic) form of the same game each player chooses a move at each node without knowing whether that node will actually be reached in the move sequence. Decisions are thus contingent on the node being reached and may be irrelevant in determining the payoffs. In the normal form, therefore, we can present the game as an $n \times m$ matrix of the $n = 3$ strategies of Player 1—right at node $x_1$, right or down at node $x_3$, and the $m = 2$ strategies of Player 2, right or down at node $x_2$. Players 1 and 2 each simultaneously choose among these alternatives not knowing the choice of the other.

McCabe et al. (2000) predict that Player 2 will move down at $x_2$, with higher frequency in the extensive than the normal form. They also predict higher rates of cooperation by Player 1 (and lower defection rates) in the extensive than normal forms. Neither own- nor other-regarding utility theory can support these predictions. The data are shown in Table 4: 46 percent of the Players 1 offer to cooperate in the extensive form, only 29 percent in the normal form. Similarly, they

TABLE 4—BRANCH CONDITIONAL OUTCOMES FOR ONE-SHOT GAME: EXTENSIVE VERSUS NORMAL FORM

| Outcome | Extensive-form frequency | Normal-form frequency |
|---------|--------------------------|-----------------------|
| ($7, $14) | $\frac{0}{26} = 0.0$ | $\frac{0}{24} = 0.0$ |
|  | $\frac{12}{26} = 0.46$ | $\frac{7}{24} = 0.29$ |
| ($8, $8) | $\frac{6}{12} = 0.50$ | $\frac{1}{7} = 0.14$ |
| ($12, $6) | $\frac{6}{12} = 0.50$ | $\frac{6}{7} = 0.86$ |

observe a 50 percent cooperative rate by Players 2 in the extensive form, but only 14 percent in the normal form.

These results and that of others cited above imply that the extensive and normal forms are not played as if they were the same games. Players' moves signal intentions that are not the same when actually experienced in extensive form as when imagined in a mental experiment corresponding to the normal form. I would argue that experience and its memory in life is an extensive process that encodes context along with outcome. The brain is not naturally adapted to solve all sequential move problems by reducing them to a single strategy vector as in a highly structured game. Apparently, we have a built-in tendency to wait, observe, then decide—a process that conserves cognitive resources by applying them only to contingencies that are realized, and avoids the need for revision, given the inevitable surprises in the less structured games of life.[70] Constructivist modeling glosses over distinctions of which we are unaware that govern the ecology of choice. Experimental designs conditioned only by constructivist thinking ill-prepare us to collect the data that can inform needed revisions in our thinking. It is both cost effective and faithful to game-theoretic assumptions in experiments to collect move data from each subject under all contingencies, but it distorts interpretability if game forms are not equivalent. The assumptions of game theory, such as those leading to the logical equivalence of the two game forms, should not be imposed on experimental designs, thereby constraining our understanding of behavior beyond those assumptions.

## K. Neuroeconomics

Neuroeconomics is concerned with studying the connections between how the mind/brain works—the internal order of the mind—and behavior in (1) individual decision-making, (2) social exchange, and (3) institutions such as markets. The working hypothesis is that the brain has evolved different, but interdependent, adaptive mechanisms for each of these tasks involving experience, memory, and perception. The tools include brain-imaging technology and the existence of patients with localized brain lesions associated with specific loss of certain mental functions.

Decision-making has drawn the attention of neuroscientists who study the deviant behavior of neurological patients with specific brain lesions, such as front lobe (ventromedial prefrontal) damage. Such patients have long been known to be challenged by tasks involving planning and coordination over time, although they score normally on batteries of psychological tests (Antonio R. Damasio, 1994). A landmark experimental study of such patients (compared with controls) in individual decision-making under uncertainty is that of Antoine Bechara et al. (1997). Starting with (fictional) endowments of $2,000, each subject on each trial draws a card from one of four freely chosen decks (A, B, C, D). In decks (A, B) each card has a payoff value of $50, whereas in decks (C, D), each is worth $100. Also, the $100 decks contain occasional large negative payoff cards, while the $50 decks have much smaller negative payoff cards. All this must be learned from single card draws in a sequence of trials, with a running tally of cumulative payoff value. A subject performs much better by learning to avoid the $100 decks in favor of the $50 decks. By period 60, normal control subjects have learned to draw only from the $50 (C, D) decks, while the brain-damaged subjects continue to sample disadvantageously the $100 (A, B) decks. Furthermore, the control subjects shift to the (C, D) decks before they are able to articulate why, in periodic questioning. Also, they pre-register emotional reactions to the (A, B) decks as measured by real-time skin conductivity test (SCT) readings. But the brain-damaged patients tend to verbally rationalize continued sampling of the (A, B) decks, and some types (with damaged amygdala) register no SCT response. Results consistent with those of Bechara et al. (1997) have been reported by Vinod Goel et al. (1997) who study patient performance in a complex financial planning task.

Over 50 years ago experiments with animal behavior demonstrated that motivation was based on relative or forgone reward—opportunity cost—and not on an absolute scale of values generated by the brain. Thus David J. Zeaman (1949) reported experiments in which rats were trained to run for a large reward-motivated goal. When shifted to a small reward, the rats responded by running more slowly than they would to the small reward only. A control group began with a small reward and shifted to a large one, and these rats immediately ran faster than if the large reward alone was applied. Monkeys similarly respond to comparisons of differential rewards. It is now established that orbito-frontal cortex (just above the eyes) neuron activity in monkeys enable them to discriminate between rewards that are directly related to the animals' relative, as distinct from absolute, preference among rewards such as cereal, apple, and raisins (in order of increasing preference in monkeys) (Leon Tremblay and Schultz, 1999).

Thus suppose A is preferred to B is preferred to C based on choice response. Then neuronal activity is greater for A than for B when the subject is viewing A and B, and similarly for B and C when comparing B and C. But the activity associated with B is much greater when compared with C than when it is compared with A. This is contrary to what one would expect to observe if A, B, and C are coded on a fixed properties scale rather than a relative scale (Tremblay and Schultz, 1999, p. 706).

These studies have a parallel significance for humans. Prospect theory proposes that the evaluation of a gamble depends not on the total asset position but focuses myopically on the opportunity cost, gain or loss, relative to one's current asset position. There is also asymmetry—the effect of a loss looms larger than the effect of a gain of the same magnitude (Kahneman and Tversky, 1979). Barbara A. Mellers et al. (1999) have shown that the emotional response to the outcome of a gamble depends on the perceived value and likelihood of the outcome and on the forgone outcome. It feels better (less bad) to receive $0 from a gamble when you forgo +$10 than when you forgo +$90. (They use the term "counterfactual" rather than "opportunity cost" to refer to the alternative that might have prevailed.) Thus, our ability to form opportunity cost comparisons receive important neurophysiological support from our emotional circuitry. Breiter et al. (2001) use these same principles in the design of a functional magnetic imaging (fMRI) study of human hemodynamic responses to both the expectation and experience of monetary gains and losses under uncertainty. They observed significant activation responses in the amygdala and orbital gyrus, with both activations increasing with the expected value of the gamble. There was also some evidence that the right hemisphere is predominantly active for gains, and the left for losses—a particularly interesting possibility inviting deeper examination, perhaps by imaging split-brain subjects in the same task. Also see Kip Smith et al. (2002).

The effect of paying subjects is informed by Thut et al. (1997) who compare brain activation under monetary rewards with the feedback of an "OK" reinforcement in a dichotomous choice task. The monetary rewards yielded a significantly higher activation of the orbitofrontal cortex and other related brain areas (see also Schultz, 2000, 2002).

The neural correlates of individual decision-making were extended, by McCabe et al. (2001), to an fMRI study of behavior in two-person strategic interactions in extensive-form trust games like those in Figures 1 to 4. The prior hypothesis, derived from reciprocity theory, the theory-of-mind literature, and supported by imaging results from individual studies of cued thought processes (P. C. Fletcher et al.,

1995), was that cooperators would show greater activation in the prefrontal cortex (specifically BA-8) and supporting circuitry, than noncooperators. The control, for comparison with the mental processes used when a subject is playing a human, is for the subject to play a computer knowing the programmed response probabilities and therefore having no need to interpret moves as intentions. The predicted activations were significantly greater, relative to controls, for cooperators than noncooperators, and are consistent with the reciprocity interpretation of behavior discussed above.

## IV. Conclusions

Cartesian constructivism applies reason to the design of rules for individual action, to the design of institutions that yield socially optimal outcomes, and constitutes the standard socioeconomic science model. But most of our operating knowledge, and ability to decide and perform is nondeliberative. Our brains conserve attentional, conceptual, and symbolic thought resources because they are scarce, and proceeds to delegate most decision-making to autonomic processes (including the emotions) that do not require conscious attention. Emergent arrangements, even if initially constructivist, must have survival properties that incorporate opportunity costs and environmental challenges invisible to constructivist modeling. This leads to an alternative, ecological concept of rationality: an emergent order based on trial-and-error cultural and biological evolutionary processes. It yields home- and socially grown rules of action, traditions and moral principles that underlie property rights in impersonal exchange, and social cohesion in personal exchange. To study ecological rationality we use rational reconstruction—for example, reciprocity or other-regarding preferences—to examine individual behavior, emergent order in human culture and institutions, and their persistence, diversity, and development over time. Experiments enable us to test propositions derived from these rational reconstructions.

The study of both kinds of rationality has been prominent in the work of experimental economists. This is made plain in the many direct tests of the observable implications of propositions derived from economic and game theory. It is also evident in the great variety of experiments that have reached far beyond the theory to ask why the tests have succeeded, failed, or performed better (under weaker conditions) than was expected. What have we learned, not as final truth, but as compelling working hypotheses for continuing examination?

1. Markets constitute an engine of productivity by supporting resource specialization through trade and creating a diverse wealth of goods and services.

2. Markets are rule-governed institutions providing algorithms that select, process, and order the exploratory messages of agents who are better informed as to their personal circumstances than that of others. As precautionary probes by agents yield to contracts, each becomes more certain of what must be given in order to receive. Out of this interaction between minds through the intermediary of rules the process aggregates the dispersed asymmetric information, converging more-or-less rapidly to competitive equilibria if they exist. Each experimental market carries its own unique mark with a different dynamic path.

3. All this information is captured in the static or time-variable supply and demand environment and must be aggregated to yield efficient clearing prices. We can never fully understand how this process

works in the world because the required information is not given, or available, to any one mind. Thus, for many, the arguments of the Scottish philosophers and of Hayek are obscure and mystical. But we can design experiments in which the information is not given to any participant, then compare market outcomes with efficient competitive outcomes and gauge a market institution's performance.

4. The resulting order is invisible to the participants, unlike the visible gains they reap. Agents discover what they need to know to achieve outcomes optimal against the constraining limits imposed by others.

5. Rules emerge as a spontaneous order—they are found—not deliberately designed by one calculating mind. Initially constructivist institutions undergo evolutionary change adapting beyond the circumstances that gave them birth. What emerges is a form of "social mind" that solves complex organization problems without conscious cognition. This "social mind" is born of the interaction among all individuals through the rules of institutions that have to date survived cultural selection processes.

6. This process accommodates tradeoffs between the cost of transacting, attending, and monitoring, and the efficiency of the allocations so that the institution itself generates an order of economy that fits the problem it evolved to solve. Hence, the hundreds of variations on the fine structure of institutions, each designed without a designer to accommodate disparate conditions, but all of them subservient to the reality of dispersed agent information.

7. We understand little about how rule systems for social interaction and markets emerge, but it is possible in the laboratory to do variations on the rules, and thus to study that which is not.

8. Markets require enforcement—voluntary or involuntary—of the rules of exchange. These are: the right possession, its transference by consent, and the performance of promises (Hume). Voluntary

enforcement occurs when people in the market reward good services with gratuities or "tips," an example, perhaps, of an emergent cultural norm in which people recognize that tips are part of an informal exchange. If self- or community-enforcement conditions are not present, the result is unintended consequences for the bad, as markets are compromised or may fail. The game of "trade" must not yield to the game of "steal."

9. Reciprocity, trust, and trustworthiness are important in personal exchange where formal markets are not worth their cost, yet there are gains from exchange to be captured. They are also important in contracting as not every margin of gain at the expense of other can be anticipated and formalized in written contracts.

10. People are not required to be selfish; rather the point of the Scottish philosophers was that people did not have to be good to produce good. Markets economize on information, understanding, rationality, numbers of agents, and virtue.

11. Markets in no way need destroy the foundation upon which they probably emerged—social exchange between family, friends, and associates. This is supported in the studies reported by Henrich (2000). Thus, individuals can be habitual social exchangers and vigorous traders as well, but as in Hayek's "two worlds" text, the ecologically rational coexistence of personal and impersonal exchange is not a self-aware Cartesian construct. Consequently, there is the ever-present danger that the rules of "personal exchange" will be applied inappropriately to govern or modify the extended order of markets. Equally dangerous, the rules of impersonal market exchange may be applied inappropriately to our cohesive social networks.

12. New brain-imaging technologies have motivated neuroeconomic studies of the internal order of the mind and its links with the spectrum of human decision from choice among fixed gambles to

choice mediated by market and other institutional rules. We are only at the beginning of this enterprise, but its promise suggests a fundamental change in how we think, observe, and model decision in all its contexts.

## Notes

1. Economists are largely untouched by Smith's first great work, which was eclipsed by the *Wealth of Nations*. Thus, one of the profession's best-known historian of economic thought, "found these two works in some measure basically inconsistent" (Jacob Viner, 1991, p. 250). For a contrary interpretation see Smith (1998). Many of the references herein to my own and coauthored work have been reprinted in Smith (1991, 2000).

2. That A implies B in no sense allows the reverse statement. But why would we economists confuse necessary with sufficient conditions? The text from Hume provides the answer. No one can consistently apply rational logical principles to everything he or she does; if there are cognitive costs in every application then the effort cost will often exceed the benefits (Smith and Ferenc Szidarovszky, 2003). Theorists live by proving theorems, and when in this mode we rarely make such errors. A missing chapter in the study of bounded rationality is its application to understanding, and accepting with a little humility, the severe limitations it imposes on our development of economic theory.

3. Douglass Cecil North (1981) has emphasized the importance of ideology in promoting economic growth.

4. In the Potlatch, some wealth—created in part by private property rights in fishing grounds—was publicly destroyed.

5. I will use the term "economic psychology" generally to refer to cognitive psychology as it has been applied to economic questions, and to a third subfield of experimental methods in economics recently product-differentiated as "behavioral economics" (Sendhil Mullainathan and Richard H. Thaler, 2001), and further differentiated into "behavioral game theory" (Colin F. Camerer, 2002); the original foundations were laid by W. Edwards, Danny Kahneman, Anatol Rapoport, Paul Slovic, and Amos Tversky, to name some of the most prominent.

6. In the nineteenth century, Bentham and John Stuart Mill were among the leading constructivists. Bentham (and the utilitarians) sought to "... remake the whole of ... [British] ... law and institutions on rational principles" (Hayek, 1960, p. 174). Mill introduced the much-abused constructivist concept of (but not the name) "natural monopoly." To Mill it was transparently wasteful and duplicative to have two or more mail carriers operating on the same route. He is the intellectual father of the U.S. and other postal monopolies around the world, their resistance to innovation, and their demise in the face of the privatization movement in some countries and the growth of superior substitutes in others. Mill could not imagine that it would be efficient for two cities to be connected by two

parallel railroad tracks (Mill, 1899, Vol. 1, pp. 131, 141–42; Vol. 2, p. 463). Mill died in 1873. I would conjecture that by that date, or soon thereafter, men with grade-school educations had become rich constructing the first parallel-route railroads. These emergent contradictions to constructivist natural monopoly are examples of what we shall call ecological rationality, as detailed below.

7. ". . . Descartes contended that all the useful human institutions were and ought to be deliberate creation(s) of conscious reason . . . a capacity of the mind to arrive at the truth by a deductive process from a few obvious and undoubtable premises" (Hayek, 1967, p. 85).

8. Behavioral economists have made a cottage industry of showing that the SSSM assumptions seem to apply almost nowhere to real decisions. This is because their research program has been a deliberate search in the tails of distributions for "Identifying the ways in which behavior differs from the standard model . . ." (Mullainathan and Thaler, 2001, Vol. II, p. 1094), a search that can only succeed.

9. Dissatisfied with the utilitarian approach because its predictions fail to account for the observed importance of instructions/procedures, we began investigating the reciprocity hypothesis in Elizabeth Hoffman et al. (1994). Mechanically, utilities can serve as intermediate placeholders for reciprocal trust, but, as surface indicators, serve poorly to generate new hypotheses designed to understand interactive processes. Good theory must be an engine for generating testable hypotheses, and utility theory runs out of fuel quickly. Utility values are seen as providing the ultimate "given" data, and the conversation stops.

10. I am reminded of a department head from Hewlett-Packard visiting our lab. I naively assumed that he would be most interested in demonstrations of some of our market experiments. Not so. He was more interested in the "trust" experiments. Why? He saw the HP management problem as one of getting teams to cooperate internally by building trust and trustworthiness, while being vigorous competitors externally. Could the trust games serve as a measurement and teaching tool for helping to solve this problem? This nicely illustrates the tension in Hayek's two-worlds quote in the text.

11. Robert B. Wilson (1992, p. 256) discusses an efficiency theorem, and suggests that the phenomenon is "perhaps unsurprising." It is, nowadays, but few believe it; also, theory has lagged well behind the evidence, and yields inadequate testable insight into the process dynamics operating in different institutions.

12. I want to acknowledge correspondence with Charles Plott and add the following: Although this is a giant victory for the economic theory of markets it simultaneously demonstrates that the theory is incomplete. The unexpectedly weak conditions under which the results obtain are good news for market performance, but not such good news for the scientific community because it demonstrates that we do not understand why markets work as they do. You do not have to have large numbers of agents, each an insignificant part of the whole—three or four buyers and as many sellers are entirely adequate in a wide range of economic environments; they do not have to have complete or perfect or common information—each can have only private information; nor is it required that individuals make decisions systematically or be economically sophisticated.

13. Throughout the paper I will use "environment" to mean the collection of agent values (preferences) that define the gains from trade; "institution" to refer to the language (messages), rules of message exchange, and contract in a market; and "behavior" for agent message choices conditional on the environment and institution (Smith, 1982).

14. If we stopped doing everything for which we do not know the reason, or for which we cannot provide a justification . . . we would probably soon be dead" (Hayek, 1988, p. 68).

15. Expected utility theory is for teaching (as Wassily Leontief once suggested), but also for the constructivist modeling of consistent choice. It seems inadequate for the prediction, or the ecological understanding, of behavior. Its inadequacy for prediction has been plainly emphasized in the many contributions of Amos Tversky and Daniel Kahneman (see their 1987 paper for an excellent summary statement), some of which have been qualified and reinterpreted in the work of Gigerenzer et al. (1999). The results are far more encouraging in the context of markets, where subjects are not consciously maximizing. See, e.g., Smith (1991, 2000) and Plott (2001). Joyce Berg et al. (1994), in a significant paper, find that the measurement of risk aversion varies with the type of market institution or procedure used in extracting risk measures from decisions. See Smith and Szidarovszky (2003) for a constructivist utilitarian treatment of decision whose reward outcome requires cognitive costs to be incurred: objective rationality is not subjectively rational, and therefore it is not optimal for the individual to apply the objectively "optimal" prescriptions.

16. "By the time we think we know something—it is part of our conscious experience—the brain has already done its work. It is old news to the brain, but fresh to 'us.' Systems built into the brain do their work automatically and largely outside of our conscious awareness. The brain finishes the work half a second before the information it processes reaches our consciousness. . . . We are clueless about how all this works and gets effected. We don't plan or articulate these actions. We simply observe the output. . . . The brain begins to cover for this 'done deal' aspect of its functioning by creating in us the illusion that the events we are experiencing are happening in real time—not before our conscious experience of deciding to do something" (Gazzaniga, 1998, pp. 63–64).

17. Hayek (1967, p. 44) notes that ". . . modern English usage does not permit generally to employ the verb 'can' [in the sense of the German *konnen*] to describe all those instances in which an individual merely 'knows how' to do a thing . . . [including] . . . the capacity to act according to rules which we may be able to discover but which we need not be able to state in order to obey them."

18. Many recognize that evolutionary processes are necessarily coevolutionary, but there is also deep denial of this, and bias, that all is due to "culture" (which is even more poorly understood than biology), leading Pinker (2002) to investigate why. Heritable abstract function can become dormant, atrophied, or malfunctional in the absence of initializing input on a developmental time schedule for the brain's vision, language, and socialization circuitry. That these processes are coevolutionary is evident in the study of twins (Nancy L. Segal, 1999). Deconstructivist reports argue that these studies exhibit many of the usual data and statistical identification problems (Arthur S. Goldberger, 1979), but the need is for positive revisionist analysis.

19. "Morality" refers to any maxim of cohesive social behavior that survives the test of time, and is prominently represented by the great "shalt not" prohibitions of the leading world religions: thou shalt not: (1) steal, (2) covet the possessions of others, commit (3) murder, (4) adultery, or (5) bear false witness. The first two define and defend property rights in the product of one's labor, and all resources accumulated by such labor, enabling the emergence of the extended order of mind through markets. The last

three commandments protect the sanctity of social exchange—the external order of the mind. These modest exclusionary constraints leave an immense scope for freedom within their bounds. Corollaries, like the Buddhist live-and-let-live version of the golden rule, are explicit in this respect: "do not unto others as you would have them not do unto you."

20. In cultural and biological evolution, order arises from mechanisms for generating variation to which is applied mechanisms for selection. I am indebted to Todd Zywicki, who, at a recent Liberty Fund conference on "Hayek, Experiment and Freedom," observed that reason is good at providing variation, but not selection. Constructivism is indeed an engine for generating variation, but is far too limited in its ability to comprehend and apply all the relevant facts to serve the process of selection, which is better left to ecological processes.

21. What experimentalists have unintentionally brought to the table is a methodology for objectively testing the Scottish-Hayekian hypotheses under scientific controls. This answers the question Milton Friedman is said to have raised concerning the validity of Hayek's theory/reasoning: "How would you know?" (I am unable to find/provide the reference). Remarkably, Hayek stated on the very edge of recognizing what experiments could do for testing his theory, then dismissed it. Thus, "We can test it ('competition as a discovery procedure') on conceptual models, and we might conceivably test it in artificially created real situations, where the facts which competition is intended to discover are already known to the observer. But in such cases it is of no practical value, so that to carry out the experiment would hardly be worth the expense" (Hayek, 1984, p. 255; also see Smith, 2002, pp. 95–96). Economic historians, e.g., North (1981), and political economists, e.g., Elinor Ostrom (1990), have long explored the intelligence and efficacy embodied in emergent socioeconomic institutions that solve, or fail to solve, problems of growth and resource management. They study "natural" ecological experiments from which we have learned immeasurably.

22. I importune students to read narrowly within economics, but widely in science. Within economics there is essentially only one model to be adapted to every application: optimization subject to constraints due to resource limitations, institutional rules, and/or the behavior of others, as in Cournot-Nash equilibria. The economic literature is not the best place to find new inspiration beyond these traditional technical methods of modeling.

23. Thus, for Hayek, "an economist who is only an economist cannot be a good economist."

24. This is illustrated by a November 6, 2002 press release by Puget Sound Energy. "PSE Proposes to End Pilot Time-of-Use Program Ahead of Schedule: PSE's time-of-use (TOU) program was created in 2000 during the energy crisis and was intended to provide financial incentives for customers to shift some of their electricity consumption to less expensive, off-peak times of the day. The program was restructured in July 2002 to reflect a calmer energy market. Since that time it has resulted in most participants' bills being slightly higher than on flat rates. . . . Reynolds (a PSE spokesman, said) 'However, when exploring new territory, you need to be able to recognize when the program is not working as you had hoped . . . and begin a rigorous analysis of the program and how it could be successfully restructured for the future energy marketplace.'" It is because no one knows what will work best that you have to open retailing up to the field experiment called "free

entry and exit." One experimental possibility is a contract that would share the inherently unknown and unpredictable savings with the customer. When a total cannot be known in advance, use a proportionality rule. New Zealand's tradable fish catch quotas were originally specified in quantities, and were redesigned as proportions of the changing quantity available (oral communication with Maurice McTigue, 2002). An advantage of laboratory experiments is that these kinds of errors are exposed, and corrective alternatives tested, at very low cost.

25. I have never been comfortable with this label because it is reminiscent of the idea that we can engineer best social arrangements, which the reader will see is not my interpretation. See footnote 20.

26. The most widely agreed-upon design failure in the California crisis was the rule preventing the distribution utilities from engaging in long-term contracts to supply power (Wilson, 2002, p. 1332). Beware this simplistic popular explanation: it is a two-wrongs-make-a-right argument: yes, of course, given that you were going to protect the monopoly power of the distribution utilities to tie the rental of the wires to the metering and sale of energy at a fixed regulated price, then one way to protect them temporarily from the consequent wholesale price volatility might be to encourage long-term contracts at a fixed average delivery cost. But suppliers will want higher prices and/or short-term contracts if they anticipate shortages—you cannot get blood out of a turnip; long contracts work to lower cost only to the extent that suppliers are surprised by high spot prices, but when it comes time to renegotiate expiring contracts they will not replicate the error. California discovered this when they intervened to sign long-term contracts, and encountered high prices. This whole argument turns the design problem on its head. You must (1) remove the legal power of the local wires monopoly to prevent competing energy suppliers from contracting with customers to discount off-peak energy, charge premiums for peak energy, and install the supporting control devices; (2) let this competition determine the dynamic price structure, and investment required to implement it; (3) simultaneously, let financial instruments evolve to hedge whatever risk is left over as prices become less volatile. Financial instruments can hedge price volatility, not load volatility. Only demand-responsive interruptible loads can relieve supply stress and provide the demand-side reserves that reduce the risk of lost load. No one mind or collective can anticipate and plan the needed mix of technologies to enable the market to manage demand. Therefore it is essential to remove all entry barriers, and allow firms to experiment through competition to discover and innovate efficient ways of organizing retail delivery systems. Claims that short-run retail demand is "notoriously" inelastic miss the point: how would you know if loan-shedding technology is inflexible? Competition and incentives to innovate have never been part of the structure.

27. People often ask, What are the limits of laboratory investigation? I think any attempt to define such limits is very likely to be bridged by the subsequent ingenuity and creativity (the primary barriers at any one time) of some experimentalist. Twenty-five years ago I could not have imagined being able to do the kinds of experiments that today have become routine in our laboratories. Experimentalists also include many of us who see no clear border separating the lab and the field.

28. The inherent difficulty in equilibrium modeling of the CDA is shown by the fact that so few have even attempted. Wilson (1987), characteristically, has had the courage and competence to log progress. Daniel Friedman (1984) uses an unconventional

no-congestion assumption to finesse Nash-Cournot analysis, concluding efficiency and a final competitive clearing price. Wilson (1987) uses standard assumptions of what is common knowledge—number of buyers (sellers), each with inelastic demand (supply) for one unit, preferences linear in payoffs, no risk aversion or wealth effects, valuations jointly distributed, and agent capacity to "compute equilibrium strategies and select one equilibrium in a way that is common knowledge" (p. 411). This is an abstract as-if-all-agents-were-game-theorists constructivist model of a thought process that no game theorist would or does use when participating in a CDA. The model itself generates its own problems, such as degeneracy in the endgame when there is only one buyer and seller left who can feasibly trade—a problem that is not a problem for the subjects, who do not know this, and see imperfectly informed buyers and sellers still attempting to trade and thereby disciplining price. Extra marginal traders provide opportunity cost end-game constraints on price. Agents need have no understanding of opportunity cost in order for their behavior to be shaped by it. Wilson recognizes these considerations: "The crucial deficiencies, however, are inescapable consequences of the game-theoretic formulation" (Wilson, 1987, p. 411). We are squarely up against the limitations—perhaps the dead-end ultimate consequences—of Cartesian constructivism. We have not a clue, any more than the so-called "naive" subjects in experiments, how it is that our brains so effortlessly solve the equilibration problem in interacting with other brains through the CDA (and other) institutions. We model not the right world to capture this important experimental finding.

29. See Jon Ketcham et al. (1984) for a comparison of CDA with the posted offer (PO) retail pricing mechanism. CDA converges more rapidly and is more efficient than PO. So why does not CDA invade and displace PO? It is the high cost of training every retail clerk to be an effective negotiator for the firm. Institutions reflect the fine structure of opportunity cost, and the loss of exchange efficiency in PO is more than offset by the distributional productive efficiency of the mass retailing innovation of the 1880s that led price policy to be centralized. As I write, those policies are being modified on the Internet where prices can be adjusted to the opportunity cost characteristics of buyers, such as how many other Internet sites they have visited (Cary Deck and Bart Wilson, 2002). Institutional changes in response to innovations like mass retailing are part of the emergence of an ecologically rational equilibrium.

30. Other markets besides the IEM are known to have efficient information-aggregating properties. Pari-mutuel racetrack markets are an example where, interestingly, the environment is much like the IEM: the settlements occur at a well-defined end-state known to all agents, unlike stock market trading where expectations float continuously with no clear value revelation endpoint. "The racetrack betting market is surprisingly efficient. Market odds are remarkably good estimates of winning probabilities. This implies [*sic*] that racetrack bettors have considerable expertise, and that the markets should be taken seriously" (Thaler and William T. Ziemba, 1988, p. 169). It is surprising to behavioral economists because their methodology is restricted to looking for deviations from the standard model. What is unusual here is that in racetracks they have found reportable evidence for efficient outcomes. For those who follow the experimental economics, IEM and similar controlled-environment market studies, efficiency is not only commonplace (if not universal), it cannot be attributed to agents with "considerable expertise." The agents are mostly naive, although they get repeat interaction experience, which, from

the evidence, clearly gives them expertise enough. But, as in the IEM and experimental markets, racetrack markets are not perfect: there are inefficiencies in the "place" and "show" options and the favorite-long-shot bias, with the latter more pronounced in the last two races of the day. Various hypotheses have been offered to explain these inefficiencies, but more significant is that computer programs have been written to arbitrage (yielding returns of some 11 percent per bet), the place, show, and long-shot inefficiencies. (It is my understanding that good profits have been accumulated on these programs, so far without neutralizing the arbitrage opportunities—let the good times roll!)

31. Space prevents me from dealing fully with the many important issues raised when a subset of agents have asymmetric advance information on product quality or value characteristics. The analysis shows that such conditions generate market failure or inefficiency. Some of these problems, however, arise because the analysis is inadequate in examining both sides of the market, and the implications of the information content of prices. Experiments have established that constructivist inefficiency is often alleviated by one of several ecologically rational response mechanisms: competition among sellers for reputations, quality (brand) signaling, product warranties, and the aggregation of private asymmetric information into public price patterns that self-correct the alleged problems. See, e.g., Plott and Louis Wilde (1982); Plott and Sunder (1982, 1988); Miller and Plott (1985); Camerer and Keith Weigelt (1988).

32. Hayek (1967, p. 318) notes that Gresham's Law is not due to Gresham nor is it a "law" in the theoretical sense, and ". . . as a mere empirical rule is practically worthless." In the 1920s when people started using dollars and other hard currencies in substitution for the depreciating mark, the claim emerged that Gresham's Law was wrong—that it was the other way around.

33. This is demonstrated by comparison experiments in which there are no government agents, but fiat money is inflated each period by the average rate that is observed in those experiments with government agents present.

34. "Prior to 1970 or so, most researchers in judgment and decision-making believed that people are pretty good decision-makers. . . . Since then, however, opinion has taken a decided turn for the worse, though the decline was not in any sense demanded by experimental results. Subjects did not suddenly become any less adept at experimental tasks nor did experimentalists begin to grade their performance against a tougher standard. Instead, researchers began selectively to emphasize some results at the expense of others." "The view that people are irrational is real in the sense that people hold it to be true. But the reality is mostly in the rhetoric" (Lola Lopes, 1991, pp. 66, 80).

35. I say "caricatures" because economics has long offered much in the way of theoretical exceptions to the core neoclassical model of self-interested market competition: externalities in choice, public good effects, and "anomalies" in choice under uncertainty requiring explanation (Friedman and L. J. Savage, 1948; Harry Markowitz, 1952). But it is the neoclassical assumption of self-interested agents that has been the most productive of theoretical results and therefore is a prominent and easy target of criticism.

36. Their most important contributions in prospect theory were in empirical tests demonstrating the relevance of two ideas suggested originally by Markowitz (1952): the idea that the theory applies to changes in wealth (income) relative to the individual's current asset state, and that people are risk preferring in losses and risk averse in gains. This much is consistent with standard expected utility theory, which requires only that the

prizes of choice can be ordered, and therefore applies either to wealth or income. Which prizes the theory is best applied to has always seemed to me to be inherently a subject for empirical determination. If applied to wealth, the theory starts to infringe on preference theory over time, long recognized as especially difficult modeling terrain.

37. As I see it experimental market economics and behavioral economics are in principle complementary. Experimental economists study market performance (rationality) given individual valuations, while cognitive psychologists study the valuations (rationality) of individuals. If the objects traded are prospects the appropriate valuations are their "cash values," whether based on expected utility, prospect theory (Kahneman and Tversky, 1979), or some other representation. Thus Plott and Jonathan T. Uhl (1981) study experimental markets in which the items traded are gambles, and report convergence to a CE defined by demand and supply based on the expected values of the gambles. But the connective interface between rationality at the individual and at the market level and how institutions modulate the interface has not been well explored. Markets do their thing with whatever are the values—rational, irrational, or nonrational—that are provided by individuals.

38. For example, the double-auction markets discussed above.

39. Experimental asset markets bubble and crash on the long path of experience to equilibrium (Smith et al., 1988; Porter and Smith, 1994). For a new study of subject experience and asset bubbles see Martin Dufwenberg et al. (2003).

40. Thus, even a ". . . monopolist . . . has to have a full general-equilibrium model of the economy" (Kenneth Arrow, 1987, p. 207). Also see footnote 30 above on racetrack market efficiency, and the inference that the bettors must therefore have considerable expertise. Thus, market rationality is automatically assumed to derive entirely from individual rationality.

41. Here is a particularly clear statement of decision as rational constructivist action: "Incentives do not operate by magic: they work by focusing attention and by prolonged deliberation" (Tversky and Kahneman, 1987, p. 90).

42. The use of cash or other reward medium in decision behavior experiments is listed by Ralph Hertwig and Andreas Ortmann (2001) as one of the key differences between psychology and economics experiments. The controversy over paying subjects, however, is rapidly being eroded as cognitive psychologists and experimental economists join with neurobiologists—including those who are informed on animal behavior models—and subjects are paid salient rewards (Gregor Thut et al., 1997; Hans C. Breiter et al., 2001; McCabe et al., 2001).

43. Kahneman clearly does not see people as irrational except in the narrow context used in economic modeling based on dominant choice. In fact he describes his empirical findings contradicting the SSSM as having been easy, thanks to the implausibility to any psychologist of the SSSM. See the Nobel Foundation interview of the 2002 Nobel Laureates in Economics at http://www.nobel.se/economics/laureates/2002/kahneman -interview.html.

44. At the macro-market level, convergence, and cases of stable and unstable equilibrium, are well predicted by the classical Walrasian adjustment model, but the paths taken, including jumps across alternative unstable equilibria, are not well predicted by the model. See the outstanding summary by Plott (2001). The disconnect with choice behavior is evident in the following: Walrasian dynamics makes ad hoc assumptions about

price adjustments in response to excess demand saying nothing about the corresponding payoff motivation of the agents who drive the price changes. Walrasian dynamics is a story about the tâtonnement mechanism in which there are no disequilibrium trades, whereas Plott's (2001) summary is about continuous double-auction trading with a great many disequilibrium trades.

45. The descriptor "fairness" has so many meanings in different contexts that I believe it is best to avoid the term entirely in experimental science except where it is explicitly modeled and the model tested in environments where subjects make decisions on the basis of the defining parameters of the model; then the descriptor "fair" and its ambiguity can be avoided altogether. This is the way it is used in the utilitarian definitions by Robert Franciosi et al. (1995), in Ernst Fehr and Klaus M. Schmidt (1999), and Bolton and Axel Ockenfels (2000). Of course it is appropriate to use the descriptor if the purpose is to see how its instructional use might have an emotive effect on behavior. The emotive content of "fairness" is clear in the important work of Edward E. Zajac (1995), who has also examined the rhetoric of fairness arguments as self-interest serving in the Florida, 2000, election controversy (Zajac, 2002).

46. KKT state that "... the phrase 'it is fair,' is simply an abbreviation for a substantial majority of the population studied thinks it is fair" (KKT, 1986, p. 201). But their main interest is in whether firm behavior is affected by community norms. Whether or not an action is "acceptable" would seem to be just as important in determining firm behavior as whether or not it is "fair." If the two terms map into different attitudes, then there is inherent ambiguity in specifying the effect on firm behavior.

47. This interpretation is consistent with asset-trading experiments using undergraduates, small businesspersons, corporation managers, and over-the-counter traders (Smith et al., 1988, Porter and Smith, 1994). Exceptions using inexperienced subjects, to my knowledge, have only been observed with advanced graduate students (McCabe and Smith, 2000).

48. This methodology is driven by the untenable belief that general theories can be derived directly from observations if you just have enough data (see Smith, 2002, and the references therein). "Perhaps the most important lesson learned from these studies is that the rules of fairness cannot be inferred either from conventional economic principles or from intuition and introspection. In the words of Sherlock Holmes in 'The Adventure of the Copper Beeches': 'Data! Data! Data! I cannot make bricks without clay'" (KKT, 1986, pp. 115–16). Neither can a predictive theory of "fairness" be inferred from any amount of the KKT data. If N "fairness" rules are discovered by trial and error modifications in the survey questionnaires, you cannot reject the hypothesis that there is an $n + 1$ variation that will identify a new one. More data will not help, as the fairness concept is used here as a word that provides no effective means of modifying standard theory to correct for its predictive flaws.

49. Experimental studies have inquired as to whether emergent norms of cooperation and constructivist incentive schemes are substitutes, the latter crowding out the former. See Iris Bohnet et al. (2001) and Fehr and Simon Gächter (2002) for studies suggesting that they are substitutes (formal rules undermine informal cooperative norms), and Sergio G. Lazzarini et al. (2002) for new results suggesting that they are complements—contracts facilitate the self-enforcement of relational elements beyond contractibility. I would hypoth-

esize that both must be true: constructivist rules ultimately must pass fitness tests of ecological rationality. Formal rules that are incompatible with informal rules will be modified or eliminated; those that are compatible will persist. Hence, at any time slice in history, both must necessarily be observed across all socioeconomic experiments.

50. "... ([A]ll early [my insertion: as in Sumar with the beginning of writing] 'lawgiving' consisted in efforts to record and make known a law that was conceived as unalterably given. A 'legislator' might endeavor to purge the law of supposed corruptions, or to restore it to its pristine purity, but it was not thought that he could make new law.... But if nobody had the power or intention to change the law... this does not mean that law did not continue to develop" (Hayek, 1973, p. 81).

51. What allowed the rule of "natural" or found law to prevail in England "... was the deeply entrenched tradition of a common law that was not conceived as the product of anyone's will but rather as a barrier to all power, including that of the king—a tradition which Edward Coke was to defend against King James I and Francis Bacon, and which Matthew Hale at the end of the seventeenth century masterly restated in opposition to Thomas Hobbes" (Hayek, 1973, p. 85; also see pp. 167, 173–74).

52. These voluntary private associations for sharing the cost of a common good—policing—were subsequently undermined by statehood, and the publicly financed local sheriff as the recognized monopoly law enforcement officer. This observation contradicts the myth that a central function of government is to "solve" the free-rider problem in the private provision of public goods. Here we have the reverse: the incentive of the cattlemen's clubs was to free ride on the general taxpayer, assigning the sheriff the task of enforcing property rights in cattle. The same free-riding occurs with school busing programs, and in publicly provided education itself in which government financing need not require government provision.

53. Later game-theoretic formulations have allowed that with two or more alternatives there may exist "standoff equilibria" that stall agreement in Coase bargaining (see Roger B. Myerson, 1991, p. 506). These cases may limit extensions of the Coase Theorem, but do not, I think, detract from its essential message that the locus of liability was irrelevant.

54. Coase (1974) also noticed that the lighthouse was frequently cited by theorists as an example of a "pure" public good. As was his style (to confront the casual parables of theory that finessed certain costs by fiat), his response in effect was, "Well, let's see what people have done who actually operate lighthouses, or who use the services of lighthouses." It turned out that early lighthouses were private enterprise, not government, solutions to a public good problem, and the alleged inevitability of free-riding was solved by the owner who contracted with port authorities to collect lighthouse fees when ships arrived portside to load or unload cargo.

55. These are the outside options or threat points in game theory.

56. The same results emerge in laboratory experiments reported by Hoffman and Matthew L. Spitzer (1985).

57. Under open range the animal owner is liable for intentional trespass, trespass of a lawful fence, and trespass by goats, whatever the circumstances, suggesting the hypothesis that goat behavior had long been recognized in pastoral norms and now captured in codified law.

58. *The Sensory Order* was not published until 1952 when Hayek revised a manuscript, originally written in the 1920s, entitled in English translation, "Contributions to a Theory of How Consciousness Develops" (noted in correspondence to me by Bruce Caldwell).

59. The interdependence between perception and memory is revealed by the different descriptions of the same event by two eyewitnesses (Gazzaniga et al., 1998, pp. 484–86).

60. Built into your brain is the maintained hypothesis that the world around you is stationary. Look at the wall and move your eyes back and forth with head still. The wall does not move. Now press your eyeball with your finger through the eyelid from the side. The wall moves as you jiggle your eyeball. Why the difference? When you flex the eye muscles and move your eyes back and forth, a copy of the signal goes to the occipital cortex to offset apparent movement of the wall so that the net perception is that of a stationary wall. This stabilizing self-ordered system for seeing also makes you vulnerable to optical illusions of motion. Moving your eyes back and forth between the tunnel gate and your airplane as it docks, you ambiguously "sense" that either the gate or the plane, or both, is in motion. The ambiguity is resolved only when the gate, or plane, stops.

61. See Terence Burnham et al. (2000), discussed below, for a study comparing the effect of using "partner" and "opponent" in a trust game.

62. It is not meaningful or helpful to talk about "experimenter effects." There are instructional and procedural effects, including the presence or absence of an experimenter, what he/she knows or does not know (as in double blind behavioral experiments), and what he/she does or does not do. All of the elementary operations used to implement an experiment are treatments that may or may not have a significant effect on observed outcomes.

63. These double blind procedures and treatment effects have been replicated by two other investigations (Catherine C. Eckel and Philip J. Grossman, 1996, and Burnham, 1998). Bolton et al. (1998), using a different double blind procedure failed to replicate the results, suggesting that procedures matter and interact with the double blind condition.

64. For a recent extension and replication of the BDM findings see Madan Pillutla et al. (2003). Also see Ortmann et al. (2000).

65. Space does not permit examining also the effect of being able to punish defection. See McCabe et al. (1996) for a more complete report of trust games with and without punishment of defection and with a wide variety of matching protocols.

66. As indicated above, the word "trust" never appears in the instructions. Of interest, however, is that the subjects use this word when you ask them open-ended questions about their analysis and perceptions of the game. "It's all a question of whether you can trust your partner." Neither do we use the word "partner."

67. Except see Smith (2002), wherein it is shown that if, in addition to the research hypothesis derived from game theory (e.g., Cournot-Nash or SPE), there is one auxiliary hypothesis (e.g., payoffs are adequate, types have been accurately defined, or subjects are sophisticated), then either the theoretical hypothesis is not falsifiable, or it has no predictive content. The belief, however, persists that the predictions of game theory are sharp and unambiguous (see, e.g., Camerer et al., 2001).

68. "Sociopaths, who comprise only 3–4 percent of the male population and less than 1 percent of the female population, are thought to account for 20 percent of the United States prison population and between 33 percent and 80 percent of the population of chronic criminal offenders. Furthermore, whereas the 'typical' U.S. burglar is estimated

to have committed a median five crimes per year before being apprehended, chronic offenders—those most likely to be sociopaths—report committing upwards of 50 crimes per year and sometimes as many as two or three hundred. Collectively, these individuals are thought to account for over 50 percent of all crimes in the U.S." (see Linda Mealy, 1995, p. 523, and pp. 587–99 for references and caveats; also David T. Lykken, 1995).

69. This thought process may explain why, in data reported by Giorgio Coricelli et al. (2000) comparing faculty with undergraduate subjects, the faculty take much longer (and earn less money) than the undergraduates to decide whether to offer cooperation, and whether to defect. Yet given knowledge of game theory, and knowing that one's counterpart has the equivalent knowledge, what is there to think about?

70. Any such natural process must be deliberately overcome, constructively, in situations where nature serves us poorly.

# References

**Acheson, James.** "The Lobster Fiefs: Economic and Ecological Effects of Territoriality in the Maine Lobster Industry." *Human Ecology*, September 1975, *2*(3), pp. 183–207.

**Anderson, Terry L., and Peter J. Hill.** "The Evolution of Property Rights: A Study of the American West." *Journal of Law and Economics*, April 1975, *18*(1), pp. 163–79.

**Arrow, Kenneth J.** "Rationality of Self and Others in an Economic System," in Robin M. Hogarth and Melvin Warren Reder, eds., *Rational choice: The contrast between economics and psychology*. Chicago: University of Chicago Press, 1987, pp. 201–16.

**Backerman, Steven R., Michael Denton, Stephen Rassenti, and Vernon L. Smith.** "Market Power in a Deregulated Electrical Industry." *Journal of Decision Support Systems*, 2001, (30), pp. 357–81.

**Banks, Jeffrey, Mark Olson, Stephen Rassenti, and Vernon L. Smith.** "Theory, Experiment and the Federal Communications Commission Spectrum Auctions." *Journal of Economic Behavior and Organization*, 2003 (forthcoming).

**Baron-Cohen, S.** *Mindblindness: An essay on autism and theory of mind.* Cambridge, MA: MIT Press, 1995.

**Bechara, Antoine, Hanna Damasio, Daniel Tranel, and Antonio R. Damasio.** "Deciding Advantageously Before Knowing the Advantageous Strategy." *Science*, February 28, 1997, *275*(5304), pp. 1293–95.

**Berg, Joyce, John Dickhaut, and Kevin McCabe.** "Risk Preference Instability Across Institutions: A Dilemma." Working paper, Carlson School of Management, University of Minnesota, 1994.

———. "Trust, Reciprocity, and Social History." *Games and Economic Behavior*, July 1995, *10*(1), pp. 122–42.

**Binswanger, Hans P.** "Attitudes Toward Risk: Experimental Measurement in Rural India." *American Journal of Agricultural Economics*, August 1980, *62*(3), pp. 395–407.

**Bohnet, Iris, Bruno S. Frey, and Steffen Huck.** "More Order with Less Law: On Contract Enforcement, Trust, and Crowding." *American Political Science Review*, March 2001, *95*(1), pp. 131–44.

**Bolton, Gary E.** "A Comparative Model of Bargaining: Theory and Evidence." *American Economic Review*, December 1991, *81*(5), pp. 1096–136.

**Bolton, Gary E., Elena Katok, and Rami Zwick.** "Dictator Game Giving: Rules of Fairness versus Acts of Kindness." *International Journal of Game Theory*, July 1998, *27*(2), pp. 269–99.

**Bolton, Gary E., and Axel Ockenfels.** "ERC: A Theory of Equity, Reciprocity, and Competition." *American Economic Review*, March 2000, *90*(1), pp. 166–93.

**Breiter, Hans C., Itzhak Aharon, Daniel Kahneman, Anders Dale, and Peter Shizgal.** "Functional Imaging of Neural Responses to Expectancy and Experience of Monetary Gains and Losses." *Neuron*, May 2001, *30*(2), pp. 619–39.

**Bronfman, Corrine, Kevin McCabe, David Porter, Stephen Rassenti, and Vernon L. Smith.** "An Experimental Examination of the Walrasian Tâtonnement Mechanism." *RAND Journal of Economics*, Winter 1996, *27*(4), pp. 681–99.

**Burnham, Terence C.** "Engineering Altruism: An Experimental Investigation of Anonymity and Gift Giving." Unpublished manuscript, Kennedy School of Government, Harvard University, 1998.

**Burnham, Terence, Kevin McCabe, and Vernon L. Smith.** "Friend-or-Foe Intentionality Priming in an Extensive Form Trust Game." *Journal of Economic Behavior and Organization*, September 2000, *43*(1), pp. 57–73.

**Camera, Gabriele, Charles Noussair, and Steven Tucker.** "Rate-of-Return Dominance and Efficiency in an Experimental Economy." *Economic Theory*, 2003 (forthcoming).

**Camerer, Colin F.** *Behavioral game theory: Experiments on strategic interaction.* Princeton, NJ: Princeton University Press, 2002.

**Camerer, Colin, and Teck-Hua Ho.** "Experience-Weighted Attraction Learning in Normal Form Games." *Econometrica*, July 1999, *67*(4), pp. 827–74.

**Camerer, Colin, Teck-Hua Ho, and Juin-Kuan Chong.** "Behavioral Game Theory: Thinking, Learning, and Teaching." Nobel Symposium on Behavioral and Experimental Economics, Stockholm, December 2001.

**Camerer, Colin, and Keith Weigelt.** "Experimental Tests of a Sequential Equilibrium Model." *Econometrica*, January 1988, *56*(1), pp. 1–36.

**Cason, Timothy, and Daniel Friedman.** "An Empirical Analysis of Price Formation in Double-Auction Markets," in D. Friedman and J. Rust, eds., *The double auction.* Redwood City, CA: Addison-Wesley, 1993, pp. 253–83.

**Chu, Yun Peng, and Ruey Ling Chu.** "The Subsistance of Preference Reversals in Simplified and Marketlike Experimental Settings: A Note." *American Economic Review*, September 1990, *80*(4), pp. 902–11.

**Coase, Ronald H.** "The Problem of Social Cost." *Journal of Law and Economics*, October 1960, *3*(1), pp. 1–44.

———. "The Lighthouse in Economics." *Journal of Law and Economics*, October 1974, *17*(2), pp. 357–76.

**Coricelli, Giorgio, Kevin McCabe, and Vernon L. Smith.** "Theory-of-Mind Mechanism in Personal Exchange," in G. Hatano, N. Okada, and H. Tanabe, eds., *Affective minds.* Amsterdam: Elsevier, 2000.

**Cosmides, Leda, and John Tooby.** "Cognitive Adaptations for Social Exchange," in Jerome H. Barkow, Leda Cosmides, and John Tooby, eds., *The adapted mind.* New York: Oxford University Press, 1992, pp. 163–228.

**Cox, James C., and David M. Grether.** "The Preference Reversal Phenomenon: Response Mode, Markets and Incentives." *Economic Theory*, April 1996, *7*(3), pp. 381–405.

**Damasio, Antonio R.** *Descartes' error: Emotion, reason, and the human brain.* New York: G. P. Putnam, 1994.

**Davis, Douglas D., and Charles A. Holt.** *Experimental economics.* Princeton, NJ: Princeton University Press, 1993.

**Deck, Cary, Kevin McCabe, and David Porter.** "Why Stable Flat Money Hyperinflates: Results from an Experimental Economy." Unpublished manuscript, Department of Economics, University of Arkansas, 2001.

**Deck, Cary, and Bart Wilson.** "Tracking Customer Search to Price Discriminate." Working paper, Interdisciplinary Center for Economic Science, George Mason University, 2002.

**Denton, Michael J., Stephen J. Rassenti, and Vernon L. Smith.** "Spot Market Mechanism Design and Competitivity Issues in Electric Power." *Journal of Economic Behavior and Organization*, April 2001, *44*(4), pp. 435–53.

**de Waal, Frans B. M.** "Food Sharing and Reciprocal Obligations Among Chimpanzees." *Journal of Human Evolution*, May 1989, *18*(5), pp. 433–59.

————. "Food Transfers Through Mesh in Brown Capuchins." *Journal of Comparative Psychology*, December 1997, *111*(4), pp. 370–78.

**Donahue, George.** "The U.S. Air Transportation System: A Bold Vision for Change." Paper prepared for the Commission on the Future of the U.S. Airspace Industry, September 19, 2002.

**Dufwenberg, Martin, Tobias Lindqvist, and Evan Moore.** "Bubbles and Experience: An Experiment on Speculation." Working paper, Department of Economics, Stockholm University, January 2003.

**Eckel, Catherine C., and Philip J. Grossman.** "Altruism in Anonymous Dictator Games." *Games and Economic Behavior*, October 1996, *76*(2), pp. 181–91.

**Ellickson, Robert C.** *Order without law: How neighbors settle disputes.* Cambridge, MA: Harvard University Press, 1991.

**Erev, Ido, and Alvin E. Roth.** "Predicting How People Play Games: Reinforcement Learning in Experimental Games with Unique, Mixed Strategy Equilibria." *American Economic Review*, September 1998, *88*(4), pp. 848–81.

**Falk, Armin, Ernst Fehr, and Urs Fischbacher.** "On the Nature of Fair Behavior." Working Paper No. 17, University of Zurich, August 1999.

**Fehr, Ernst, and Simon Gächter.** "Do Incentive Contracts Crowd Out Voluntary Cooperation?" Working Paper No. 34, University of Zurich, April 2002.

**Fehr, Ernst, and Klaus M. Schmidt.** "A Theory of Fairness, Competition, and Cooperation." *Quarterly Journal of Economics*, August 1999, *114*(3), pp. 817–68.

**Fiske, Alan Page.** *Structures of social life: The four elementary forms of human relations.* New York: Free Press, 1991.

**Fletcher, P. C., F. Happé, U. Frith, S. C. Baker, R. J. Dolan, R. S. J. Frakowiak, and C. D. Frith.** "Other Minds in the Brain: A Functional Imaging Study of 'Theory of Mind' in Story Comprehension." *Cognition*, November 1995, *57*(2), pp. 109–28.

**Forsythe, Robert, Joel L. Horowitz, N. E. Savin, and Martin Sefton.** "Fairness in Simple Bargaining Experiments." *Games and Economic Behavior,* May 1994, *6*(3), pp. 347–69.

**Forsythe, Robert, Forrest Nelson, George R. Neumann, and Jack Wright.** "Anatomy of an Experimental Political Stock Market." *American Economic Review,* December 1992, *82*(5), pp. 1142–61.

**Forsythe, Robert, Thomas A. Rietz, and Thomas W. Ross.** "Wishes, Expectations and Actions: A Survey on Price Formation in Election Stock Markets." *Journal of Economic Behavior and Organization,* May 1999, *39*(1), pp. 83–110.

**Fouraker, Lawrence E., and Sidney Siegel.** *Bargaining behavior.* New York: McGraw-Hill, 1963.

**Franciosi, Robert, Praveen Kujal, Roland Michelitsch, Vernon Smith, and Gang Deng.** "Fairness: Effect on Temporary and Equilibrium Prices in Posted-Offer Markets." *Economic Journal,* July 1995, *105*(431), pp. 938–50.

**Freuchen, Peter.** *Peter Freuchen's book of the eskimos.* Cleveland, OH: World Publishing Co., July 1961.

**Friedman, Daniel.** "On the Efficiency of Double Auction Markets." *American Economic Review,* March 1984, *74*(1), pp. 60–72.

———. "The Double Auction Market Institution: A Survey," in D. Friedman and J. Rust, eds., *The double auction market: Institutions, theory, and evidence.* Reading, MA: Addison-Wesley Publishing Co., 1993, pp. 3–25.

**Friedman, Milton, and L. J. Savage.** "The Utility Analysis of Choices Involving Risk." *Journal of Political Economy,* August 1948, *56*(4), pp. 279–304.

**Fuster, Joaquin M.** *Memory in the cerebral cortex: An empirical approach to neural networks in the human and nonhuman primate.* Cambridge, MA: MIT Press, 1999.

**Gazzaniga, Michael S.** *The mind's past.* Berkeley, CA: University of California Press, 1998.

**Gazzaniga, Michael S., Richard B. Ivry, and G. Mangun.** *Cognitive neuroscience: The biology of the mind.* New York: Norton, 1998.

**Gigerenzer, Gerd, Peter M. Todd, and the ABC Research Group.** *Simple heuristics that make us smart.* New York: Oxford, 1999.

**Goel, Vinod, Jordan Grafman, Jinous Tajik, Sheldon Gana, and David Danto.** "A Study of the Performance of Patients with Frontal Lobe Lesions in a Financial Planning Task." *Brain,* October 1997, *120*(10), pp. 1805–22.

**Goldberger, Arthur S.** "Heritability." *Economica,* November 1979, *46*(184), pp. 327–47.

**Hawkes, Kristen.** "Showing Off: Tests of an Hypothesis about Men's Foraging Goals." *Ethology and Sociobiology,* January 1991, *12*(1), pp. 29–54.

**Hayek, Friedrich A.** *The sensory order: An inquiry into the foundations of theoretical psychology.* Chicago: University of Chicago Press, 1952.

———. *The constitution of liberty.* Chicago: University of Chicago Press, 1960.

———. *Studies in philosophy, politics and economics.* Chicago: University of Chicago Press, 1967.

———. *Law, legislation, and liberty, volume I, rules and order.* Chicago: University of Chicago Press, 1973.

———. "Competition as a Discovery Procedure," in *The essence of Hayek.* Stanford, CA: Hoover Institution Press, 1984, pp. 254–65.

———. *The fatal conceit: The errors of socialism.* Chicago: University of Chicago Press, 1988.

————. "Adam Smith (1723–1790): His Message in Today's Language," in *The trend of economic thinking: Essays on political economists and economic history*. Chicago: University of Chicago Press, 1991, pp. 119–24.

Henrich, Joseph. "Does Culture Matter in Economic Behavior? Ultimatum Game Bargaining Among the Machiguenga of the Peruvian Amazon." *American Economic Review*, September 2000, *90*(4), pp. 973–79.

Hertwig, Ralph, and Andreas Ortmann. "Experimental Practices in Economics: A Methodological Challenge for Psychologists?" *Behavioral and Brain Sciences*, June 2001, *24*(3), pp. 383–451.

Hoffman, Elizabeth, Kevin A. McCabe, Keith Shachat, and Vernon L. Smith. "Preferences, Property Rights, and Anonymity in Bargaining Games." *Games and Economic Behavior*, November 1994, *7*(3), pp. 346–80.

Hoffman, Elizabeth, Kevin A. McCabe, and Vernon L. Smith. "On Expectations and the Monetary Stakes in Ultimatum Games." *International Journal of Game Theory*, 1996a, *25*(3), pp. 289–301.

————. "Social Distance and Other-Regarding Behavior in Dictator Games." *American Economic Review*, June 1996b, *86*(3), pp. 653–60.

————. "The Impact of Exchange Context on the Activation of Equity in Ultimatum Games." *Experimental Economics*, June 2000, *3*(1), pp. 5–9.

Hoffman, Elizabeth, and Matthew L. Spitzer. "Entitlements, Rights, and Fairness: An Experimental Examination of Subjects' Concepts of Distributive Justice." *Journal of Legal Studies*, June 1985, *14*(2), pp. 259–97.

Hogarth, Robin M., and Melvin Warren Reder. *Rational choice: The contrast between economics and psychology*. Chicago: University of Chicago Press, 1987.

Holt, Charles. "Industrial Organization: A Survey of Laboratory Research," in J. Kagel and A. Roth, eds., *The handbook of experimental economics*. Princeton, NJ: Princeton University Press, 1995, pp. 349–443.

Hume, David. *A treatise of human nature*. London: Penguin Books, 1985 (first published in 1739).

Kachelmeier, Steven J., and Mohamed Shehata. "Examining Risk Preferences under High Monetary Incentives: Evidence from the People's Republic of China." *American Economic Review*, December 1992, *82*(5), pp. 1120–41.

Kagan, Jerome. *Galen's prophecy: Temperament in human nature*. New York: Basic Books, 1994.

Kagan, Jerome, and Sharon Lamb. *The emergence of morality in young children*. Chicago: University of Chicago Press, 1987.

Kagel, John H., and Alvin E. Roth, eds. *The handbook of experimental economics*. Princeton, NJ: Princeton University Press, 1995.

Kahneman, Daniel, Jack L. Knetsch, and Richard Thaler. "Fairness as a Constraint on Profit Seeking: Entitlements in the Market." *American Economic Review*, September 1986, *76*(4), pp. 728–41.

————. "Fairness and the Assumptions of Economics," in R. Thaler, ed., *Quasi rational economics*. New York: Russell Sage Foundation, 1991, pp. 220–35.

Kahneman, Daniel, and Amos Tversky. "Prospect Theory: An Analysis of Decision Under Risk." *Econometrica*, March 1979, *47*(2), pp. 263–91.

**Kaplan, Hillard, and Kim Hill.** "Food Sharing among Ache Foragers: Tests of Explanatory Hypotheses." *Current Anthropology*, April 1985, *26*(2), pp. 223–46.

**Ketcham, Jon, Vernon L. Smith, and Arlington Williams.** "A Comparison of Posted-Offer and Double-Auction Pricing Institutions." *Review of Economic Studies*, October 1984, *51*(4), pp. 595–614.

**Knowlton, Barbara J., Jennifer A. Mangels, and Larry R. Squire.** "A Neostriatal Habit Learning System in Humans." *Science*, September 6, 1996, *273*(5280), pp. 1399–402.

**Lazzarini, Sergio G., Gary Miller, and Todd Zenger.** "Order with Some Law: Complementarity vs. Substitution of Formal and Informal Arrangements." Interdisciplinary Conference on Trust and Reciprocity in Experimental Economics, Washington University, St. Louis, October 11–12, 2002.

**Ledyard, John D.** "The Scope of the Hypothesis of Bayesian Equilibrium." *Journal of Economic Theory*, June 1986, *39*(1), pp. 59–82.

**Lopes, Lola.** "The Rhetoric of Irrationality." *Theory and Psychology*, 1991, *1*(1), pp. 65–82.

**Lykken, David T.** *The antisocial personalities*. Hillsdale, NJ: Lawrence Erlbaum Associates, 1995.

**Markowitz, Harry.** "The Utility of Wealth." *Journal of Political Economy*, April 1952, *60*(2), pp. 151–58.

**McCabe, Kevin A., Daniel Houser, Lee Ryan, Vernon L. Smith, and Theodore Trouard.** "A Functional Imaging Study of Cooperation in Two-person Reciprocal Exchange." *Proceedings of the National Academy of Sciences*, September 25, 2001, *98*(20), pp. 11832–35.

**McCabe, Kevin A., Stephen J. Rassenti, and Vernon L. Smith.** "Smart Computer-Assisted Markets," *Science*, October 1991, *254*(5031), pp. 534–38.

———. "Designing a Uniform-Price Double Auction: An Experimental Evaluation," in D. Friedman and J. Rust, eds., *The double auction market: Institutions, theory, and evidence.* Reading, MA: Addison-Wesley Publishing Co., 1993, pp. 307–32.

———. "Game Theory and Reciprocity in Some Extensive Form Experimental Games." *Proceedings of the National Academy of Sciences*, September 16, 1996, *93*(23), pp. 13421–28.

**McCabe, Kevin A., Mary L. Rigdon, and Vernon L. Smith.** "Positive Reciprocity and Intentions in Trust Games." *Journal of Economic Behavior and Organization*, 2003 (forthcoming).

**McCabe, Kevin A., and Vernon L. Smith.** "A Comparison of Naïve and Sophisticated Subject Behavior with Game Theoretic Predictions." *Proceedings of the National Academy of Sciences*, March 28, 2000, *97*(7), pp. 3777–81.

———. "Goodwill Accounting and the Process of Exchange," in G. Gigerenzer and R. Selten, eds., *Bounded rationality: The adaptive toolbox.* Cambridge, MA: MIT Press, 2001, pp. 319–40.

**McCabe, Kevin A., Vernon L. Smith, and Michael LePore.** "Intentionality Detection and 'Mind-reading': Why Does Game Form Matter?" *Proceedings of the National Academy of Sciences*, April 11, 2000, *97*(8), pp. 4404–09.

**Mealy, Linda.** "The Sociobiology of Sociopathy: An Integrated Evolutionary Model." *Behavioral and Brain Sciences*, September 1995, *18*(3), pp. 523–99.

**Mellers, Barbara A., A. Schwartz, and I. Ritov.** "Emotion-Based Choice." *Journal of Experimental Psychology: General*, March 1999, *128*(1), pp. 1–14.

**Milgrom, Paul R., and Robert J. Weber.** "A Theory of Auctions and Competitive Bidding." *Econometrica*, September 1982, *50*(5), pp. 1089–122.

**Mill, John Stuart.** *Principles of political economy, with some of their applications to social philosophy, volumes 1 and 2.* London: Colonial Press, 1899.

**Miller, Ross M.** "Don't Let Your Robots Grow Up to Be Traders." Working paper, Miller Risk Advisors, 2002.

**Miller, Ross M., and Charles R. Plott.** "Product Quality Signaling in Experimental Markets." *Econometrica,* July 1985, *53*(4), pp. 837–72.

**Mullainathan, Sendhil, and Richard H. Thaler.** "Behavioral Economics." *International encyclopedia of the social and behavioral sciences, volume II.* Oxford: Pergamon, 2001, pp. 1094–99.

**Myerson, Roger B.** *Game theory: Analysis of conflict.* Cambridge, MA: Harvard University Press, 1991.

**North, Douglass Cecil.** *Structure and change in economic history.* New York: Norton, 1981.

**Olson, Mark, Stephen Rassenti, Vernon L. Smith, and Mary Rigdon.** "Market Design and Motivated Human Trading Behavior in Electricity Markets." *Institute of Industrial Engineering Transactions*, 2003 (forthcoming).

**Ortmann, Andreas, John Fitzgerald, and Carl Boeing.** "Trust, Reciprocity, and Social History: A Re-examination." *Experimental Economics,* June 2000, *3*(3), pp. 81–100.

**Ostrom, Elinor.** *Governing the commons: The evolution of institutions for collective action.* Cambridge: Cambridge University Press, 1990.

**Pillutla, Madan, Deepak Malhotra, and J. Keith Murnighan.** "Attributions of Trust and the Calculus of Reciprocity." *Journal of Experimental Social Psychology*, 2003 (forthcoming).

**Pinker, Steven.** *The language instinct.* New York: W. Morrow and Co., 1994.

———. *The blank slate: The modern denial of human nature.* New York: Viking, 2002.

**Plott, Charles R.** "Research on Pricing in a Gas Transportation Network." Office of Economic Policy Technical Report No. 88–2. Federal Energy Regulatory Commission, Washington, DC, July 1988.

———. "Equilibrium, Equilibration, Information and Multiple Markets: From Basic Science to Institutional Design." Nobel Symposium, Behavioral and Experimental Economics, Grand Hotel Saltsjobaden, December 4–6, 2001.

**Plott, Charles R., and Shyam Sunder.** "Efficiency of Experimental Security Markets with Insider Information: An Application of Rational-Expectations Models." *Journal of Political Economy*, August 1982, *90*(4), pp. 663–98.

———. "Rational Expectations and the Aggregation of Diverse Information in Laboratory Securities Markets." *Econometrica*, September 1988, *56*(5), pp. 1085–118.

**Plott, Charles R., and Jonathan T. Uhl.** "Competitive Equilibrium with Middlemen: An Empirical Study." *Southern Economic Journal*, April 1981, *47*(4), pp. 1063–71.

**Plott, Charles R., and Louis Wilde.** "Professional Diagnosis vs. Self-Diagnosis: An Experimental Examination of Some Special Features of Markets with Uncertainty," in V. L. Smith, ed., *Research in experimental economics, volume 2.* Greenwich, CT: JAI Press, 1982, pp. 63–112.

**Porter, David, and Vernon L. Smith.** "Stock Market Bubbles in the Laboratory." *Applied Mathematical Finance,* December 1994, *1,* pp. 111–27.

**Rabin, Matthew.** "Incorporating Fairness into Game Theory and Economics." *American Economic Review,* December 1993, *83*(5), pp. 1281–302.

**Rapoport, Amnon.** "Order of Play in Strategically Equivalent Games in Extensive Form." *International Journal of Game Theory,* 1997, *26*(1), pp. 113–36.

**Rassenti, Stephen, Vernon L. Smith, and R. Bulfin.** "A Combinatorial Auction Mechanism for Airport Time Slot Allocation." *Bell Journal of Economics,* Autumn 1982, *13*(2), pp. 402–17.

**Rassenti, Stephen, Vernon L. Smith, and Bart J. Wilson.** "Using Experiments to Inform the Privatization/Deregulation Movement in Electricity." *Cato Journal,* Winter 2002, *21*(3), pp. 515–44.

———. "Controlling Market Power and Price Spikes in Electricity Networks: Demand-side Bidding." *Proceedings of the National Academy of Sciences,* March 2003, *100*(5), pp. 2998–3003.

**Rosenthal, Robert W.** "Games of Perfect Information, Predatory Pricing and the Chain-Store Paradox." *Journal of Economic Theory,* August 1981, *25*(1), pp. 92–100.

**Satterthwaite, Mark.** "Strategy-Proof Allocation Mechanisms," in J. Eatwell, M. Milgate, and P. Newman, eds., *The new Palgrave, volume 4.* London: Macmillan, 1987, pp. 518–20.

**Schotter, Andrew, Keith Weigelt, and Charles Wilson.** "A Laboratory Investigation of Multiperson Rationality and Presentation Effects." *Games and Economic Behavior,* May 1994, *6*(3), pp. 445–68.

**Schultz, Wolfram.** "Multiple Reward Signals in the Brain." *Nature Reviews: Neuroscience,* December 2000, *1*(3), pp. 199–207.

———. "Getting Formal with Dopamine and Reward." *Neuron,* October 2002, *36*(2), pp. 241–63.

**Schwartz, T., and J. S. Ang.** "Speculative Bubbles in the Asset Market: An Experimental Study." Paper presented at the American Finance Association meeting, Atlanta, December, 1989.

**Segal, Nancy L.** *Entwined lives: Twins and what they tell us about human behavior.* New York: Plume, 1999.

**Selten, Reinhard.** "Reexamination of the Perfectness Concept for Equilibrium Points in Extensive Games." *International Journal of Game Theory,* 1975, *4*, pp. 25–55.

**Siegel, Sidney.** "Theoretical Models of Choice and Strategy Behavior." *Psychometrika,* 1959, *24*, pp. 303–16.

**Siegel, Sidney, and Lawrence E. Fouraker.** *Bargaining and group decision making: Experiments in bilateral monopoly.* New York: McGraw-Hill, 1960.

**Simon, Herbert Alexander.** *The sciences of the artificial, 3rd ed.* Cambridge, MA: MIT Press, 1981, 1996.

**Smith, Adam.** *The theory of moral sentiments.* Indianapolis, IN: Liberty Classics, 1759 (republished in 1982).

———. *An enquiry into the nature and causes of the wealth of nations.* Indianapolis, IN: Liberty Classics, 1776 (republished in 1981).

**Smith, Kip, John Dickhaut, Kevin McCabe, and José V. Pardo.** "Neuronal Substrates for Choice Under Ambiguity, Risk, Gains, and Losses." *Management Science,* June 2002, *48*(6), pp. 711–18.

**Smith, Vernon L.** "An Experimental Study of Competitive Market Behavior." *Journal of Political Economy*, April 1962, *70*(12), pp. 111–37.

———. "Experimental Economics: Induced Value Theory." *American Economic Review*, May 1976 (*Papers and Proceedings*), *66*(2), pp. 274–79.

———. "Relevance of Laboratory Experiments to Testing Resource Allocation Theory," in Jan Kmenta and James Bernard Ramsey, eds., *Evaluation of econometric models*. New York: Academic Press, 1980, pp. 345–77.

———. "Microeconomic Systems as an Experimental Science." *American Economic Review*, December 1982, *72*(5), pp. 923–55.

———. "Experimental Methods in the Political Economy of Exchange." *Science*, October 10, 1986, *234*(4773), pp. 167–73.

———. *Papers in experimental economics*. Cambridge: Cambridge University Press, 1991.

———. "The Two Faces of Adam Smith." *Southern Economic Journal*, July 1998, *65*(1), pp. 1–19.

———. *Bargaining and market behavior: Essays in experimental economics*. Cambridge: Cambridge University Press, 2000.

———. "Method in Experiment: Rhetoric and Reality." *Journal of Experimental Economics*, 2002.

**Smith, Vernon L., Gerry L. Suchanek, and Arlington W. Williams.** "Bubbles, Crashes and Endogenous Expectations in Experimental Spot Asset Markets." *Econometrica*, September 1988, *56*(5), pp. 1119–51.

**Smith, Vernon L., and Ferenc Szidarovszky.** "Monetary Rewards and Decision Cost in Strategic Interactions," in M. Augier and J. March, eds., *Models of a man: Essays in memory of Herbert A. Simon*. Cambridge, MA: MIT Press, 2003 (forthcoming).

**Smith, Vernon L., Arlington W. Williams, Kenneth Bratton, and Michael G. Vannoni.** "Competitive Market Institutions: Double Auctions vs. Sealed Bid-Offer Auctions." *American Economic Review*, March 1982, *72*(1), pp. 58–77.

**Soper, Barry, and Gary Gigiolotti.** "Intransitive Cycles: Rational Choice or Random Error?" *Theory and Decision*, 1993, *35*, pp. 311–36.

**Sunder, Shyam.** "Market as Artifact: Aggregate Efficiency from Zero Intelligence Traders," in M. Augier and J. March, eds., *Models of a man: Essays in memory of Herbert A. Simon*. Cambridge, MA: MIT Press, 2003 (forthcoming).

**Thaler, Richard H., and William T. Ziemba.** "Parimutuel Betting Markets: Racetracks and Lotteries." *Journal of Economics Perspectives*, Spring 1988, *2*(2), pp. 161–74.

**Thut, Gregor, Wolfram Schultz, Ulrich Roelcke, Matthias Nieuhusmeier, John Missimer, R. Paul Maguire, and Klaus L. Leenders.** "Activation of the Human Brain by Monetary Reward." *NeuroReport*, January 1997, *8*(5), pp. 1225–28.

**Tremblay, Leon, and Wolfram Schultz.** "Relative Reward Preference in Primate Orbitofrontal Cortex." *Nature*, April 22, 1999, *39*, pp. 466–83.

**Tversky, Amos, and Daniel Kahneman.** "Rational Choice and the Framing of Decisions," in Robin M. Hogarth and Melvin Warren Reder, eds., *Rational choice: The contrast between economics and psychology*. Chicago: University of Chicago Press, 1987, pp. 67–94.

**Umbeck, John.** "The California Gold Rush: A Study of Emerging Property Rights." *Explorations in Economic History*, July 1977, *14*(3), pp. 197–226.

**Vickrey, William.** "Counterspeculation, Auctions, and Competitive Sealed Tenders." *Journal of Finance*, March 1961, *16*(1), pp. 8–37.

**Viner, Jacob.** "Adam Smith," in D. Irvin, ed., *Essays on the intellectual history of economics*. Princeton, NJ: Princeton University Press, 1991, pp. 248–61.

**Williams, Arlington, and Vernon L. Smith.** "Simultaneous Trading in Two Competitive Markets." Unpublished manuscript, Indiana University Department of Economics, Bloomington, Indiana, 1986.

**Williams, Arlington W., Vernon L. Smith, John O. Ledyard, and Steven Gjerstad.** "Concurrent Trading in Two Experimental Markets with Demand Interdependence." *Economic Theory*, November 2000, *16*(3), pp. 511–28.

**Wilson, Robert B.** "On Equilibria of Bid-Ask Markets," in George R. Feiwal, ed., *Arrow and the ascent of modern economic theory*. New York: New York University Press, 1987, pp. 375–414.

———. "Strategic Analysis of Auctions," in Robert J. Aumann and Sergi Hart, eds., *Handbook of game theory*. Amsterdam: North-Holland, 1992, pp. 227–79.

———. "Design of Efficient Auction Procedures," in D. Friedman and J. Rust, eds., *The double auction market: Institutions, theory, and evidence*. Reading, MA: Addison-Wesley Publishing Co., 1993, pp. 125–52.

———. "Architecture of Power Markets." *Econometrica*, July 2002, *70*(4), pp. 1299–1340.

**Zajac, Edward E.** *Political economy of fairness*. Cambridge, MA: MIT Press, 1995.

———. "What Fairness-and-Denial Research Could Have Told the Florida Supreme Court (and Can Tell the Rest of Us)." *Independent Review*, Winter 2002, *6*(3), pp. 377–97.

**Zeaman, David J.** "Response Latency as a Function of the Amount of Reinforcement." *Experimental Psychology*, 1949, *39*, pp. 466–83.

# CHAPTER 6

✸

# ELINOR C. OSTROM

Elinor C. Ostrom was awarded the Sveriges Riksbank Prize in Economic Sciences in Memory of Alfred Nobel in 2009, along with Oliver E. Williamson, for their respective contributions to demonstrating that "economic analysis can shed light on most forms of social organization." Ostrom was recognized for "her analysis of economic governance, especially the commons." Challenging conventional wisdom that "common property is poorly managed and should be either regulated by central authorities or privatized," she gathered numerous field studies in the areas of user-managed fish stocks, pastures, woods, lakes, and groundwater basins and concluded that resource users commonly cultivate refined mechanisms for decision-making and rule enforcement to resolve conflicts. In Ostrom's analysis, individuals are capable of effectively managing common property through rules and institutions that encourage fair administration of shared resources. The Nobel Committee credited Ostrom's and Williamson's seminal research in previously neglected nonmarket contexts with bringing economic governance "from the fringe to the forefront of scientific attention."

# BEYOND MARKETS *and* STATES: POLYCENTRIC GOVERNANCE *of* COMPLEX ECONOMIC SYSTEMS

## ELINOR C. OSTROM

Contemporary research on the outcomes of diverse institutional arrangements for governing common-pool resources (CPRs) and public goods at multiple scales builds on classical economic theory while developing new theory to explain phenomena that do not fit in a dichotomous world of "the market" and "the state." Scholars are slowly shifting from positing simple systems to using more complex frameworks, theories, and models to understand the diversity of puzzles and problems facing humans interacting in contemporary societies. The humans we study have complex motivational structures and establish diverse private-for-profit, governmental, and community institutional arrangements that operate at multiple scales to generate productive and innovative as well as destructive and perverse outcomes (Douglass C. North 1990, 2005).

In this article, I will describe the intellectual journey that I have taken the last half century from when I began graduate studies in the late 1950s. The early efforts to understand the polycentric water industry in California were formative for me. In addition to working with Vincent Ostrom and Charles M. Tiebout as they formulated the concept of polycentric systems for governing metropolitan areas, I studied the efforts of a large group of private and public water producers facing the problem of an overdrafted groundwater basin on the coast and watching saltwater intrusion threaten the possibility of long term use. Then, in the 1970s, I participated with colleagues in the study of polycentric police industries serving US metropolitan areas to find that the dominant theory underlying massive reform proposals was incorrect. Metropolitan areas served by a combination of large and small producers could achieve economies of scale in the production of some police services and avoid *dis*economies of scale in the production of others.

These early empirical studies led over time to the development of the Institutional Analysis and Development (IAD) framework. A common framework consistent with game theory enabled us to undertake a variety of empirical studies including a meta-analysis of a large number of existing case studies on common-pool resource systems around the world. Carefully designed experimental studies in the lab have enabled us to test precise combinations of structural variables to find that isolated, anonymous individuals overharvest from common-pool resources. Simply allowing communication, or "cheap talk," enables participants to reduce overharvesting and increase joint payoffs contrary to game theoretical predictions. Large studies of irrigation systems in Nepal and forests around the world challenge the presumption that governments always do a better job than users in organizing and protecting important resources.

Currently, many scholars are undertaking new theoretical efforts. A core effort is developing a more general theory of individual choice that recognizes the central role of trust in coping with social dilemmas. Over time, a clear set of findings from the microsituational level have emerged regarding structural factors affecting the likelihood of increased cooperation. Due to the complexity of broader field settings, one needs to develop more configural approaches to the study of factors that enhance or detract from the emergence and robustness of self-organized efforts within multilevel, polycentric systems. Further, the application of empirical studies to the policy world leads one to stress the importance of fitting institutional rules to a specific social-ecological setting. "One size fits all" policies are not effective. The frameworks and empirical work that many scholars have undertaken in recent decades provide a better foundation for policy analysis. With this brief overview, let us now discuss the journey itself.

# I. The Earlier World View of Simple Systems

In the mid-twentieth century, the dominant scholarly effort was to try to fit the world into simple models and to criticize institutional arrangements that did not fit. I will briefly review the basic assumptions that were made at that time but have been challenged by scholars around the world, including the work of Herbert A. Simon (1955) and V. Ostrom (2008).

## A. Two Optimal Organizational Forms

The market was seen as the optimal institution for the production and exchange of private goods. For nonprivate goods, on the other hand, one needed "the" government to impose rules and taxes to force self-interested individuals to contribute necessary resources and refrain from self-seeking activities. Without a hierarchical government to induce compliance, self-seeking citizens and officials would fail to generate efficient levels of public goods, such as peace and security, at multiple scales (Thomas Hobbes [1651] 1960; Woodrow Wilson 1885). A single governmental unit, for example, was strongly recommended to reduce the "chaotic" structure of metropolitan governance, increase efficiency, limit conflict among governmental units, and best serve a homogeneous view of the public (William Anderson and Edward W. Weidner 1950; Luther Gulick 1957; H. Paul Friesema 1966). This dichotomous view of the world explained patterns of interaction and outcomes related to markets for the production and exchange of strictly private goods (Armen A. Alchian 1950), but it has not adequately accounted for internal dynamics within private firms (Oliver E. Williamson 1975, 1986). Nor does it adequately deal with the wide diversity of institutional arrangements that humans craft to govern, provide, and manage public goods and common-pool resources.

## B. Two Types of Goods

In his classic definitional essay, Paul Samuelson (1954) divided goods into two types. Pure private goods are both excludable (individual A can be excluded from consuming private goods unless paid for) and rival-rous (whatever individual A consumes, no one else can consume). Public goods are both nonexcludable (impossible to keep those who have not paid for a good from consuming it) and nonrivalrous (whatever individual A consumes does not limit the consumption by others). This basic division was consistent with the dichotomy of the institutional world into private property exchanges in a market setting and government-owned property organized by a public hierarchy. The people of the world were viewed primarily as consumers or voters.

## C. One Model of the Individual

The assumption that all individuals are fully rational was generally accepted in mainstream economics and game theory. Fully rational individuals are presumed to know (i) all possible strategies available in a particular situation, (ii) which outcomes are linked to each strategy given the likely behavior of others in a situation, and (iii) a rank order for each of these outcomes in terms of the individual's own preferences as measured by utility. The rational strategy for such an individual in every situation is to maximize expected utility. While utility was originally conceived of as a way of combining a diversity of external values on a single internal scale, in practice it has come to be equated with one externalized unit of measure—such as expected profits. This model of the individual has fruitfully generated useful and empirically validated predictions about the results of exchange transactions related to goods with specific attributes in a competitive market but not in a diversity of social dilemmas. I will return to a discussion of the theory of individual behavior in Section VIIA.

## II. Early Efforts to Develop a Fuller Understanding of Complex Human Systems

The mid-twentieth-century worldviews of simple systems have slowly been transformed as a result of extensive empirical research and the development of a framework consistent with game theoretical models for the analysis of a broad array of questions.

### A. Studying Polycentric Public Industries

Undertaking empirical studies of how citizens, local public entrepreneurs, and public officials engage in diverse ways of providing, producing, and managing public service industries and common property regimes at multiple scales has generated substantial knowledge that is not explained by two models of optimal organizational forms. V. Ostrom, Tiebout, and Robert Warren (1961) introduced the concept of polycentricity in their effort to understand whether the activities of a diverse array of public and private agencies engaged in providing and producing of public services in metropolitan areas were chaotic, as charged by other scholars—or potentially a productive arrangement.

> "Polycentric" connotes many centers of decision-making that are formally independent of each other. Whether they actually function independently, or instead constitute an interdependent system of relations, is an empirical question in particular cases. To the extent that they take each other into account in competitive relationships, enter into various contractual and cooperative undertakings or have recourse to central mechanisms to resolve conflicts, the various political jurisdictions in a metropolitan area may function in a coherent manner with consistent and predictable patterns of interacting behavior. To the extent that this is so, they may be said to function as a "system."
>
> —V. Ostrom, Tiebout, and Warren 1961: 831–32

Drawing on the concept of a public service industry (Joe S. Bain 1959; Richard Caves 1964; V. Ostrom and Elinor Ostrom 1965), several studies of water industry performance were carried out in diverse regions of California during the 1960s (V. Ostrom 1962; Louis F. Weschler 1968; Warren 1966; E. Ostrom 1965). Substantial evidence was found that multiple public and private agencies had searched out productive ways of organizing water resources at multiple scales contrary to the view that the presence of multiple governmental units without a clear hierarchy was chaotic. Further, evidence pointed out three mechanisms that increase productivity in polycentric metropolitan areas: (i) small to medium sized cities are more effective than large cities in monitoring performance of their citizens and relevant costs, (ii) citizens who are dissatisfied with service provision can "vote with their feet" and move to jurisdictions that come closer to their preferred mix and costs of public services, and (iii) local incorporated communities can contract with larger producers and change contracts if not satisfied with the services provided, while neighborhoods inside a large city have no voice.

In the 1970s, the earlier work on effects of diverse ways of organizing the provision of water in metropolitan areas was extended to policing and public safety. These studies directly addressed whether substantial economies of scale existed in the production of police services for urban neighborhoods as asserted in calls for reform (Daniel L. Skoler and June M. Hetler 1970). Not a *single* case was found where a large centralized police department outperformed smaller departments serving similar neighborhoods in regard to multiple indicators. A series of studies was conducted in Indianapolis (E. Ostrom et al. 1973), Chicago (E. Ostrom and Gordon P. Whitaker 1974), and St. Louis (E. Ostrom and Roger B. Parks 1973; E. Ostrom 1976) and then replicated in Grand Rapids, Michigan (Samir IsHak 1972) and Nashville, Tennessee (Bruce D. Rogers and C. McCurdy Lipsey 1974).

We found that while many police departments served the 80 metropolitan areas that we also studied, duplication of services by more than one department to the same set of citizens rarely occurred (E. Ostrom, Parks, and Whitaker 1978). Further, the widely held belief that a multiplicity of departments in a metropolitan area was less efficient was *not* found. In fact, the "most efficient producers supply more output for given inputs in high multiplicity metropolitan areas than do the efficient producers in metropolitan areas with fewer producers" (E. Ostrom and Parks 1999: 287). Metropolitan areas with large numbers of autonomous direct service producers achieved higher levels of technical efficiency (ibid.: 290). Technical efficiency was also enhanced in those metropolitan areas with a small number of producers providing indirect services such as radio communication and criminal laboratory analyses. We were able to reject the theory underlying the proposals of the metropolitan reform approach. We demonstrated that complexity is not the same as chaos in regard to metropolitan governance. That lesson has carried forth as we have undertaken further empirical studies of polycentric governance of resource and infrastructure systems across the world (Krister Andersson and E. Ostrom 2008; E. Ostrom, Larry Schroeder, and Susan Wynne 1993).

## B. Doubling the Types of Goods

Studying how individuals cope with diverse public problems in the world led us to reject Samuelson's twofold classification of goods. James Buchanan (1965) had already added a third type of good, which he called "club goods." In relation to these kinds of goods, it was feasible for groups of individuals to create private associations (clubs) to provide themselves with nonrivalrous but small-scale goods and services that they could enjoy while excluding nonmembers from participation and consumption of benefits.

In light of further empirical and theoretical research, we proposed additional modifications to the classification of goods to identify fundamental differences that affect the incentives facing individuals (V. Ostrom and E. Ostrom 1977).

(i) Replacing the term "rivalry of consumption" with "subtractability of use."

(ii) Conceptualizing subtractability of use and excludability to vary from low to high rather than characterizing them as either present or absent.

(iii)  Overtly adding a very important fourth type of good—common-pool resources—that shares the attribute of subtractability with private goods and difficulty of exclusion with public goods (V. Ostrom and E. Ostrom 1977). Forests, water systems, fisheries, and the global atmosphere are all common-pool resources of immense importance for the survival of humans on this earth.

(iv)  Changing the name of a "club" good to a "toll" good since many goods that share these characteristics are provided by small-scale public as well as private associations.

Figure 1 provides an overview of four broad types of goods that differentially affect the problems individuals face in devising institutions to enable them to provide, produce, and consume diverse goods. These four broad types of goods contain many subtypes of goods that vary substantially in regard to many attributes. For example, a river and a forest are both common-pool resources. They differ substantially, however, in regard to the mobility of the resource units produced, the ease of measurement, the time scale for regeneration, and other attributes. Specific common-pool resources also differ in regard to spatial extent, number of users, and many other factors.

When one engages in substantial fieldwork, one confronts an immense diversity of situations in which humans interact. Riding as an observer in a patrol car in the central district of a large American city at midnight on a Saturday evening, one sees different patterns of human

FIGURE 1. FOUR TYPES OF GOODS

| | | Subtractability of Use | |
|---|---|---|---|
| | | High | Low |
| Difficulty of excluding potential beneficiaries | High | *Common-pool resources*: groundwater basins, lakes, irrigation systems, fisheries, forests, etc. | *Public goods*: peace and security of a community, national defense, knowledge, fire protection, weather forecasts, etc. |
| | Low | *Private goods*: food, clothing, automobiles, etc. | *Toll goods*: theaters, private clubs, daycare centers, etc. |

*Source:* Adapted from E. Ostrom 2005: 24.

interaction than in a suburb on a weekday afternoon when school is letting out. In both cases, one observes the production of a public good—local safety—by an official of a local government. Others, who are involved in each situation, differ in regard to age, sobriety, why they are there, and what they are trying to accomplish. And this context affects the strategies of the police officer one is observing.

Contrast observing the production of a public good to watching private water companies, city utilities, private oil companies, and local citizens meeting in diverse settings to assess who is to blame for overdrafting their groundwater basin causing massive saltwater intrusion, and what to do next. These individuals all face the same problem—the overdraft of a common-pool resource—but their behavior differs substantially when they meet monthly in a private water association, when they face each other in a courtroom, and when they go to the legislature and eventually to the citizens to sponsor a Special Replenishment District. These and many other situations observed in irrigation systems and forests in multiple countries do not closely resemble the standard models of a market or a hierarchy.

## III. Developing a Framework for Analyzing the Diversity of Human Situations

The complexity and diversity of the field settings we have studied has generated an extended effort by colleagues associated with the Workshop in Political Theory and Policy Analysis (the Workshop) to develop the IAD framework (V. Ostrom 1975; Larry L. Kiser and E. Ostrom 1982; Michael McGinnis 1999a, b, 2000; E. Ostrom 1986, 2005). The framework contains a nested set of building blocks that social scientists can use in efforts to understand human interactions and outcomes across diverse settings. The IAD builds on earlier work on *transactions* (John R. Commons

[1924] 1968), *logic of the situation* (Karl R. Popper 1961), *collective structures* (Floyd H. Allport 1962), *frames* (Irving Goffman 1974), and *scripts* (Roger C. Schank and Robert P. Abelson 1977). The approach also draws inspiration from the work of Arthur Koestler (1973) and Simon (1981, 1995) who both challenged the assumption that human behavior and outcomes are entirely based on a small set of irreducible building blocks.

While the terms frameworks, theories, and models are used interchangeably by many scholars, we use these concepts in a nested manner to range from the most general to the most precise set of assumptions made by a scholar. The IAD *framework* is intended to contain the most general set of variables that an institutional analyst may want to use to examine a diversity of institutional settings including human interactions within markets, private firms, families, community organizations, legislatures, and government agencies. It provides a metatheoretical language to enable scholars to discuss any particular theory or to compare theories.

A specific *theory* is used by an analyst to specify which working parts of a framework are considered useful to explain diverse outcomes and how they relate to one another. Microlevel theories including game theory, microeconomic theory, transaction cost theory, and public goods/common-pool resource theories are examples of specific theories compatible with the IAD framework. *Models* make precise assumptions about a limited number of variables in a theory that scholars use to examine the formal consequences of these specific assumptions about the motivation of actors and the structure of the situation they face.

The IAD framework is designed to enable scholars to analyze systems that are composed of a cluster of variables, each of which can then be unpacked multiple times depending on the question of immediate interest. At the core of the IAD framework is the concept of an action situation affected by external variables (see Figure 2). The broadest categories of external factors affecting an action situation at a particular time include:

(i)  Biophysical conditions, which may be simplified in some analyses to be one of the four types of goods defined in Figure 1.

(ii)  Attributes of a community, which may include the history of prior interactions, internal homogeneity or heterogeneity of key attributes, and the knowledge and social capital of those who may participate or be affected by others.

(iii)  Rules-in-use, which specify common understanding of those involved related to who must, must not, or may take which actions affecting others subject to sanctions (Sue E. S. Crawford and E. Ostrom 2005). The rules-in-use may evolve over time as those involved in one action situation interact with others in a variety of settings (E. Ostrom 2008; E. Ostrom and Xavier Basurto forthcoming; Robert Boyd and Peter J. Richerson 1985) or self-consciously change the rules in a collective choice or constitutional-choice setting.

The set of external variables impacts an action situation to generate patterns of interactions and outcomes that are evaluated by participants in the action situation (and potentially by scholars) and feedback on both the external variables and the action situation.

FIGURE 2. A FRAMEWORK FOR INSTITUTIONAL ANALYSIS

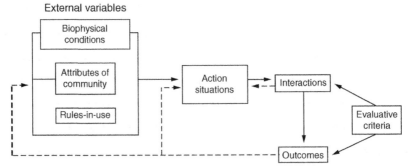

*Source:* Adapted from E. Ostrom 2005: 15.

The internal working parts of an action situation are overtly consistent with the variables that a theorist uses to analyze a formal game.[1] This has meant that colleagues have been able to use formal game theory models consistent with the IAD framework to analyze simplified but interesting combinations of theoretical variables and derive testable conclusions from them (see James M. Acheson and Roy Gardner 2005; Gardner et al. 2000; Franz Weissing and E. Ostrom 1993) as well as agent-based models (ABMs) (Wander Jager and Marco A. Janssen 2002; Janssen 2008). It is not feasible to develop a formal game (or even an ABM) to analyze the more complex empirical settings with many variables of relevance affecting outcomes and of importance for institutional analysis. It is possible, however, to use a common set of structural elements to develop structured coding forms for data collection and analysis. And one can design experiments using a common set of variables for many situations of interest to political economists and then examine why particular behavior and outcomes occur in some situations and not in others.

To specify the structure of a game and predict outcomes, the theorist needs to posit the:

(i) characteristics of the actors involved (including the model of human choice adopted by the theorist);

(ii) positions they hold (e.g., first mover or row player);

(iii) set of actions that actors can take at specific nodes in a decision tree;

(iv) amount of information available at a decision node;

(v) outcomes that actors jointly affect;

(vi) set of functions that map actors and actions at decision nodes into intermediate or final outcomes; and

(vii) benefits and costs assigned to the linkage of actions chosen and outcomes obtained.

FIGURE 3. THE INTERNAL STRUCTURE OF AN ACTION SITUATION

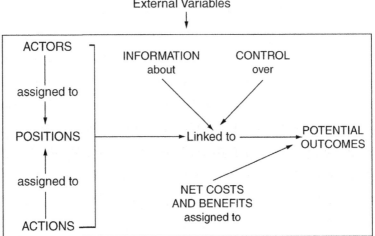

*Source:* Adapted from E. Ostrom 2005: 33.

These are also the internal working parts of an action situation as shown in Figure 3. As discussed below, using a common framework across a wide diversity of studies has enabled a greater cumulation of understanding of interactions and outcomes in very complex environments. The IAD framework overtly embeds a particular situation of interest in a broader setting of external variables, some of which can be self-consciously revised over time.

## IV. Are Rational Individuals Helplessly Trapped in Social Dilemmas?

The classic assumptions about rational individuals facing a dichotomy of organizational forms and of goods hide the potentially productive efforts of individuals and groups to organize and solve social dilemmas such as the overharvesting of common-pool resources and the underprovision of local public goods. The classic models have been used to view those who are involved in a prisoner's dilemma game or other social dilemmas as always trapped in the situation without capabilities to change the structure themselves. This analytical step was a retrogressive step in the theories used to analyze the human condition. Whether or not the individuals, who are in a situation, have capacities to transform the external variables affecting their own situation varies dramatically from one situation to the next. It is an empirical condition that varies from situation to situation rather than a logical universality. Public investigators purposely keep prisoners separated so they cannot communicate. The users of a common-pool resource are not so limited.

When analysts perceive the human beings they model as being trapped inside perverse situations, they then assume that other human beings external to those involved—scholars and public officials—are able to analyze the situation, ascertain why counterproductive outcomes are reached, and posit what changes in the rules-in-use will enable participants to improve outcomes. Then, external officials are expected to impose an optimal set of rules on those individuals involved. It is assumed that the momentum for change must come from outside the situation rather than from the self-reflection and creativity of those within a situation to restructure their own patterns of interaction. As Richard Sugden has described this approach:

> Most modern economic theory describes a world presided over by *a government* (not, significantly, by governments), and sees this world through the government's eyes. The government is supposed to have the responsibility, the will and the power to restructure society in whatever way maximizes social welfare; like the US Cavalry in a good Western, the government stands ready to rush to the rescue whenever the market "fails," and the economist's job is to advise it on when and how to do so. Private individuals,

in contrast, are credited with little or no ability to solve collective problems among themselves. This makes for a distorted view of some important economic and political issues.

—Sugden 1986: 3; emphasis in original

Garrett Hardin's (1968) portrayal of the users of a common-pool resource—a pasture open to all—being trapped in an inexorable tragedy of overuse and destruction has been widely accepted since it was consistent with the prediction of no cooperation in a prisoner's dilemma or other social dilemma games. It captured the attention of scholars and policymakers across the world. Many presumed that all common-pool resources were owned by no one. Thus, it was thought that government officials had to impose new external variables (e.g., new policies) to prevent destruction by users who could not do anything other than destroy the resources on which their own future (as well as the rest of our futures) depended.

## A. Scholars from Diverse Disciplines Examine Whether Resource Users Are Always Trapped

Dramatic incidents of overharvested resources had captured widespread attention, while studies by anthropologists, economic historians, engineers, historians, philosophers, and political scientists of local governance of smaller to medium scale common-pool resources over long periods of time were *not* noticed by many theorists and public officials (see Robert McC. Netting 1972; Bonnie J. McCay and Acheson 1987; E. Walter Coward 1980). Cumulation of the knowledge contained in these studies did not occur, due to the fact that the studies were written by scholars in diverse disciplines focusing on different types of resources located in many countries.

Fortunately, the National Research Council (NRC) established a committee in the mid-1980s to assess diverse institutional arrangements for effective conservation and utilization of jointly managed resources. The NRC committee brought scholars from multiple disciplines together and used the IAD framework in an effort to begin to identify common variables in cases where users had organized or failed to organize (Ronald J. Oakerson 1986; NRC 1986). Finding multiple cases where resource users were successful in organizing themselves challenged the presumption that it was *impossible* for resource users to solve their own problems of overuse. The NRC report opened up the possibility of a diversity of studies using multiple methods. The NRC effort also stimulated an extended research program at the Workshop that involved coding and analyzing case studies of common-pool resources written by other scholars.

## B. Meta-analyses of Common-Pool Resource Cases

In an effort to learn more than just the existence of multiple cases where resource users had self-organized, colleagues at the Workshop undertook a meta-analysis of existing case studies that were identified as a result of the activities of the NRC panel.[2] Because of our prior studies of complex urban systems and the development of a framework and common language for linking the parts of complex systems, we could use the framework to help organize our efforts. The IAD framework became the foundation for designing a coding manual that was used to record a consistent set of variables for each common-pool resource study.

This was an immense effort. More than two years was devoted to developing the final coding manual (E. Ostrom et al. 1989). A key problem was the minimal overlap of variables identified by case study authors from diverse disciplines. The team had to read and screen over 500 case studies in order to identify a small set of cases that recorded information about the actors, their strategies, the condition of the resource, and the rules-in-use.[3] A common set of variables was recorded for 44 subgroups of fishers who harvested from inshore fisheries (Edella Schlager 1990, 1994) and 47 irrigation systems that were managed either by farmers or by a government (Shui Yan Tang 1992, 1994).

Of the 47 irrigation systems included in the analysis, 12 were managed by governmental agencies of which only 40 percent ($n = 7$) had high performance. Of the 25 farmer-managed, over 70 percent ($n = 18$) had high performance (Tang 1994: 234). Rule conformance was a key variable affecting the adequacy of water over time (Tang 1994: 229). None of the inshore fishery groups analyzed by Schlager were government managed and 11 (25 percent) were not organized in any way. The other 33 subgroups had a diversity of informal rules to define who was allowed to fish in a particular location and how harvesting was restricted (Schlager 1994: 260).

In addition to finding significant levels of cooperation, we found some support for earlier theoretical predictions of no cooperation in particular settings.

> In CPR dilemmas where individuals do not know one another, cannot communicate effectively, and thus cannot develop agreements, norms, and sanctions, aggregate predictions derived from models of rational individuals in a noncooperative game receive substantial support. These are sparse environments and full rationality appears to be a reasonable assumption in them.
>
> —E. Ostrom, Gardner, and James A. Walker 1994: 319

On the other hand, the capacity to overcome dilemmas and create effective governance occurred far more frequently than expected and depended upon the structure of the resource itself and whether the rules-in-use developed by users were linked effectively to this structure (William Blomquist et al. 1994). In all self-organized systems, we found that users had created boundary rules for determining who could use the resource, choice rules related to the allocation of the flow of resource units, and active forms of monitoring and local sanctioning of rule breakers (ibid.: 301). On the other hand, we did not find a single case where harvesters used the "grim trigger" strategy—a form of punishment that was posited in many theoretical arguments for how individuals could solve repeated dilemmas (Prajit K. Dutta 1990: 264).

## C. The Bundles of Property Rights Related to Common-Pool Resources

Resource economists have used the term "common property resource" to refer to fisheries and water resources (H. Scott Gordon 1954; Anthony D. Scott 1955; Frederick W. Bell 1972). Combining the term "property" with "resource" introduced considerable confusion between the nature of a good and the absence or presence of a property regime (Siegfried V. Ciriacy-Wantrup and Richard C. Bishop 1975). A common-pool resource can be owned and managed as government property, private property, community property, or owned by no one (Daniel W. Bromley 1986). A further reason for the lack of awareness about property systems developed by local users was that many scholars presumed that unless users possessed alienation rights—the right to sell their property—they did not have any property rights (Alchian and Harold Demsetz 1973; Terry L. Anderson and Peter J. Hill 1990; Richard Posner 1975).

Schlager and E. Ostrom (1992) drew on the earlier work of Commons ([1924] 1968) to conceptualize property rights systems as containing *bundles* of rights rather than a single right. The meta-analysis of existing field cases helped to identify five property rights that individuals using a common-pool resource might cumulatively have: (i) access—the right to enter a specified property,[4] (ii) withdrawal—the right to harvest specific products from a resource, (iii) management—the right to transform the resource and regulate internal use patterns, (iv) exclusion—the right to decide who will have access, withdrawal, or management rights, and (v) alienation—the right to lease or sell any of the other four rights. Conceiving of property rights bundles is now widely accepted by scholars who have studied diverse property rights systems around the world (David J. Brunckhorst 2000; P. Degnbol and McCay 2007; Jouni Paavola and W. Neil Adger 2005; Paul B. Trawick 2001; James A. Wilson et al. 1994).

## D. Linking the Internal Parts of an Action Situation to External Rules

Actors who have specific property rights to a resource also face more fundamental rules that affect the structure of the action situations they are in. In our meta-analysis, we found an incredible array of specific rules used in different settings (e.g., who could withdraw how many resource units at what location and time, what information was required of all users, what costs and benefits were attached to which actions, etc.). As we attempted to find a consistent way of coding and analyzing this rich diversity of specific rules described by case authors, we turned again to the IAD framework. Since we had identified seven working parts of a game or action situation itself, it seemed reasonable to think of seven broad types of rules operating as external variables affecting the individual working parts of action situations (see Figure 4). The seven types of rules are:

(i)  Boundary rules that specify how actors were to be chosen to enter or leave these positions;

(ii) Position rules that specify a set of positions and how many actors hold each one;

(iii) Choice rules that specify which actions are assigned to an actor in a position;

(iv) Information rules that specify channels of communication among actors and what information must, may, or must not be shared;

(v) Scope rules that specify the outcomes that could be affected;

(vi) Aggregation rules (such as majority or unanimity rules) that specify how the decisions of actors at a node were to be mapped to intermediate or final outcomes; and

(vii) Payoff rules that specify how benefits and costs were to be distributed to actors in positions (Crawford and E. Ostrom 2005).

A useful way of thinking about institutional rules is to conceptualize what part of an action situation is affected by a rule (see Figure 4).

FIGURE 4. RULES AS EXOGENOUS VARIABLES DIRECTLY AFFECTING THE ELEMENTS OF AN ACTION SITUATION

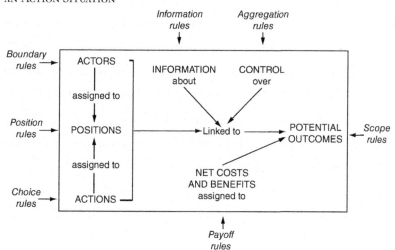

*Source:* Adapted from E. Ostrom 2005: 189.

Conceptualizing seven broad types of rules (rather than one or two) has been upsetting to scholars who wanted to rely on simple models of interactions among humans. In addition to finding seven broad types of rules, however, we also found multiple variants of each type. For example, we found 27 boundary rules described by case study authors as used in at least one common-pool resource setting (E. Ostrom 1999: 510). Some rules specified diverse forms of residence, organizational memberships, or personal attributes that are ascribed or acquired. Similarly, we found 112 different choice rules that were usually composed of two parts—an allocation formula specifying where, when, or how resource units could be harvested and a specific basis for the implementation of the formula (such as the amount of land held, historical use patterns, or assignment through lottery) (ibid.: 512).

## E. Long-Surviving Resource Institutions

After working for several years with colleagues to code cases of successful and failed systems, I thought my next task would be to undertake careful statistical analysis to identify which specific rules were associated with successful systems. I had not yet fully absorbed the incredible number and diversity of rules that the team had recorded. In 1988, I spent a sabbatical leave in a research group organized by Reinhard Selten at the Center for Interdisciplinary Research at Bielefeld University. I struggled to find rules that worked across ecological, social, and economic environments, but the specific rules associated with success or failure varied extensively across sites. Finally, I had to give up the idea that *specific* rules might be associated with successful cases.

Moving up a level in generality, I tried to understand the broader institutional regularities among the systems that were sustained over a long period of time and were absent in the failed systems. I used the term "design principle" to characterize these regularities. I did not mean that the fishers, irrigators, pastoralists, and others overtly had these principles in their minds when they developed systems that survived for long periods of time. My effort was to identify a set of core underlying lessons that characterized the long sustained regimes as contrasted to the cases of failure (E. Ostrom 1990).[5]

Since the design principles are described extensively in E. Ostrom (1990, 2005), I will mention only a brief updated list as developed by Michael Cox, Gwen Arnold, and Sergio Villamayor-Tomás (2009):

1A. *User Boundaries:* Clear and locally understood boundaries between legitimate users and nonusers are present.

1B. *Resource Boundaries:* Clear boundaries that separate a specific common-pool resource from a larger social-ecological system are present.

2A. *Congruence with Local Conditions:* Appropriation and provision rules are congruent with local social and environmental conditions.

2B. *Appropriation and Provision:* Appropriation rules are congruent with provision rules; the distribution of costs is proportional to the distribution of benefits.

3. *Collective Choice Arrangements:* Most individuals affected by a resource regime are authorized to participate in making and modifying its rules.

4A. *Monitoring Users:* Individuals who are accountable to or are the users monitor the appropriation and provision levels of the users.

4B. *Monitoring the Resource:* Individuals who are accountable to or are the users monitor the condition of the resource.

5. *Graduated Sanctions:* Sanctions for rule violations start very low but become stronger if a user repeatedly violates a rule.

6. *Conflict Resolution Mechanisms:* Rapid, low cost, local arenas exist for resolving conflicts among users or with officials.

7. *Minimal Recognition of Rights:* The rights of local users to make their own rules are recognized by the government.

8. *Nested Enterprises:* When a common-pool resource is closely connected to a larger social-ecological system, governance activities are organized in multiple nested layers.

The design principles appear to synthesize core factors that affect the probability of long term survival of an institution developed by the users of a resource. Cox, Arnold, and Villamayor-Tomás (2009) analyzed over 100 studies by scholars who assessed the relevance of the principles as an explanation of the success or failure of diverse common-pool resources. Two-thirds of these studies confirm that robust resource systems are characterized by most of the design principles and that failures are not. The authors of some studies that found the design principles inadequate tended to interpret them very rigidly and felt that successful systems were characterized by more flexibility. In three instances, the initial wording of the design principles was too general and did not distinguish between ecological and social conditions. Thus, I have adopted the improvements to principles 1, 2, and 4 suggested by Cox and coauthors.

## V. Conducting Experiments to Study Common-Pool Resource Problems

The existence of a large number of cases where users had overcome social dilemmas in order to sustain long term use of common-pool resources successfully challenged the presumption that this was impossible. Many variables simultaneously affect these outcomes in the field. Developing game theoretical models of common-pool resource situations (Weissing and E. Ostrom 1993; E. Ostrom and Gardner 1993) has been one strategy we have used to assess the theoretical outcomes of a set of variables we have observed in the field. We have also thought it was important to examine the effect of precise combinations of variables in an experimental setting.

## A. Common-Pool Resource Experiments in University Laboratories

Roy Gardner and James Walker joined me in an extended effort to build and test well-specified, game theoretical models consistent with the IAD framework (see E. Ostrom, Walker, and Gardner 1992; E. Ostrom, Gardner, and Walker 1994). The initial CPR experiments started with a static, baseline situation that was as simple as could be specified without losing crucial aspects of the appropriation problems facing harvesters in the field. We used a quadratic payoff production function based on Gordon's (1954) classic model. The initial resource endowment $w$ for each of eight subjects was a set of tokens that the subject could allocate between Market 1 (which had a fixed return) and Market 2 (which functioned as a common-pool resource with a return affected by the actions of all subjects in the experiment). Subjects received aggregated information so they did not know each individual's actions. Each subject $i$ could invest a portion $x_i$ of his/her endowment in the common resource (Market 2) and the remaining portion would then be invested in Market 1. The payoff function we used (E. Ostrom, Gardner, and Walker 1994: 110) was:

(1) $$u_i(x) = we \qquad \text{if } x_i = 0$$

(2) $$w(e - x_i) + (x_i / \Sigma x_i) F(\Sigma x_i) \qquad \text{if } x_i > 0.$$

The baseline experiment was a commons dilemma in which the game-theoretic outcome involved substantial overuse of a resource while a much better outcome could be reached if subjects were to reduce their joint allocation. The prediction from noncooperative game theory was that subjects would invest according to the Nash equilibrium—8 tokens each for a total of 64 tokens. Subjects could earn considerably more if they reduced their allocation to a total of 36 tokens in the common-pool resource. Subjects in baseline experiments with multiple decision rounds substantially overinvested—they invested even more tokens than predicted, so the joint outcome was worse than the predicted Nash equilibrium.[6]

Building off prior public goods research (Isaac and Walker 1988), we then conducted a series of face-to-face communication experiments in which the same payoff function was retained. After an initial ten rounds without communication, subjects were told they could communicate with each other in a group setting before returning to their terminals to make their own private decisions. This provided an opportunity for "cheap talk." The same outcome was predicted in these experiments as in the baseline since a subject could promise to cooperate but no external "third party" ensured that the promise was fulfilled.

Subjects used face-to-face communication to discuss strategies to gain the best outcomes and then to agree—if possible—on what each subject should invest. They learned about their aggregate investments after each round, but not the decision of individual subjects. This gave them information as to whether the total investments were greater than agreed upon. In many rounds, subjects kept their promises to each other. In other rounds, some defections did occur. Subjects used information about the aggregate investment levels to scold their unknown fellow subjects if the total investment was higher than they had agreed upon. The opportunity for repeated face-to-face communication was extremely successful in increasing joint returns. Findings from communication experiments are consistent with a large number of studies of the impact of face-to-face communication on the capacity of subjects to solve a variety of social dilemma problems (see E. Ostrom and Walker 1991; John M. Orbell, Alphons van de Kragt, and Robyn M. Dawes 1988; David Sally 1995; Daniel Balliet 2010).

In many field settings, resource users have devised a variety of formal or informal ways of sanctioning one another if rules are broken, even though this behavior is not consistent with the theory of norm-free, complete rationality (Jon Elster 1989: 40–41). It was thus important to see if subjects in a controlled experimental setting would actually use their own assets to financially punish other subjects. After subjects played ten rounds of the baseline common-pool resource game, they were told that in the subsequent rounds they would have an opportunity to pay a fee in order to impose a fine on another subject. We found much more sanctioning occurred in this design than the zero level predicted.[7] Subjects did increase gross benefits through their sanctioning but substantially reduced net returns due to the overuse of costly sanctions.[8] Sanctioning was primarily directed at those who defected, but a few sanctions appeared to be directed at low contributors as a form of revenge by those who had fined themselves. In a further design, subjects were given a chance to communicate and decide whether or not to adopt a sanctioning system of their own. Subjects who decided to adopt their own sanctioning system achieved the highest returns achieved in any of the common-pool resource laboratory experiments—90 percent of optimal after the fines related to the small number of defections were subtracted (E. Ostrom, Walker, and Gardner 1992).

The predictions of noncooperative game theory are roughly supported only when participants in a laboratory experiment do not know the reputation of the others involved in a common-pool resource dilemma and cannot communicate with them. On the other hand, when subjects communicate face-to-face, they frequently agree on joint strategies and keep to their agreements—substantially increasing their net returns. Further, communication to decide on and design a sanctioning system enables those choosing this option to achieve close to optimal returns.

## B. Studying Common-Pool Resources in Field Experiments

A series of field experiments have now been conducted by colleagues in Colombia to assess whether experienced villagers who are dependent on resources make decisions about the "time spent in a forest" in a design that is mathematically consistent with those reported on above. Juan-Camilo Cardenas (2000) conducted field experiments in rural schoolhouses with over 200 users of local forests. He modified the design of the common-pool resource experiments without, and with, face-to-face communication so that villagers were asked to make decisions regarding "harvesting trees." The outcomes of these experiments were broadly consistent with the findings obtained with university students.

In a different design, Cardenas, John K. Stranlund, and Cleve E. Willis (2000) ran ten rounds of baseline experiments with resource users from five villages who were then given a chance to communicate face-to-face for the next set of experiments. In five additional villages, participants were told after the baseline rounds that a new regulation would go into force that mandated them to spend no more than the optimal time in the forest each round. The probability of an inspection was 1/16 per round—a low but realistic probability for monitoring rule conformance in rural areas in developing countries. If the person was over the limit imposed, a penalty was subtracted from that person's payoff, but the penalty was not revealed to the others. Subjects in this experimental condition increased their withdrawal levels when compared to the outcomes obtained when face-to-face communication was allowed and no rule was imposed. Other scholars have also found that externally imposed regulation that would theoretically lead to higher joint returns "crowded out" voluntary behavior to cooperate (see Bruno S. Frey and Felix Oberholzer-Gee 1997; Andrew F. Reeson and John G. Tisdell 2008).

Fehr and Andreas Leibbrandt (2008) conducted an interesting set of public goods experiments with fishers who harvest from an "open access" inland lake in northeastern Brazil. They found that a high percentage (87 percent) of fishers contributed in the first period of the field experiment and that contributions leveled off in the remaining periods. Fehr and Leibbrandt examined the mesh size of the nets used by individual fishermen and found that those who contributed more in the public goods experiment used nets with bigger mesh sizes. Larger mesh sizes allow young fish to escape, grow larger, and reproduce at a higher level than if they are caught when they are still small. In other words, cooperation in the field experiment was consistent with observed cooperation related to a real CPR dilemma. They conclude that the "fact that our laboratory measure for other-regarding preferences predicts field behavior increases our confidence about the behavioral relevance of other-regarding preferences gained from laboratory experiments" (ibid.: 17).

In summary, experiments on CPRs and public goods have shown that many predictions of the conventional theory of collective action do not hold. More cooperation occurs than predicted, "cheap talk" increases cooperation, and subjects invest in sanctioning free riders. Experiments also establish that motivational heterogeneity exists in harvesting or contribution decisions as well as decisions on sanctioning.

# VI. Studying Common-Pool Resource Problems in the Field

Having conducted extensive meta-analyses of case studies and experiments, we also needed to undertake field studies where we could draw on the IAD framework to design questions to obtain consistent information about key theoretically important variables across sites.

## A. Comparing Farmer and Government-Managed Irrigation Systems in Nepal

An opportunity to visit Nepal in 1988 led to the discovery of a large number of written studies of farmer built and maintained irrigation systems as well as some government constructed and managed systems. Ganesh Shivakoti, Paul Benjamin, and I were able to revise the CPR coding manual so as to include variables of specific relevance to understanding irrigation systems in a new coding manual for the Nepal Irrigation and Institutions (NIIS) project. We coded existing cases and again found numerous "missing variables" not discussed by the original author. Colleagues made several trips to Nepal to visit previously described systems in written case studies to fill in missing data and verify the data in the original study. While in the field, we were able to add new cases to the data set (Benjamin et al. 1994).

In undertaking analysis of this large dataset, Wai Fung Lam (1998) developed three performance measures that could be applied to all systems: (i) the physical condition of irrigation systems, (ii) the quantity of water available to farmers at the tail end of a system at different seasons of the year, and (iii) the agricultural productivity of the systems. Controlling for environmental differences among systems, Lam found that irrigation systems governed by the farmers themselves perform significantly better on all three performance measures. On the farmer governed systems, farmers communicate with one another at annual meetings and informally on a regular basis, develop their own agreements, establish the positions of monitors, and sanction those who do not conform to their own rules. Consequently, farmer managed systems are likely to grow more rice, distribute water more equitably, and keep their systems in better repair than government systems. While farmer systems do vary in performance, few perform as poorly as government systems—holding other relevant variables constant.

Over time, colleagues have visited and coded still further irrigation systems in Nepal. The earlier findings regarding the higher level of performance of farmer managed systems was again confirmed using the expanded database containing 229 irrigation systems (Neeraj N. Joshi et al. 2000; Shivakoti and E. Ostrom 2002). Our findings are not unique to Nepal. Scholars have carefully documented effective farmer designed and operated systems in many countries including Japan (Masahiko Aoki 2001), India (Ruth Meinzen-Dick 2007; Pranab K. Bardhan 2000), and Sri Lanka (Norman T. Uphoff 1991).

## B. Studying Forests around the World

In 1992, Dr. Marilyn Hoskins, who headed the Forest, Trees and People Program at the Food and Agriculture Organization (FAO) of the United Nations, asked colleagues at the Workshop to draw on our experience in studying irrigation systems to develop methods for assessing the impact of diverse forest governance arrangements in multiple countries. Two years of intense development and review by ecologists and social scientists around the world led to the development of ten research protocols to obtain reliable information about users and forest governance as well as about the ecological conditions of sampled forests. A long-term collaborative research network—the International Forestry Resources and Institutions (IFRI) research program—was established with centers now located in Bolivia, Colombia, Guatemala, India, Kenya, Mexico, Nepal, Tanzania, Thailand, Uganda, and the United States, with new centers being established in Ethiopia and China (see Clark Gibson, Margaret McKean, and E. Ostrom 2000; Poteete and E. Ostrom 2004; Eva Wollenberg et al. 2007). IFRI is unique among efforts to study forests as it is the only interdisciplinary long-term monitoring and research program studying forests in multiple countries owned by governments, private organizations, and communities.

Forests are a particularly important form of common-pool resource given their role in climate change–related emissions and carbon sequestration (Josep G. Canadell and Michael R. Raupach 2008), the biodiversity they contain, and their contribution to rural livelihoods in developing countries. A "favorite" policy recommendation for protecting forests and biodiversity is government owned protected areas (J. Terborgh 1999). In an effort to examine whether government ownership of protected areas is a necessary condition for improving forest density, Tanya Hayes (2006) used IFRI data to compare the rating of forest density (on a five point scale) assigned to a forest by the forester or ecologist who had supervised the forest mensuration of trees, shrubs, and groundcover in a random sample of forest plots.[9] Of the 163 forests included in the analysis, 76 were government owned forests *legally designated* as *protected forests* and 87 were public, private, or communally owned forested lands used for a diversity of purposes. No statistical difference existed between the forest density in officially designated protected areas versus other forested areas. Gibson, John Williams, and E. Ostrom (2005) examined the monitoring behavior of 178 forest user groups and found a strong correlation between the level of monitoring and a forester's assessment of forest density even when controlling for whether users were formally organized, whether the users were heavily dependent on a forest, and the level of social capital within a group.

Ashwini Chhatre and Arun Agrawal (2008) have now examined the changes in the condition of 152 forests under diverse governance arrangements as affected by the size of the forest, collective action around forests related to improvement activities, size of the user group, and the dependence of local users on a forest. They found that "forests with a higher probability of regeneration are likely to be small to medium in size with low levels of subsistence dependence, low commercial value, high levels of local enforcement, and strong collective action for improving the quality of the forest" (ibid.: 1327). In a second major analysis, Chhatre and Agrawal (2009) focus on factors that affect tradeoffs and synergies between the level of carbon storage in forests and their contributions to livelihoods. They find that larger forests are more effective in enhancing both carbon and livelihoods outcomes, particularly when local communities also have high levels of rulemaking autonomy. Recent studies by Eric Coleman (2009) and Coleman and Brian Steed (2009) also find that a major variable affecting forest conditions is the investment by local users in monitoring. Further, when local users are given harvesting rights, they are more likely to monitor illegal uses themselves. Other focused studies also stress the relationship between local monitoring and better forest conditions (Rucha Ghate and Harini Nagendra 2005; E. Ostrom and Nagendra 2006; Abwoli Y. Banana and William Gombya-Ssembajjwe 2000; Edward Webb and Shivakoti 2008).

The legal designation of a forest as a protected area is *not* by itself related to forest density. Detailed field studies of monitoring and enforcement as they are conducted on the ground, however, illustrate the challenge of achieving high levels of forest regrowth without active involvement of local forest users (see Mateus Batistella, Scott Robeson, and Emilio F. Moran 2003; Agrawal 2005; Andersson, Gibson, and Fabrice Lehoucq 2006; Catherine M. Tucker 2008). Our research shows that forests under different property regimes—government, private, communal—sometimes meet enhanced social goals such as biodiversity protection, carbon storage, or improved livelihoods. At other times, these property regimes fail to provide such goals. Indeed, when governments adopt top-down decentralization policies leaving local officials and users in the dark, stable forests may become subject to deforestation (Banana et al. 2007). Thus, it is not the general type of forest governance that is crucial in explaining forest conditions; rather, it is how a particular governance arrangement fits the local ecology, how specific rules are developed and adapted over time, and whether users consider the system to be legitimate and equitable (for a more detailed overview of the IFRI research program, see Poteete, Janssen, and E. Ostrom 2010: chap. 5).

## VII. Current Theoretical Developments

Given the half century of our own extensive empirical research and that of many distinguished scholars (e.g., Jean-Marie Baland and Jean-Philippe Platteau 2005; Fikret Berkes 2007; Berkes, Johan Colding, and Carl Folke 2003; Colin W. Clark 2006; Graham R. Marshall 2008; Thomas C. Schelling 1960, 1978, 1984), where are we now? What have we learned? We now know that the earlier theories of rational, but helpless, individuals who are trapped in social dilemmas are not supported by a large number of studies using diverse methods (Nicolas Faysse 2005; Poteete, Janssen, and E. Ostrom 2010). On the other hand, we cannot be overly optimistic and presume that dilemmas will always be solved by those involved. Many groups have struggled and failed (Tom

Dietz, E. Ostrom, and Paul Stern 2003). Further, simple policy prescriptions to turn over resources to a government, to privatize, or more recently to decentralize, may also fail (Berkes 2007; William A. Brock and Stephen R. Carpenter 2007; Meinzen-Dick 2007).

We thus face the tough task of further developing our theories to help understand and predict when those involved in a common-pool resource dilemma will be able to self-organize and how various aspects of the broad context they face affect their strategies, the short term success of their efforts, and the long term robustness of their initial achievements. We need to develop a better theoretical understanding of human behavior as well as of the impact of the diverse contexts that humans face.

## A. Developing a More General Theory of the Individual

As discussed earlier in Section III, efforts to explain phenomena in the social world are organized at three levels of generality. Frameworks, such as the IAD that have been used to organize diverse efforts to study common-pool resources, are metatheoretical devices that help provide a general language for describing relationships at multiple levels and scales. Theories are efforts to build understanding by making core assumptions about specific working parts of frequently encountered phenomena and predicting general outcomes. Models are very specific working examples of a theory—and they are frequently confused with being theories themselves. As Alchian (1950) pointed out long ago, what is called "rational choice theory" is not a broad *theory* of human behavior but rather a useful *model* to predict behavior in a particular situation—a highly competitive market for private goods. Predictions derived from the rational choice model are empirically supported in open markets for private goods and other competitive environments (Charles A. Holt 2007; Vernon L. Smith and Walker 1993; Debra Satz and John Ferejohn 1994). Thus, it is a useful model to retain for predicting outcomes in competitive settings related to excludable and divisible outcomes.

While it is not possible yet to point to a single *theory* of human behavior that has been successfully formulated and tested in a variety of settings, scholars are currently positing and testing assumptions that are likely to be at the core of future developments (Smith 2003, 2010). These relate to (i) the capability of boundedly rational individuals to learn fuller and more reliable information in repeated situations when reliable feedback is present, (ii) the use of heuristics in making daily decisions, and (iii) the preferences that individuals have related to benefits for self as well as norms and preferences related to benefits for others (see Poteete, Janssen, and E. Ostrom 2010: chap. 9; E. Ostrom 1998).

The assumption that individuals have complete information about all actions available to them, the likely strategies that others will adopt, and the probabilities of specific consequences that will result from their own choices must be rejected in any but the very simplest of repeated settings. When boundedly rational individuals do interact over time, it is reasonable to assume that they learn more accurate information about the actions they can take and the likely actions of other individuals (Selten 1990; Simon 1955, 1999). Some highly complex common-pool resource environments, however, approach mathematical chaos (J. Wilson et al. 1994) in which resource users cannot gain complete information about all likely combinations of future events.

In many situations, individuals use rules of thumb—heuristics—that they have learned over time that work relatively well in a particular setting. Fishers end up "fishing for knowledge" (J. Wilson 1990) where using heuristics over time enables them to recognize diverse clues of environmental processes that they need to take into account when making their own decisions. When individuals do interact repeatedly, it is possible to learn heuristics that approach "best response" strategies and achieve close to local optima (Gerd Gigerenzer and Selten 2001).

In eras of rapid change or sudden shocks, however, heuristics may not enable individuals to achieve high payoffs.

Individuals also learn norms—internal valuations that are negative or positive related to specific actions such as lying or being brave in particular situations (Crawford and E. Ostrom 2005). The strength of an internal commitment (Amartya K. Sen 1977) may be represented in the size of the internal weight that an individual assigns to actions and outcomes in a particular setting. Among individual norms are those related to valuing outcomes achieved by others (James Cox and Cary Deck 2005; J. Cox, Klarita Sadiraj, and Vjollca Sadiraj 2008; James Andreoni 1989; Gary E. Bolton and Axel Ockenfels 2000). Fehr and Klaus Schmidt (1999) propose that individuals dislike unequal outcomes of interactions and thus have an internal norm of "inequity aversion." Robert Axelrod (1986) posits that individuals who adopt meta norms related to whether others follow the norms that have evolved in a group increase the probability that norms will be followed. Leibbrandt, Uri Gneezy, and John List (2010) show that individuals who regularly work in teams are more likely to adopt norms and trust each other more than individuals working alone. Norman Frohlich and Joe A. Oppenheimer (1992) posit that many individuals adopt norms of fairness and justice. Not all individuals have the same norms or perceptions of a situation (Umut Ones and Louis Putterman 2007) and may differ substantially in whether they consider a way of sharing costs to be fair (Catherine Eckel and Philip J. Grossman 1996).

Simply assuming that humans adopt norms, however, is not sufficient to predict behavior in a social dilemma, especially in very large groups with no arrangements for communication. Even with strong preferences to follow norms, "observed behavior may vary by context because the perception of the 'right thing' would change" (Angela de Oliveira, Rachel Croson, and Eckel 2009: 19). Various aspects of the context in which individuals interact affect how individuals learn about the situation they are in and about the others with whom they are interacting. Individual differences do make a difference, but the context of interactions also affects behavior over time (Walker and E. Ostrom 2009). Biologists recognize that an organism's appearance and behavior are affected by the environment in which it develops.

> For example, some plants produce large, thin leaves (which enhance photosynthetic photon harvest) in low light, and narrow, thicker leaves (which conserve water) in high light; certain insects develop wings only if they live in crowded conditions (and hence are likely to run out of adequate food in their current location). Such environmentally contingent development is so commonplace that it can be regarded as a universal property of living things.
> —David W. Pfennig and Cris Ledón-Rettig 2009: 268

Social scientists also need to recognize that individual behavior is strongly affected by the context in which interactions take place rather than being simply a result of individual differences.

## B. The Central Role of Trust in Coping with Dilemmas

Even though Kenneth J. Arrow (1974) long ago pointed to the crucial role of trust among participants as the most efficient mechanism to enhance transactional outcomes, collective action theory has paid more attention to payoff functions than to how individuals build trust that others are reciprocators of costly cooperative efforts. Empirical studies, however, confirm the important role of trust in overcoming social dilemmas (Bo Rothstein 2005). As illustrated in Figure 5, the updated theoretical assumptions of learning and norm-adopting individuals can be used as the foundation for understanding how individuals may gain

FIGURE 5. MICROSITUATIONAL AND BROADER CONTEXTS OF SOCIAL DILEMMAS
AFFECT LEVELS OF TRUST AND COOPERATION

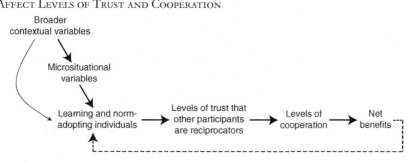

*Source:* Poteete, Janssen, and Ostrom 2010: 227.

increased levels of trust in others, leading to more cooperation and higher benefits with feedback mechanisms that reinforce positive or negative learning. Thus, it is not only that individuals adopt norms but also that the structure of the situation generates sufficient information about the likely behavior of others to be trustworthy reciprocators who will bear their share of the costs of overcoming a dilemma. Thus, in some contexts, one can move beyond the presumption that rational individuals are helpless in overcoming social dilemma situations.

## C. The Microsituational Level of Analysis

Asserting that context makes a difference in building or destroying trust and reciprocity is not a sufficient theoretical answer to how and why individuals sometimes solve and sometimes fail to solve dilemmas. Individuals interacting in a dilemma situation face two contexts: (i) a microcontext related to the specific attributes of an action situation in which individuals are directly interacting and (ii) the broader context of the social-ecological system in which groups of individuals make decisions. A major advantage of studies conducted in an experimental lab or in field experiments is that the researcher designs the micro setting in which the experiment is conducted. Thus, empirical results are growing (and are summarized in Poteete, Janssen, and E. Ostrom 2010) to establish that the following attributes of microsituations affect the level of cooperation that participants achieve in social dilemma settings (including both public goods and common-pool resource dilemmas).

(i) Communication is feasible with the full set of participants. When face-to-face communication is possible, participants use facial expressions, physical actions, and the way that words are expressed to judge the trustworthiness of the others involved.

(ii) Reputations of participants are known. Knowing the past history of other participants, who may not be personally known prior to interaction, increases the likelihood of cooperation.

(iii) High marginal per capita return (MPCR). When MPCR is high, each participant can know that their own contributions make a bigger difference than with low MPCR, and that others are more likely to recognize this relationship.

(iv) Entry or exit capabilities. If participants can exit a situation at low cost, this gives them an opportunity not to be a sucker, and others can recognize that cooperators may leave (and enter other situations) if their cooperation is not reciprocated.

(v) Longer time horizon. Participants can anticipate that more could be earned through cooperation over a long time period versus a short time.

(vi) Agreed-upon sanctioning capabilities. While external sanctions or imposed sanctioning systems may reduce cooperation, when participants themselves agree to a sanctioning system they frequently do not need to use sanctions at a high volume, and net benefits can be improved substantially.

Other microsituational variables are being tested in experiments around the world. The central core of the findings is that when individuals face a social dilemma in a microsetting, they are more likely to cooperate when situational variables increase the likelihood of gaining trust that others will reciprocate.

## D. The Broader Context in the Field

Individuals coping with common-pool resource dilemmas in the field are also affected by a broader set of contextual variables related to the attributes of the social-ecological system (SES) in which they are interacting. A group of scholars in Europe and the United States are currently working on the further development of a framework that links the IAD and its interactions and outcomes at a micro level with a broader set of variables observed in the field.[10] As illustrated in Figure 6, one can think of individuals interacting in an Action Situation generating Interactions and Outcomes that are affected by and affect a Resource System, Resource Units, Governance System, and Users who affect and are affected by Social, Economic, and Political Settings, and Related Ecosystems (see E. Ostrom 2007, 2009). Figure 6 provides an overview of the highest tier of variables that exist in all field settings. The highest tier can be unpacked several times when one is trying to analyze specific questions related to SESs in the field, but there is not enough time or space to undertake a thorough unpacking in this article.

Experimental researchers have reached a higher level of agreement about the impact of microsituational variables on the incentives, levels of trust, and behavior of individuals in dilemma situations than exists among field researchers. Few SES variables have a fully independent impact on the action situations that participants face and their likely behavior. The SES variables that are most important differ depending on which interactions (such as monitoring, conflict, lobbying, self-organization) or longer term outcomes (such as overharvesting, regeneration

FIGURE 6. ACTION SITUATIONS EMBEDDED IN BROADER SOCIAL-ECOLOGICAL SYSTEMS

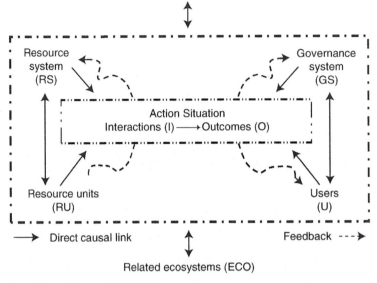

*Source:* Adapted from E. Ostrom 2007: 15182.

of biodiversity, resilience of an ecological system to human and nature induced disturbances) one wishes to predict. A set of ten variables have been identified across many field studies as impacting the likelihood of users self-organizing in order to overcome a common-pool resource dilemma (E. Ostrom 2009; Basurto and E. Ostrom 2009). These include: the size, productivity, and predictability of the resource system, the extent of mobility of the resource units, the existence of collective choice rules that the users may adopt authoritatively in order to change their own operational rules, and four attributes of users (the number, the existence of leadership/entrepreneurship, knowledge about the SES, and the importance of the SES to the users). Linking the broader contextual variables and microcontextual variables is one of the major tasks facing scientists who work across disciplinary lines to understand how both social and ecological factors affect human behavior.[11]

## VIII. Complexity and Reform

The economic and social sciences have significantly moved ahead over the past five decades since scholars posited two optimal organizational forms, two types of goods, and one model of the individual. Extensive empirical research documents the diversity of settings in which individuals solve common-pool resource problems on their own, when these solutions are sustainable over long periods of time, and how larger institutional arrangements enhance or detract from the capabilities of individuals at smaller scales to solve problems efficiently and sustainably (see, for example, Agrawal and Gibson 2001; Gibson et al. 2005; Schlager and Blomquist 2008). While there is not yet a single well-developed theory that explains all of the diverse outcomes obtained in microsettings, such as the experimental lab, or broader contextual settings of fisheries, irrigation systems, forests, lakes, and other common-pool resources, considerable agreement does exist. Nor do we have a single normative theory of justice that can unambiguously be applied to all settings (Sen 2009).

Building trust in one another and developing institutional rules that are well matched to the ecological systems being used are of central importance for solving social dilemmas. The surprising but repeated finding that users of resources that are in relatively good condition—or even improving—do invest in various ways of monitoring one another relates to the core problem of building trust.

Unfortunately, policy analysts, public officials, and scholars who still apply simple mathematical models to the analysis of field settings have not yet absorbed the central lessons articulated here. All too often a single policy prescription—such as Individual Transferable Quotas (ITQs)—is recommended for all resources of a particular type, such as all fisheries. While several ITQ systems are working successfully, the time and effort needed to tailor the broad theoretical concept of an ITQ system into an operational system in a particular location involves multiple years of hard work by the fishers involved as well as the government officials (see Clark 2006; Tracy Yandle 2007; Yandle and Christopher Dewees 2003; Thráinn Eggertsson 1990).

Other scholars propose government-owned protected areas as the "only" way to ensure that biodiversity is protected around the world (Terborgh 1999). Careful studies of protected areas have found, however, that the frequent eviction of indigenous peoples who had lived in a region for multiple centuries prior to the establishment of the park in their territory has not produced the positive results expected. Using remote sensing, Jianguo Liu et al. (2001) assessed that the rate of loss and fragmentation of high-quality habitat after the Wolong Nature Reserve was established in southwestern China was much higher than before the reserve was created. Daniel Brockington and James Igoe (2006) reviewed 250 reports on protected areas and the level of evictions from them and conclude that "forced relocation inflicts considerable material and psychological harm. But it is not just damaging for its material effects, rather for the reshaping of landscape and memory it imposes" (ibid.: 246). David Barton Bray and colleagues (2004) made a detailed study of another type of reform that created a forested landscape that was inhabited and productively used. Using Landsat images, they found a very "low incidence of net deforestation, 0.01% for the 1984–2000 period, the lowest recorded deforestation rate for southeastern Mexico" (ibid.: 333) based on a reform that created common property institutions.

A positive development of recent research is that more scholars are carefully assessing diverse policies adopted for the governance of common-pool resources (Brian R. Copeland and M. Scott Taylor 2009). In light of a comparative study of private, community, and state governed common-pool resources, R. Quentin Grafton (2000) found each to be successful when well matched to local settings and involving the active participation of local users.

> Each is capable of preventing resource degradation and ensuring the on-going flow of benefits to resource users. A comparison of the bundle of rights of the three regimes suggests that a common factor in ensuring successful governance of CPRs is the active participation of resource users in the management of the flow of benefits from the resources.
>
> —Grafton 2000: 515

Jeremy S. Brooks et al. (2006) reviewed data generated by 124 conservation projects and found that allowing local users to harvest and sell some products and involving communities in the design and administration of a project were all important factors for successful outcomes. Moving away from the presumption that *the* government must solve all common-pool resource problems while recognizing the important role of governments is a big step forward. Hopefully, in the future, more national officials will learn to work with local and regional officials, nongovernmental organizations, and local groups of citizens.

The most important lesson for public policy analysis derived from the intellectual journey I have outlined here is that humans have a more complex motivational structure and more capability to solve social dilemmas than posited in earlier rational-choice theory. Designing institutions to force (or nudge) entirely self-interested individuals to achieve better outcomes has been the major goal posited by policy analysts for governments to accomplish for much of the past half century. Extensive empirical research leads me to argue that instead, a core goal of public policy should be to facilitate the development of institutions that bring out the best in humans. We need to ask how diverse polycentric institutions help or hinder the innovativeness, learning, adapting, trustworthiness, levels of cooperation of participants, and the achievement of more effective, equitable, and sustainable outcomes at multiple scales (Theo Toonen 2010).

To explain the world of interactions and outcomes occurring at multiple levels, we also have to be willing to deal with complexity instead of rejecting it. Some mathematical models are very useful for explaining outcomes in particular settings. We should continue to use simple models where they capture enough of the core underlying structure and incentives that they usefully predict outcomes. When the world we are trying to explain and improve, however, is not well described by a simple model, we must continue to improve our frameworks and theories so as to be able to understand complexity and not simply reject it.

## Notes

1. I am much appreciative of the many hours of productive discussions that I had with Reinhard Selten in the early 1980s as we started to develop the IAD framework about the internal working parts of a formal game that could be used in the framework.

2. This meta-analysis effort is described in chapter 4 of Amy Poteete, Janssen, and E. Ostrom (2010).

3. Scholars across disciplines tend to use very different vocabularies and theoretical frameworks when they describe empirical settings. Other scholars, who have used meta-analysis, have also needed to screen many publications to obtain consistent data about human-used resource systems. Adcharaporn Pagdee, Yeon-Su Kim, and P.J. Daugherty (2006) report screening over 100 articles in order to analyze 31 cases related to forest management. Thomas K. Rudel (2008) reported that he had screened nearly 1,200 studies for a meta-analysis of 268 cases of tropical forest cover change.

4. The concept of access rights has puzzled some scholars. An everyday example of an access right is the buying of a permit to enter a public park. This assigns the holder of a

permit the right to enter and enjoy hiking and other nonharvesting activities for a defined period of time.

5. The term "design principle" has confused many readers. Perhaps I should have used the term "best practices" to describe the rules and structure of robust institutions.

6. In simple, repeated public goods experiments, subjects initially tended to contribute at a higher level than predicted by the Nash equilibrium (R. Mark Isaac et al. 1984, 1985, 1994; Isaac and Walker 1988; Gerald Marwell and Ruth E. Ames 1979) and outcomes slowly approach the predicted Nash equilibrium from a higher level. In common-pool resource games, on the other hand, subjects initially achieved outcomes that were much worse than the Nash equilibrium that they then slowly approached from below (see also Marco Casari and Charles R. Plott 2003).

7. See Joseph Henrich et al. (2006) in which field experiments were conducted in multiple countries testing whether a much broader set of participants would also use punishments in public goods experiments. See also Henrich et al. (2004) for the reports of earlier field experiments of social dilemmas in 15 small communities.

8. Similar findings exist for public goods experiments where punishers typically punish low contributors (Toshio Yamagishi 1986; Ernst Fehr and Simon Gächter 2002).

9. Extensive forest mensuration is conducted at every IFRI site at the same time that information is obtained about forest users, their activities and organization, and about governance arrangements. Comparing forest measures across ecological zones is misleading since the average diameter at breast height in a forest is strongly affected by precipitation, soils, elevation, and other factors that vary dramatically across ecological zones. Thus, we ask the forester or ecologist who has just supervised the collection of forest data to rate the forest on a five-point scale from very sparse to very abundant.

10. Scholars at the Stockholm Environment Institute, the International Institute for Applied Systems Analysis, Delft University of Technology, the University of Zurich, the Nordland Research Institute of Bodø University College, the Potsdam Institute for Climate Impact Research (PIK), Humboldt University, Marburg University, and the EU NeWATER project located at the University of Osnabrück have had several meetings in Europe to begin plans for using a common framework (initially developed by E. Ostrom 2007) to study a variety of resource systems. Scholars at the Workshop in Bloomington and the Center for the Study of Institutional Diversity at Arizona State University will also participate in this effort. A core problem identified by these scholars is the lack of cumulation across studies on diverse natural resource systems as well as humanly engineered resources.

11. See James I. Stewart (2009) for an important study that links size of group, acceptance of norms of cooperation, and support of property rights in 25 mining camps in the American Southwest.

# References

**Acheson, James M., and Roy Gardner.** 2005. "Spatial Strategies and Territoriality in the Maine Lobster Industry." *Rationality and Society*, 17(3): 309–41.

**Agrawal, Arun.** 2005. *Environmentality: Technologies of Government and the Making of Subjects.* Durham, NC: Duke University Press.

**Agrawal, Arun, and Clark Gibson, ed.** 2001. *Communities and the Environment: Ethnicity, Gender, and the State in Community-Based Conservation.* New Brunswick, NJ: Rutgers University Press.

**Alchian, Armen A.** 1950. "Uncertainty, Evolution, and Economic Theory." *Journal of Political Economy*, 58(3): 211–21.

**Alchian, Armen A., and Harold Demsetz.** 1973. "The Property Rights Paradigm." *Journal of Economic History*, 33(1): 16–27.

**Allport, Floyd H.** 1962. "A Structuronomic Conception of Behavior: Individual and Collective." *Journal of Abnormal and Social Psychology*, 64(1): 3–30.

**Anderson, Terry L., and Peter J. Hill.** 1990. "The Race for Property Rights." *Journal of Law and Economics*, 33(1): 177–97.

**Anderson, William, and Edward W. Weidner.** 1950. *American City Government.* New York: Henry Holt.

**Andersson, Krister P., and Elinor Ostrom.** 2008. "Analyzing Decentralized Resource Regimes from a Polycentric Perspective." *Policy Sciences*, 41(1): 71–93.

**Andersson, Krister P., Clark C. Gibson, and Fabrice Lehoucq.** 2006. "Municipal Politics and Forest Governance: Comparative Analysis of Decentralization in Bolivia and Guatemala." *World Development*, 34(3): 576–95.

**Andreoni, James.** 1989. "Giving with Impure Altruism: Applications to Charity and Ricardian Equivalence." *Journal of Political Economy*, 97(6): 1447–58.

**Aoki, Masahiko.** 2001. *Toward a Comparative Institutional Analysis.* Cambridge, MA: MIT Press.

**Arrow, Kenneth J.** 1974. *The Limits of Organization.* New York: Norton.

**Axelrod, Robert.** 1986. "An Evolutionary Approach to Norms." *American Political Science Review*, 80(4): 1095–111.

**Bain, Joe S.** 1959. *Industrial Organization.* New York: Wiley.

**Baland, Jean-Marie, and Jean-Philippe Platteau.** 2005. *Halting Degradation of Natural Resources: Is There a Role for Rural Communities?* Oxford: Clarendon Press.

**Balliet, Daniel.** 2010. "Communication and Cooperation in Social Dilemmas: A Meta-Analytic Review." *Journal of Conflict Resolution*, 54(1): 39–57.

**Banana, Abwoli Y., and William Gombya-Ssembajjwe.** 2000. "Successful Forest Management: The Importance of Security of Tenure and Rule Enforcement in Ugandan Forests." In *People and Forests: Communities, Institutions, and Governance*, ed. Clark C. Gibson, Margaret A. McKean, and Elinor Ostrom, 87–98. Cambridge, MA: MIT Press.

**Banana, Abwoli, Nathan D. Vogt, Joseph Bahati, and William Gombya-Ssembajjwe.** 2007. "Decentralized Governance and Ecological Health: Why Local Institutions Fail to Moderate Deforestation in Mpigi District of Uganda." *Scientific Research and Essays*, 2(10): 434–45.

**Bardhan, Pranab.** 2000. "Irrigation and Cooperation: An Empirical Analysis of 48 Irrigation Communities in South India." *Economic Development and Cultural Change*, 48(4): 847–65.

**Basurto, Xavier, and Elinor Ostrom.** 2009. "Beyond the Tragedy of the Commons." *Economia delle fonti di energia e dell'ambiente*, 52(1): 35–60.

**Batistella, Mateus, Scott Robeson, and Emilio F. Moran.** 2003. "Settlement Design, Forest Fragmentation, and Landscape Change in Rondônia, Amazônia." *Photogrammetric Engineering and Remote Sensing*, 69(7): 805–12.

**Bell, Frederick W.** 1972. "Technological Externalities and Common-Property Resources: An Empirical Study of the U.S. Northern Lobster Fishery." *Journal of Political Economy*, 80(1): 148–58.

**Benjamin, Paul, Wai Fung Lam, Elinor Ostrom, and Ganesh Shivakoti.** 1994. *Institutions, Incentives, and Irrigation in Nepal.* Burlington, VT: Associates in Rural Development.

**Berkes, Fikret.** 2007. "Community-Based Conservation in a Globalized World." *Proceedings of the National Academy of Sciences*, 104(39): 15188–93.

**Berkes, Fikret, Johan Colding, and Carl Folke.** 2003. *Navigating Social-Ecological Systems: Building Resilience for Complexity and Change.* Cambridge, UK: Cambridge University Press.

**Blomquist, William, Edella Schlager, Shui Yan Tang, and Elinor Ostrom.** 1994. "Regularities from the Field and Possible Explanations." In *Rules, Games, and Common-Pool Resources*, ed. Elinor Ostrom, Roy Gardner, and James Walker, 301–18. Ann Arbor, MI: University of Michigan Press.

**Bolton, Gary E., and Axel Ockenfels.** 2000. "ERC: A Theory of Equity, Reciprocity, and Competition." *American Economic Review*, 90(1): 166–93.

**Boyd, Robert, and Peter J. Richerson.** 1985. *Culture and the Evolutionary Process.* Chicago: University of Chicago Press.

**Bray, David Barton, Edward A. Ellis, Natalia Armijo-Canto, and Christopher T. Beck.** 2004. "The Institutional Drivers of Sustainable Landscapes: A Case Study of the 'Mayan Zone' in Quintana Roo, Mexico." *Land Use Policy*, 21(4): 333–46.

**Brock, William A., and Stephen R. Carpenter.** 2007. "Panaceas and Diversification of Environmental Policy." *Proceedings of the National Academy of Sciences*, 104(39): 15206–11.

**Brockington, Daniel, and James Igoe.** 2006. "Eviction for Conservation: A Global Overview." *Conservation and Society*, 4(3): 424–70.

**Bromley, Daniel W.** 1986. "Closing Comments at the Conference on Common Property Resource Management." In *Proceedings of the Conference on Common Property Resource Management*, 591–98. Washington, DC: National Academies Press.

**Brooks, Jeremy S., Margaret A. Franzen, Christopher M. Holmes, Mark N. Grote, and Monique Borgerhoff Mulder.** 2006. "Testing Hypotheses for the Success of Different Conservation Strategies." *Conservation Biology*, 20(5): 1528–38.

**Brunckhorst, David J.** 2000. *Bioregional Planning: Resource Management beyond the New Millennium.* Amsterdam: Harwood Academic.

**Buchanan, James M.** 1965. "An Economic Theory of Clubs." *Economica*, 32(125): 1–14.

**Canadell, Josep G., and Michael R. Raupach.** 2008. "Managing Forests for Climate Change Mitigation." *Science*, 320(5882): 1456–57.

**Cardenas, Juan-Camilo.** 2000. "How Do Groups Solve Local Commons Dilemmas? Lessons from Experimental Economics in the Field." *Environment, Development and Sustainability*, 2(3–4): 305–22.

**Cardenas, Juan-Camilo, John Stranlund, and Cleve Willis.** 2000. "Local Environmental Control and Institutional Crowding-Out." *World Development*, 28(10): 1719–33.

**Casari, Marco, and Charles R. Plott.** 2003. "Decentralized Management of Common Property Resources: Experiments with a Centuries-Old Institution." *Journal of Economic Behavior and Organization*, 51(2): 217–47.

**Caves, Richard.** 1964. *American Industry: Structure, Conduct, Performance*. Englewood Cliffs, NJ: Prentice-Hall.

**Chhatre, Ashwini, and Arun Agrawal.** 2008. "Forest Commons and Local Enforcement." *Proceedings of the National Academy of Sciences*, 105(36): 13286–91.

———. 2009. "Trade-offs and Synergies between Carbon Storage and Livelihood Benefits from Forest Commons." *Proceedings of the National Academy of Sciences*, 106(42): 17667–70.

**Ciriacy-Wantrup, S. V., and Richard C. Bishop.** 1975. "'Common Property' as a Concept in Natural Resources Policy." *Natural Resources Journal*, 15(4): 713–27.

**Clark, Colin W.** 2006. *The Worldwide Crisis in Fisheries: Economic Models and Human Behavior*. Cambridge, UK: Cambridge University Press.

**Coleman, Eric A.** 2009. "Institutional Factors Affecting Biophysical Outcomes in Forest Management." *Journal of Policy Analysis and Management*, 28(1): 122–46.

**Coleman, Eric A., and Brian C. Steed.** 2009. "Monitoring and Sanctioning in the Commons: An Application to Forestry." *Ecological Economics*, 68(7): 2106–13.

**Commons, John R.** 1968. *Legal Foundations of Capitalism*. Madison, WI: University of Wisconsin Press. (Orig. Pub. 1924).

**Copeland, Brian R., and M. Scott Taylor.** 2009. "Trade, Tragedy, and the Commons." *American Economic Review*, 99(3): 725–49.

**Coward, E. Walter.** 1980. *Irrigation and Agricultural Development in Asia*. Ithaca, NY: Cornell University Press.

**Cox, James C., and Cary A. Deck.** 2005. "On the Nature of Reciprocal Motives." *Economic Inquiry*, 43(3): 623–35.

**Cox, James C., Klarita Sadiraj, and Vjollca Sadiraj.** 2008. "Implications of Trust, Fear, and Reciprocity for Modeling Economic Behavior." *Experimental Economics*, 11(1): 1–24.

**Cox, Michael, Gwen Arnold, and Sergio Villamayor-Tomás.** 2009. "A Review and Reassessment of Design Principles for Community-Based Natural Resource Management." Unpublished.

**Crawford, Sue E. S., and Elinor Ostrom.** 2005. "A Grammar of Institutions." In *Understanding Institutional Diversity*, 137–74. Princeton, NJ: Princeton University Press.

**Degnbol, Poul, and Bonnie J. McCay.** 2007. "Unintended and Perverse Consequences of Ignoring Linkages in Fisheries Systems." *ICES Journal of Marine Science*, 64(4): 793–97.

**de Oliveira, Angela C. M., Rachel T. A. Croson, and Catherine Eckel.** 2009. "Are Preferences Stable across Domains? An Experimental Investigation of Social Preferences in the Field." CBEES Working Paper 2008–3.

**Dietz, Thomas, Elinor Ostrom, and Paul C. Stern.** 2003. "The Struggle to Govern the Commons." *Science*, 302(5652): 1907–12.

**Dutta, Prajit K.** 1999. *Strategies and Games: Theory and Practice.* Cambridge, MA: MIT Press.

**Eckel, Catherine C., and Philip J. Grossman.** 1996. "The Relative Price of Fairness: Gender Differences in a Punishment Game." *Journal of Economic Behavior and Organization*, 30(2): 143–58.

**Eggertsson, Thrainn.** 1990. *Economic Behavior and Institutions.* Cambridge, UK: Cambridge University Press.

**Elster, Jon.** 1989. *Solomonic Judgements: Studies in the Limitations of Rationality.* Cambridge, UK: Cambridge University Press.

**Faysse, Nicolas.** 2005. "Coping with the Tragedy of the Commons: Game Structure and Design of Rules." *Journal of Economic Surveys*, 19(2): 239–61.

**Fehr, Ernst, and Simon Gächter.** 2002. "Altruistic Punishment in Humans." *Nature*, 415(6868): 137–40.

**Fehr, Ernst, and Andreas Leibbrandt.** 2008. "Cooperativeness and Impatience in the Tragedy of the Commons." IZA Discussion Paper 3625.

**Fehr, Ernst, and Klaus M. Schmidt.** 1999. "A Theory of Fairness, Competition, and Cooperation." *Quarterly Journal of Economics*, 114(3): 817–68.

**Frey, Bruno S., and Felix Oberholzer-Gee.** 1997. "The Cost of Price Incentives: An Empirical Analysis of Motivation Crowding-Out." *American Economic Review*, 87(4): 746–55.

**Friesema, H. Paul.** 1966. "The Metropolis and the Maze of Local Government." *Urban Affairs Review*, 2(2): 68–90.

**Frohlich, Norman, and Joe A. Oppenheimer.** 1992. *Choosing Justice: An Experimental Approach to Ethical Theory.* Berkeley, CA: University of California Press.

**Gardner, Roy, Andrew Herr, Elinor Ostrom, and James A. Walker.** 2000. "The Power and Limitations of Proportional Cutbacks in Common-Pool Resources." *Journal of Development Economics*, 62(2): 515–33.

**Ghate, Rucha, and Harini Nagendra.** 2005. "Role of Monitoring in Institutional Performance: Forest Management in Maharashtra, India." *Conservation and Society*, 3(2): 509–32.

**Gibson, Clark C., Margaret McKean, and Elinor Ostrom, ed.** 2000. *People and Forests: Communities, Institutions, and Governance.* Cambridge, MA: MIT Press.

**Gibson, Clark C., John T. Williams, and Elinor Ostrom.** 2005. "Local Enforcement and Better Forests." *World Development*, 33(2): 273–84.

**Gibson, Clark C., Krister Andersson, Elinor Ostrom, and Sujai Shivakumar.** 2005. *The Samaritan's Dilemma: The Political Economy of Development Aid.* Oxford: Oxford University Press.

**Gigerenzer, Gerd, and Reinhard Selten, ed.** 2001. *Bounded Rationality: The Adaptive Toolbox.* Cambridge, MA: MIT Press.

**Goffman, Erving.** 1974. *Frame Analysis: An Essay on the Organization of Experience.* Cambridge, MA: Harvard University Press.

**Gordon, H. Scott.** 1954. "The Economic Theory of a Common-Property Resource: The Fishery." *Journal of Political Economy*, 62(2): 124–42.

**Grafton, R. Quentin.** 2000. "Governance of the Commons: A Role for the State?" *Land Economics*, 76(4): 504–17.

**Gulick, Luther.** 1957. "Metropolitan Organization." *The ANNALS of the American Academy of Political and Social Science*, 314(1): 57–65.

**Hardin, Garrett.** 1968. "The Tragedy of the Commons." *Science,* 162(3859): 1243–48.

**Hayes, Tanya M.** 2006. "Parks, People, and Forest Protection: An Institutional Assessment of the Effectiveness of Protected Areas." *World Development*, 34(12): 2064–75.

**Henrich, Joseph, Robert Boyd, Samuel Bowles, Colin Camerer, Ernst Fehr, and Herbert Gintis, ed.** 2004. *Foundations of Human Sociality: Economic Experiments and Ethnographic Evidence from Fifteen Small-Scale Societies.* Oxford: Oxford University Press.

**Henrich, Joseph, Richard McElreath, Abigail Barr, Jean Ensminger, Clark Barrett, Alexander Bolyanatz, Juan-Camilo Cardenas, et al.** 2006. "Costly Punishment across Human Societies." *Science*, 312(5781): 1767–70.

**Hobbes, Thomas.** 1651. *Leviathan or the Matter, Forme and Power of a Commonwealth Ecclesiasticall and Civil.* Ed. Michael Oakeshott. Oxford: Basil Blackwell, 1960.

**Holt, Charles A.** 2007. *Markets, Games, and Strategic Behavior.* Boston: Pearson Addison Wesley.

**Isaac, R. Mark, and James M. Walker.** 1988. "Communication and Free-Riding Behavior: The Voluntary Contribution Mechanism." *Economic Inquiry*, 26(4): 585–608.

**Isaac, R. Mark, Kenneth F. McCue, and Charles R. Plott.** 1985. "Public Goods Provision in an Experimental Environment." *Journal of Public Economics*, 26(1): 51–74.

**Isaac, R. Mark, James M. Walker, and Susan H. Thomas.** 1984. "Divergent Evidence on Free Riding: An Experimental Examination of Possible Explanations." *Public Choice*, 43(2): 113–49.

**Isaac, R. Mark, James M. Walker, and Arlington W. Williams.** 1994. "Group Size and the Voluntary Provision of Public Goods: Experimental Evidence Utilizing Large Groups." *Journal of Public Economics*, 54(1): 1–36.

**IsHak, Samir.** 1972. "Consumers' Perception of Police Performance: Consolidation vs. Deconcentration: The Case of Grand Rapids, Michigan." PhD diss. Indiana University.

**Jager, Wander, and Marco A. Janssen.** 2002. "Using Artificial Agents to Understand Laboratory Experiments of Common-Pool Resources with Real Agents." In *Complexity and Ecosystem Management: The Theory and Practice of Multi-Agent Systems*, ed. Marco A. Janssen, 75–102. Cheltenham, UK: Elgar.

**Janssen, Marco A.** 2008. "Evolution of Cooperation in a One-Shot Prisoner's Dilemma Based on Recognition of Trustworthy and Untrustworthy Agents." *Journal of Economic Behavior and Organization*, 65(3–4): 458–71.

**Joshi, Neeraj N., Elinor Ostrom, Ganesh P. Shivakoti, and Wai Fung Lam.** 2000. "Institutional Opportunities and Constraints in the Performance of Farmer-Managed Irrigation Systems in Nepal." *Asia-Pacific Journal of Rural Development*, 10(2): 67–92.

**Kiser, Larry L., and Elinor Ostrom.** 1982. "The Three Worlds of Action: A Metatheoretical Synthesis of Institutional Approaches." In *Strategies of Political Inquiry*, ed. Elinor Ostrom, 179–222. Beverly Hills, CA: Sage.

**Koestler, Arthur.** 1973. "The Tree and the Candle." In *Unity through Diversity: A Festschrift for Ludwig von Bertalanffy*, ed. William Gray and Nicholas D. Rizzo, 287–314. New York: Gordon and Breach Science Publishers.

**Lam, Wai Fung.** 1998. *Governing Irrigation Systems in Nepal: Institutions, Infrastructure, and Collective Action*. Oakland, CA: ICS Press.

**Leibbrandt, Andreas, Uri Gneezy, and John List.** 2010. "Ode to the Sea: The Socio-Ecological Underpinnings of Social Norms." Unpublished.

**Liu, Jianguo, Marc Linderman, Zhiyun Ouyang, Li An, Jian Yang, and Hemin Zhang.** 2001. "Ecological Degradation in Protected Areas: The Case of Wolong Nature Reserve for Giant Pandas." *Science*, 292(5514): 98–101.

**Marshall, Graham R.** 2008. "Nesting, Subsidiarity, and Community-Based Environmental Governance beyond the Local Level." *International Journal of the Commons*, 2(1): 75–97.

**Marwell, Gerald, and Ruth E. Ames.** 1979. "Experiments on the Provision of Public Goods I: Resources, Interest, Group Size, and the Free Rider Problem." *American Journal of Sociology*, 84(6): 1335–60.

**McCay, Bonnie J., and James M. Acheson.** 1987. *The Question of the Commons: The Culture and Ecology of Communal Resources*. Tucson, AZ: University of Arizona Press.

**McGinnis, Michael D., ed.** 1999a. *Polycentric Governance and Development: Readings from the Workshop in Political Theory and Policy Analysis*. Ann Arbor, MI: University of Michigan Press.

———. 1999b. *Polycentricity and Local Public Economies: Readings from the Workshop in Political Theory and Policy Analysis*. Ann Arbor, MI: University of Michigan Press.

———. 2000. *Polycentric Games and Institutions: Readings from the Workshop in Political Theory and Policy Analysis*. Ann Arbor, MI: University of Michigan Press.

**Meinzen-Dick, Ruth.** 2007. "Beyond Panaceas in Water Institutions." *Proceedings of the National Academy of Sciences*, 104(39): 15200–05.

**National Research Council.** 1986. *Proceedings of the Conference on Common Property Resource Management*. Washington, DC: National Academies Press.

**Netting, Robert McC.** 1972. "Of Men and Meadows: Strategies of Alpine Land Use." *Anthropological Quarterly*, 45(3): 132–44.

**North, Douglass C.** 1990. *Institutions, Institutional Change and Economic Performance*. Cambridge, UK: Cambridge University Press.

———. 2005. *Understanding the Process of Economic Change*. Princeton, NJ: Princeton University Press.

**Oakerson, Ronald J.** 1986. "A Model for the Analysis of Common Property Problems." In *Proceedings of the Conference on Common Property Resource Management*, 13–30. Washington, DC: National Academies Press.

**Ones, Umut, and Louis Putterman.** 2007. "The Ecology of Collective Action: A Public Goods and Sanctions Experiment with Controlled Group Formation." *Journal of Economic Behavior and Organization*, 62(4): 495–521.

Orbell, John M., Alphons van de Kragt, and Robyn M. Dawes. 1988. "Explaining Discussion-Induced Cooperation." *Journal of Personality and Social Psychology*, 54(5): 811–19.

Ostrom, Elinor. 1965. "Public Entrepreneurship: A Case Study in Ground Water Basin Management." PhD diss. University of California, Los Angeles.

———. 1976. "Size and Performance in a Federal System." *Publius: The Journal of Federalism*, 6(2): 33–73.

———. 1986. "An Agenda for the Study of Institutions." *Public Choice*, 48(1): 3–25.

———. 1990. *Governing the Commons: The Evolution of Institutions for Collective Action*. Cambridge, UK: Cambridge University Press.

———. 1998. "A Behavioral Approach to the Rational Choice Theory of Collective Action." *American Political Science Review*, 92(1): 1–22.

———. 1999. "Coping with Tragedies of the Commons." *Annual Review of Political Science*, 2: 493–535.

———. 2005. *Understanding Institutional Diversity*. Princeton, NJ: Princeton University Press.

———. 2007. "A Diagnostic Approach for Going beyond Panaceas." *Proceedings of the National Academy of Sciences*, 104(39): 15181–87.

———. 2008. "Developing a Method for Analyzing Institutional Change." In *Alternative Institutional Structures: Evolution and Impact*, ed. Sandra S. Batie and Nicholas Mercuro, 48–76. New York: Routledge.

———. 2009. "A General Framework for Analyzing the Sustainability of Social-Ecological Systems." *Science*, 325(5939): 419–22.

Ostrom, Elinor, and Xavier Basurto. Forthcoming. "Crafting Analytical Tools to Study Institutional Change." *Journal of Institutional Economics*.

Ostrom, Elinor, and Roy Gardner. 1993. "Coping with Asymmetries in the Commons: Self-Governing Irrigation Systems Can Work." *Journal of Economic Perspectives*, 7(4): 93–112.

Ostrom, Elinor, and Harini Nagendra. 2006. "Insights on Linking Forests, Trees, and People from the Air, on the Ground, and in the Laboratory." *Proceedings of the National Academy of Sciences*, 103(51): 19224–31.

Ostrom, Elinor, and Roger B. Parks. 1973. "Suburban Police Departments: Too Many and Too Small?" In *The Urbanization of the Suburbs*, ed. Louis H. Masotti and Jeffrey K. Hadden, 367–402. Beverly Hills, CA: Sage.

———. 1999. "Neither Gargantua nor the Land of Lilliputs: Conjectures on Mixed Systems of Metropolitan Organization." In *Polycentricity and Local Public Economies: Readings from the Workshop in Political Theory and Policy Analysis*, ed. Michael D. McGinnis, 284–305. Ann Arbor, MI: University of Michigan Press.

Ostrom, Elinor, and James Walker. 1991. "Communication in a Commons: Cooperation without External Enforcement." In *Laboratory Research in Political Economy*, ed. Thomas R. Palfrey, 287–322. Ann Arbor, MI: University of Michigan Press.

Ostrom, Elinor, and Gordon P. Whitaker. 1974. "Community Control and Governmental Responsiveness: The Case of Police in Black Neighborhoods. In *Improving the Quality of Urban Management*, ed. Willis Hawley and David Rogers, 303–34. Beverly Hills, CA: Sage.

**Ostrom, Elinor, Roy Gardner, and James Walker.** 1994. *Rules, Games, and Common-Pool Resources.* Ann Arbor, MI: University of Michigan Press.

**Ostrom, Elinor, Roger B. Parks, and Gordon P. Whitaker.** 1978. *Patterns of Metropolitan Policing.* Cambridge, MA: Ballinger.

**Ostrom, Elinor, Larry Schroeder, and Susan Wynne.** 1993. *Institutional Incentives and Sustainable Development: Infrastructure Policies in Perspective.* Boulder, CO: Westview Press.

**Ostrom, Elinor, James Walker, and Roy Gardner.** 1992. "Covenants with and without a Sword: Self-Governance Is Possible." *American Political Science Review,* 86(2): 404–17.

**Ostrom, Elinor, Arun Agrawal, William Blomquist, Edella Schlager, and S. Y. Tang.** 1989. *CPR Coding Manual.* Bloomington, IN: Indiana University, Workshop in Political Theory and Policy Analysis.

**Ostrom, Elinor, William Baugh, Richard Guarasci, Roger B. Parks, and Gordon P. Whitaker.** 1973. *Community Organization and the Provision of Police Services.* Beverly Hills, CA: Sage.

**Ostrom, Elinor, Thomas Dietz, Nives Dolšak, Paul C. Stern, Susan Stonich, and Elke U. Weber, ed.** 2002. *The Drama of the Commons.* Washington, DC: National Academies Press.

**Ostrom, Vincent.** 1962. "The Political Economy of Water Development." *American Economic Review,* 52(2): 450–58.

———. 1975. "Language, Theory and Empirical Research in Policy Analysis." *Policy Studies Journal,* 3(3): 274–82.

———. 2008. *The Intellectual Crisis in American Public Administration.* 3rd ed. Tuscaloosa, AL: University of Alabama Press.

**Ostrom, Vincent, and Elinor Ostrom.** 1965. "A Behavioral Approach to the Study of Intergovernmental Relations." *The ANNALS of the American Academy of Political and Social Science,* 359(1): 137–46.

———. 1977. "Public Goods and Public Choices." In *Alternatives for Delivering Public Services: Toward Improved Performance,* ed. Emanuel S. Savas, 7–49. Boulder, CO: Westview Press.

**Ostrom, Vincent, Charles M. Tiebout, and Robert Warren.** 1961. "The Organization of Government in Metropolitan Areas: A Theoretical Inquiry." *American Political Science Review,* 55(4): 831–42.

**Paavola, Jouni, and W. Neil Adger.** 2005. "Institutional Ecological Economics." *Ecological Economics,* 53(3): 353–68.

**Pagdee, Adcharaporn, Yeon-Su Kim, and P. J. Daugherty.** 2006. "What Makes Community Forest Management Successful: A Meta-Study from Community Forests throughout the World." *Society & Natural Resources,* 19(1): 33–52.

**Pfennig, David W., and Cris Ledon-Rettig.** 2009. "The Flexible Organism." *Science,* 325(5938): 268–69.

**Popper, Karl R.** 1961. *The Poverty of Historicism.* New York: Harper & Row.

**Posner, Richard.** 1975. "Economic Analysis of Law." In *Economic Foundation of Property Law,* ed. Bruce A. Ackerman. Boston, MA: Little, Brown and Co.

**Poteete, Amy R., and Elinor Ostrom.** 2004. "In Pursuit of Comparable Concepts and Data about Collective Action." *Agricultural Systems,* 82(3): 215–32.

Poteete, Amy R., Marco Janssen, and Elinor Ostrom. 2010. *Working Together: Collective Action, the Commons, and Multiple Methods in Practice*. Princeton, NJ: Princeton University Press.

Reeson, Andrew F., and John G. Tisdell. 2008. "Institutions, Motivations and Public Goods: An Experimental Test of Motivational Crowding." *Journal of Economic Behavior and Organization*, 68(1): 273–81.

Rogers, Bruce D., and C. McCurdy Lipsey. 1974. "Metropolitan Reform: Citizen Evaluations of Performance in Nashville-Davidson County, Tennessee." *Publius: The Journal of Federalism*, 4(4): 19–34.

Rothstein, Bo. 2005. *Social Traps and the Problem of Trust*. Cambridge, UK: Cambridge University Press.

Rudel, Thomas K. 2008. "Meta-Analyses of Case Studies: A Method for Studying Regional and Global Environmental Change." *Global Environmental Change*, 18(1): 18–25.

Sally, David. 1995. "Conservation and Cooperation in Social Dilemmas: A Meta-Analysis of Experiments from 1958 to 1992." *Rationality and Society*, 7(1): 58–92.

Samuelson, Paul A. 1954. "The Pure Theory of Public Expenditure." *Review of Economics and Statistics*, 36(4): 387–89.

Satz, Debra, and John Ferejohn. 1994. "Rational Choice and Social Theory." *Journal of Philosophy*, 91(2): 71–87.

Schank, Roger C., and Robert P. Abelson. 1977. *Scripts, Plans, Goals, and Understanding: An Inquiry in Human Knowledge Structures*. Hillsdale, NJ: Lawrence Erlbaum Associates.

Schelling, Thomas C. 1960. *The Strategy of Conflict*. Oxford: Oxford University Press.

———. 1978. *Micromotives and Macrobehavior*. New York: Norton.

———. 1984. *Choice and Consequence: Perspectives of an Errant Economist*. Cambridge, MA: Harvard University Press.

Schlager, Edella. 1990. "Model Specification and Policy Analysis: The Governance of Coastal Fisheries." PhD diss. Indiana University.

———. 1994. "Fishers' Institutional Responses to Common-Pool Resource Dilemmas." In *Rules, Games, and Common-Pool Resources*, ed. Elinor Ostrom, Roy Gardner, and James Walker, 247–65. Ann Arbor, MI: University of Michigan Press.

Schlager, Edella, and William Blomquist. 2008. *Embracing Watershed Politics*. Boulder, CO: University Press of Colorado.

Schlager, Edella, and Elinor Ostrom. 1992. "Property-Rights Regimes and Natural Resources: A Conceptual Analysis." *Land Economics*, 68(3): 249–62.

Scott, Anthony. 1955. "The Fishery: The Objectives of Sole Ownership." *Journal of Political Economy*, 63(2): 116–24.

Selten, Reinhard. 1990. "Bounded Rationality." *Journal of Institutional and Theoretical Economics*, 146(4): 649–58.

Sen, Amartya K. 1977. "Rational Fools: A Critique of the Behavioral Foundations of Economic Theory." *Philosophy and Public Affairs*, 6(4): 317–44.

———. 2009. *The Idea of Justice*. Cambridge, MA: Harvard University Press.

Shivakoti, Ganesh, and Elinor Ostrom, ed. 2002. *Improving Irrigation Governance and Management in Nepal*. Oakland, CA: ICS Press.

Simon, Herbert A. 1955. "A Behavioural Model of Rational Choice." *Quarterly Journal of Economics*, 69(1): 99–188.

———. 1981. *The Sciences of the Artificial*. 2nd ed. Cambridge, MA: MIT Press.

————. 1995. "Near Decomposability and Complexity: How a Mind Resides in a Brain." In *The Mind, the Brain, and Complex Adaptive Systems*, ed. Harold J. Morowitz and Jerome L. Singer, 25–44. Reading, MA: Addison-Wesley.

————. 1999. "The Potlatch between Economics and Political Science." In *Competition and Cooperation: Conversations with Nobelists About Economics and Political Science*, ed. James E. Alt, Margaret Levi, and Elinor Ostrom, 112–19. New York: Russell Sage Foundation.

Skoler, Daniel L., and June M. Hetler. 1971. "Government Restructuring and Criminal Administration: The Challenge of Consolidation." In *Crisis in Urban Government. A Symposium: Restructuring Metropolitan Area Government*. Silver Spring, MD: Thomas Jefferson.

Smith, Vernon L. 2003. "Constructivist and Ecological Rationality in Economics." *American Economic Review*, 93(3): 465–508.

————. 2010. "Theory and Experiment: What Are the Questions?" *Journal of Economic Behavior and Organization*, 73(1): 3–15.

Smith, Vernon L., and James M. Walker. 1993. "Rewards, Experience and Decision Costs in First Price Auctions." *Economic Inquiry*, 31(2): 237–45.

Stewart, James I. 2009. "Cooperation When N Is Large: Evidence from the Mining Camps of the American West." *Journal of Economic Behavior and Organization*, 69(3): 213–25.

Sugden, Robert. 1986. *The Economics of Rights, Co-Operation and Welfare*. Oxford: Blackwell.

Tang, Shui Yan. 1992. *Institutions and Collective Action: Self-Governance in Irrigation*. San Francisco: ICS Press.

————. 1994. "Institutions and Performance in Irrigation Systems." In *Rules, Games, and Common-Pool Resources*, ed. Elinor Ostrom, Roy Gardner, and James Walker, 225–45. Ann Arbor, MI: University of Michigan Press.

Terborgh, John. 1999. *Requiem for Nature*. Washington, DC: Island Press.

Toonen, Theo. 2010. "Resilience in Public Administration: The Work of Elinor and Vincent Ostrom from a Public Administration Perspective." *Public Administration Review*, 70(2): 193–202.

Trawick, Paul B. 2001. "Successfully Governing the Commons: Principles of Social Organization in an Andean Irrigation System." *Human Ecology*, 29(1): 1–25.

Tucker, Catherine M. 2008. *Changing Forests: Collective Action, Common Property, and Coffee in Honduras*. Berlin: Springer.

Uphoff, Norman T., Priti Ramamurthy and Roy Steiner. 1991. *Managing Irrigation: Analyzing and Improving the Performance of Bureaucracies*. New Delhi: Sage.

Walker, James, and Elinor Ostrom. 2009. "Trust and Reciprocity as Foundations for Cooperation." In *Whom Can We Trust?: How Groups, Networks, and Institutions Make Trust Possible*, ed. Karen S. Cook, Margaret Levi, and Russell Hardin, 91–124. New York: Russell Sage Foundation.

Warren, Robert O. 1966. *Government of Metropolitan Regions: A Reappraisal of Fractionated Political Organization*. Davis, CA: University of California, Institute of Governmental Affairs.

Webb, Edward L., and Ganesh Shivakoti, ed. 2008. *Decentralization, Forests and Rural Communities: Policy Outcomes in South and Southeast Asia*. New Delhi: Sage India.

**Weissing, Franz, and Elinor Ostrom.** 1993. "Irrigation Institutions and the Games Irrigators Play: Rule Enforcement on Government and Farmer-Managed Systems." In *Games in Hierarchies and Networks: Analytical and Empirical Approaches to the Study of Governance Institutions*, ed. Fritz W. Scharpf, 387–428. Frankfurt, Germany: Campus Verlag.

**Weschler, Louis F.** 1968. *Water Resources Management: The Orange County Experience.* Davis, CA: University of California, Institute of Governmental Affairs.

**Williamson, Oliver E.** 1975. *Markets and Hierarchies: Analysis and Antitrust Implications.* New York: Free Press.

———. 1986. "The Economics of Governance: Framework and Implications." In *Economics as a Process: Essays in the New Institutional Economics*, ed. Richard N. Langlois, 171–202. Cambridge, UK: Cambridge University Press.

**Wilson, James A.** 1990. "Fishing for Knowledge." *Land Economics*, 66(1): 12–29.

**Wilson, James A., James M. Acheson, Mark Metcalfe, and Peter Kleban.** 1994. "Chaos, Complexity, and Community Management of Fisheries." *Marine Policy*, 18(4): 291–305.

**Wilson, Woodrow.** 1885. *Congressional Government: A Study in American Politics.* Boston: Houghton Mifflin.

**Wollenberg, Eva, Leticia Merino, Arun Agrawal, and Elinor Ostrom.** 2007. "Fourteen Years of Monitoring Community-Managed Forests: Learning from IFRI's Experience." *International Forestry Review*, 9(2): 670–84.

**Yamagishi, Toshio.** 1986. "The Provision of a Sanctioning System as a Public Good." *Journal of Personality and Social Psychology*, 51(1): 110–16.

**Yandle, Tracy.** 2007. "Understanding the Consequence of Property Rights Mismatches: A Case Study of New Zealand's Marine Resources." *Ecology and Society*, 12(2). http://www.ecologyandsociety.org/vol12/iss2/art27/.

**Yandle, Tracy, and Christopher M. Dewees.** 2003. "Privatizing the Commons... Twelve Years Later: Fishers' Experiences with New Zealand's Market-Based Fisheries Management." In *The Commons in the New Millennium: Challenges and Adaptation*, ed. Nives Dolsak and Elinor Ostrom, 101–27. Cambridge, MA: MIT Press.

# CONCLUSION: PURSUING RESEARCH
## *in the* MAINLINE TRADITION

PETER J. BOETTKE, STEFANIE HAEFFELE-BALCH,
AND VIRGIL HENRY STORR

---

The Nobel Laureates in Economics featured in this volume—
F. A. Hayek, James M. Buchanan, Ronald H. Coase, Douglass C. North, Vernon L. Smith, and Elinor C. Ostrom—represent
key figures within mainline economics.

Each of these six authors drew inspiration from Adam Smith.
Often they explicitly acknowledged their debt to him. For instance,
James M. Buchanan drew inspiration from Smith's emphasis on institutions. As Buchanan (2001: 290) notes, "to Adam Smith, the 'laws
and institutions,' the political-legal framework within which persons
interact, one with another, are important and necessary elements in the
inclusive 'constitution' for the political economy." Similarly, Hayek's
work on spontaneous orders and the use of knowledge within economic systems builds on Smith's discussion of how the invisible hand
promotes prosperity under the division of labor. As Hayek (1978:
124–25) explains, "Adam Smith's decisive contribution was the account
of a self-generating order which formed itself spontaneously if the
individuals were restrained by appropriate rules of law."

Following Adam Smith, these Nobel Laureates in Economics
advanced a view of the economy that stressed (1) the cognitive and

epistemic limits as well as the limits to human generosity that individuals face as they negotiate the world, (2) the importance of formal and informal institutions as guides to human activity, and (3) the potential of social cooperation in the absence of central direction. Each recognized that human beings are error-prone and have limited knowledge and cognitive capacities but are nonetheless aided by social rules and norms, which serve as guideposts that allow them to interact and exchange with one another in socially beneficially ways.

Moreover, the economists featured here offered serious critiques of mainstream economics and argued for continued work within the mainline tradition. In practice, this has meant for them an emphasis on human fallibility, the role of institutions, and the possibility of the beneficial emergent orders, as well as a preference for thick over thin descriptions and an openness to multidisciplinary and interdisciplinary projects and methods.

Mainline economics advances thick rather than thin descriptions of the world. Recall Gilbert Ryle's (1971) now famous example of the two boys who are rapidly contracting the eyelids of their right eyes. One of the boys, he explains, is merely twitching. The blinking of his right eye is an involuntary response to some external stimuli. It is not meant to convey anything to those around him. The other boy is winking at a coconspirator. The blinking of his right eye is intentional and meant to convey something to his accomplice. A thin description of these two acts, Ryle explains, would not allow us to distinguish between them. A thin description would only note that the boy quickly closed and then opened his right eye. A thick description, on the other hand, would offer the kind of details about the boy, his background, and the context in which the twitch/wink has occurred that are needed to properly interpret the act. As he (ibid.: 482) describes, "thick description is a many-layered sandwich, of which only the bottom slice is catered by the thinnest description."

The preference for thick over thin descriptions has led mainline economists to be open to working within multiple disciplines and with multiple methods. Emily Chamlee-Wright (2010: 27–29) utilizes a helpful metaphor to shed light on why this openness is important. Social science's effort to understand the world, she suggests, is like trying to put together an extremely complex puzzle. Unlike a typical puzzle, however, the social scientist has no picture to serve as a guide as she puts together the puzzle pieces. Moreover, the pieces are three-dimensional, are not easily manipulated, and are too large to fit on a single table. In fact, sometimes the puzzle is the size of a town, sometimes as large as the whole world. Further complicating matters, the puzzle pieces are moving. This movement is both exogenous (as if large cranes are picking up the pieces and moving them around) and endogenous (as if the pieces are moving of their own accord). Endogenous change means that the puzzle is no longer inanimate but rather is filled with pieces that can make decisions, act on their desires, potentially persuade others to follow them, and, possibly, learn from their experiences. In other words, there is activity within the puzzle. As Chamlee-Wright (ibid.) notes, there are multiple ways of going about studying society, including building simple models (more closely representing the small, manageable puzzle), taking a sample and studying it in the lab, examining it from an aerial view, or getting on the ground (or inside the puzzle) to examine things up close and talk to people. Each of these strategies for "solving the puzzle" has its limitations. None alone will offer a complete picture of what is going on in the puzzle. By combining multiple strategies, however, a richer image might result.

The economists selected for this volume were able to offer thick descriptions of the world by working in multiple fields and utilizing multiple methods. Hayek, for instance, contributed to multiple disciplines in addition to economics, including philosophy, history, law, the history of ideas, and psychology, through his research on the limited cognition of human beings, constructivism, and the importance of institutions. Similarly, Buchanan made significant contributions to economics, political science, and political philosophy through highlighting the limits to political action and emphasizing the importance of constitutional political economy. Ronald H. Coase utilized on-the-ground observations to fuel his research on firms and contributed to legal theory in addition to economic theory. Douglass C. North combined economics and history, through archival research, to examine historical institutions and social change. Vernon L. Smith pioneered experimental economics and has contributed to economics as well as psychology. He has not only demonstrated, with his idea of ecological rationality, that the market has greater "efficiency" than standard theory predicts but has also shown that humans exhibit more cooperative behavior than standard theory predicts. And, Elinor C. Ostrom combined multiple disciplines—such as economics, political science, and the natural sciences—and multiple methods—such as fieldwork, game theory, experiment economics, and so on—in her research on commons and self-governing institutions. Ostrom and her coauthors champion this multiple method methodology in the book *Working Together* (Poteete, Janssen, and Ostrom 2010).

Adam Smith's writings asked and attempted to answer the most important questions of not only his time but all times: How can we live together peacefully and prosperously? To pursue research in the mainline tradition is to advance research that is thick in description, that is interdisciplinary, and that uses multiple methods to answer that important question. Our six mainline Nobel Laureates in Economics took up Smith's challenge and rearticulated, updated, developed, and, in some cases, corrected Smith's response. We would do well to follow their lead as we attempt to understand the world.

# References

**Buchanan, James M.** 2001. "Adam Smith As Inspiration." In *Ideas, Persons & Events, The Collected Works of James M. Buchanan.* Vol. 19. Indianapolis, IN: Liberty Fund.

**Chamlee-Wright, Emily.** 2010. *The Cultural and Political Economy of Recovery: Social Learning in a Post-Disaster Environment.* New York: Routledge.

**Hayek, F. A.** 1978. *New Studies in Philosophy, Politics, Economics and the History of Ideas.* London: Routledge.

**Poteete, Amy R., Marco A. Janssen, and Elinor Ostrom.** 2010. *Working Together: Collective Action, the Commons, and Multiple Methods in Practice.* Princeton, NJ: Princeton University Press.

**Ryle, Gilbert.** 1971. *Collected Papers.* Vol. 2, *Collected Essays 1929–1968.* London: Hutchinson.

**Storr, Virgil Henry.** 2010. "The Facts of the Social Sciences Are What People Believe and Think." In *Handbook on Contemporary Austrian Economics,* ed. Peter J. Boettke, 30–40. Northampton, MA: Edward Elgar Publishing.

# FURTHER READINGS
## *in* MAINLINE ECONOMICS

Scholars associated with the F. A. Hayek Program for Advanced Study in Philosophy, Politics, and Economics at the Mercatus Center at George Mason University have written a great deal on the key themes within mainline economics. Below is a selection of those books and articles.

### On the Cognitive and Epistemic Limits That Individuals Face

**Boettke, Peter J.** 2010. *Calculation and Coordination: Essays on Socialism and Transitional Political Economy.* New York: Routledge.

**Coyne, Christopher J.** 2008. *After War: The Political Economy of Exporting Democracy.* Stanford, CA: Stanford University Press.

————. 2013. *Doing Bad by Doing Good: Why Humanitarian Action Fails.* Stanford, CA: Stanford University Press.

**Lavoie, Don.** 2015. *Rivalry and Central Planning: The Social Calculation Debate Considered.* Arlington, VA: Mercatus Center. (Orig. Pub. 1985).

**Wagner, Richard E.** 2010. *Mind, Society and Human Action: Time and Knowledge in a Theory of Social Economy.* New York: Routledge.

### On the Formal and Informal Institutions
### That Guide and Direct Human Activity

**Boettke, Peter J., ed.** 2005. "Forum Series on the Role of Institutions in Promoting Economic Grown." *The Review of Austrian Economics,* 18(3–4).

————, ed. 2011. "Special Issue on the Work of James Buchanan." *Journal of Economic Behavior & Organization*, 57(2).

**Boudreaux, Karol, and Paul Dragos Aligica.** 2007. *Paths to Property: Approaches to Institutional Change in International Development*. London: Institute of Economic Affairs.

**Lavoie, Don.** 2015. *National Economic Planning: What Is Left?* Arlington, VA: Mercatus Center. (Orig. Pub. 1985).

**White, Lawrence H.** 1999. *The Theory of Monetary Institutions*. Malden, MA: Wiley-Blackwell.

## On the Possibility of Social Cooperation
## without Central Direction

**Boettke, Peter J., ed.** 2005. "Polycentric Political Economy: A Festschrift for Elinor & Vincent Ostrom." *Journal of Economic Behavior & Organization*, 80(2).

**Leeson, Peter T.** 2009. *The Invisible Hook: The Hidden Economics of Pirates*. Princeton, NJ: Princeton University Press.

————. 2014. *Anarchy Unbound: Why Self-Governance Works Better Than You Think*. Cambridge: Cambridge University Press.

**Storr, Virgil Henry, Stefanie Haeffele-Balch, and Laura E. Grube.** 2015. *Community Revival in the Wake of Disaster: Lessons in Local Entrepreneurship*. London: Palgrave Macmillan.

**Stringham, Edward Peter.** 2015. *Private Governance: Creating Order in Economics and Social Life*. Oxford: Oxford University Press.

## On Using Multiple Disciplines and Methods
## in the Social Sciences

**Chamlee-Wright, Emily.** 2014. *The Cultural Foundations of Economics Development: Urban Female Entrepreneurship in Ghana*. New York: Routledge. (Orig. Pub. 1997).

————. 2013. *The Cultural and Political Economy of Recovery: Social Learning in a Post-Disaster Environment*. New York: Routledge.

**Lavoie, Don, and Emily Chamlee-Wright.** 2000. *Culture and Enterprise: The Development, Representation and Morality of Business*. New York: Routledge.

**Skarbek, David.** 2014. *Social Order of the Underground: How Prison Gangs Govern the American Penal System*. Oxford: Oxford University Press.

**Wagner, Richard E.** 2007. *Fiscal Sociology and the Theory of Public Finance: An Exploratory Essay*. Northampton, MA: Edward Elgar Publishing.

## On Thick, Rather Than Thin, Descriptions

**Aligica, Paul Dragos.** 2014. *Institutional Diversity and Political Economy: The Ostroms and Beyond*. Oxford: Oxford University Press.

**Boettke, Peter J.** 2012. *Living Economics: Yesterday, Today, and Tomorrow.* Oakland, CA: The Independent Institute.

**Dekker, Erwin.** 2016. *The Viennese Students of Civilization: The Meaning and Context of Austrian Economics Reconsidered.* Cambridge: Cambridge University Press.

**Storr, Virgil Henry.** 2012. *Understanding the Culture of Markets.* New York: Routledge.

**White, Lawrence H.** 2012. *The Clash of Economic Ideas: The Great Policy Debates and Experiments of the Last Hundred Years.* Cambridge: Cambridge University Press.

Also, there are several textbooks and reference volumes that extend mainline economics:

**Boettke, Peter J., ed.** 2010. *Handbook on Contemporary Austrian Economics.* Northampton, MA: Edward Elgar Publishing.

**Boettke, Peter J., and Christopher J. Coyne, eds.** 2015. *The Oxford Handbook of Austrian Economics.* Oxford: Oxford University Press.

**Grube, Laura E., and Virgil Henry Storr, eds.** 2015. *Culture and Economic Action.* Northampton, MA: Edward Elgar Publishing.

**Heyne, Paul, Peter J. Boettke, and David Prychitko.** 2013. *The Economic Way of Thinking.* 13th ed. Upper Saddle River, NJ: Prentice Hall.

**Kasper, Wolfgang, Manfred E. Streit, and Peter J. Boettke.** 2012. *Institutional Economics: Property, Competition, and Policies.* 2nd ed. Northampton, MA: Edward Elgar Publishing.

# INDEX